ORANGE, BLACK & BLUE

The Greatest Philadelphia Flyers Stories Never Told

By Chuck Gormley

SPORTS CHALLENGE
Network Publishing

WWW.SPORTSCHALLENGENETWORK.COM

ORANGE, BLACK & BLUE
The Greatest Philadelphia Flyers Stories Never Told

Digital composition and design
by Ilene Griff Design

This book is published with permission granted by The Philadelphia Flyers.

Publisher
Sports Challenge Network
Philadelphia, PA 19102
www.sportschallengenetwork.com
email: sales@sportschallengenetwork.com

To my loving wife, Denise,
my soulmate and true companion
and
To Sean, Tom, Ryan and Kayla,
whose enthusiasm kept this book alive

In Memory of
Dutch Culbertson
and
Roger Neilson

CONTENTS

FOREWORD

I HATED THE PHILADELPHIA FLYERS.

In 1982, I was a young goaltender playing for my hometown Brandon Wheat Kings, and working my summer job washing cars. I had grown up watching the Broad Street Bullies beat my father Bryan's teams, both physically and on the scoreboard. Then one day in June, my mother telephoned to tell me that I had been drafted in the 6th round, by the team I despised most in the entire National Hockey League, the Philadelphia Flyers.

In spite of my misgivings, it didn't take long for me to develop the utmost respect and admiration for this organization and its win-at-all-costs attitude. My relationship with the Flyers turned out to be a match made in heaven.

Throughout my 20 years as a player and in management with the Philadelphia Flyers, I lived the "never take a back seat to anybody" culture. In all the years I pulled on the orange and black jersey, I always knew how fortunate I was to be playing in Philadelphia. I had the most any athlete could ask for — the opportunity to play for an organization where winning is demanded, and expected.

I truly believe that virtually every player who was ever a part of the Philadelphia Flyers became a better player and definitely a better competitor because of the culture and environment the Flyers created. I know that I did. This is the environment that shaped me, and I will forever be grateful for it.

In my opinion, there is no greater franchise in professional sports than the Philadelphia Flyers, and there is no greater privilege for any professional athlete than to play for the Flyers.

I only wish I had been able to help bring the Stanley Cup back to Philadelphia, especially when we came so close in the 1987 finals. The city, the organization and every one of my extraordinary teammates deserved it.

It's truly an honor to have been asked to write this foreword by one of the top sports writers in Philadelphia. Throughout my playing career, Chuck was always diligent, objective and fair. His questions reflected his sophisticated knowledge of the game of hockey.

I hope you enjoy reading this book as much as I have. It brought back a lot of memories for me, and it will give you real insight into what it is like to be a part of the Flyers family.

— Ron Hextall

ACKNOWLEDGMENTS

UNLIKE RON HEXTALL, I GREW UP LOVING THE FLYERS.

In the spring of 1974, when I was 10, my parents bought our first color television so we could watch the Stanley Cup playoffs in living color.

On May 19, 1974, after the Flyers won their first of two Stanley Cups, my Dad loaded all of us – six children and as many friends as could fit — into our olive green Rambler and drove us up and down the streets of Collingdale, a small suburb of Philadelphia. The car horn never worked after that wild night.

As a street hockey-playing teenager, I lost my front tooth to a high stick, never imagining I would someday talk to players who thought nothing of losing a mouthful of teeth and returning in the same game.

For the past 21 years I have had the privilege of covering the Flyers as a beat writer for the Courier-Post in Cherry Hill, New Jersey and in the following pages you will meet many of the extraordinary men I have gotten to know during that time.

From the moment Dave Poulin introduced me to every member of the 1988-89 Flyers, I have been impressed by the professionalism, honesty and integrity of hockey players and in return I have tried to provide those same qualities in my written words.

This book would not be possible without the time and cooperation of the Philadelphia Flyers organization. Chairman Ed Snider, president Peter Luukko, senior vice president Bob Clarke, general manager Paul Holmgren, senior vice president of business operations Shawn Tilger, senior director of communications Zack Hill, archive manager Brian McBride and interns Antonio Cima, David Weibrecht and Jasen Hurka all contributed to this book in some way and for that I am grateful.

I would also like to thank the dozens of players and coaches who delved deep into their memory banks for stories that had never before been put to paper. The trust they have placed in me over the years will never be compromised.

I'd like to extend a special thanks to Eli Kowalski, the publisher of this book, for his enthusiasm and professionalism throughout the process, and to my newspaper colleagues who for years have sat alongside me on press row.

Most importantly, I'd like to thank my beautiful wife, Denise, whose untold sacrifices throughout our marriage have allowed me to succeed in a profession I love. And to our four wonderful children, Sean, Tom, Ryan and Kayla, who for the past year have woken up and gone to bed with their Dad sitting in front of his laptop.

Finally, I would like to thank you for picking up this book. I hope you enjoy reading it as much as I enjoyed writing it.

Game On!

— Chuck Gormley

It cost $12 million to build the Spectrum, but hockey boards were not delivered until just before the Flyers' home opener.

CHAPTER 1

BIRTH OF THE BULLIES

1967–1973

A look at how the Flyers evolved from a timid expansion team to the most feared in NHL history.

FROM THE SCRAP HEAP

JOE WATSON CAN STILL RECALL THE SOUNDS OF TWISTED metal.

It was late September, 1967 and Watson, an unassuming 23-year-old defenseman from Smithers, British Columbia, was getting a backseat look at the City of Brotherly Love.

"A driver picked me up at the airport and we were crossing over the Penrose Avenue Bridge on the way to the Spectrum, which was still being built," recalled Watson, an original member of the Flyers.

"We passed all these smelly refineries and at the foot of the bridge was this big scrap heap. I asked the guy, 'What's that?'"

"The mafia owns that place," the driver said, "and when they want to get rid of people they put them in those cars and grind them up."

Welcome to Philadelphia, the city that loves you back.

A few minutes later, when Watson arrived at the corner of Broad Street and Pattison Avenue, he found the Flyers' new brick-faced home finished on the outside, but mostly a shell on the inside.

Seats were still being installed during the Flyers' first practice at the Spectrum and no glass had been installed surrounding the ice surface.

"The workers had never heard the sound of shooting pucks," Watson recalled, "and when a few went into the stands they thought they were getting shot."

13

Lew Angotti, a 29-year-old center who had played for the New York Rangers and Chicago Blackhawks before being claimed by the Flyers in the expansion draft, looked around the building and wondered if he'd been sent to hockey purgatory.

"All of us wondered if hockey was ever going to survive in Philadelphia," Angotti said. "The building wasn't close to being ready and it really scared the players. We said, 'Aw, Geez! We're an expansion team and we're not even going to play our first game here.'"

EVERYBODY LOVES A PARADE

Contrary to popular belief, the first parade in Flyers history did not attract more than 2 million spectators. Twenty might be a better estimate.

Once all of the players had arrived from their Canadian outposts, the Flyers and the City of Philadelphia organized a Welcome Parade introducing 25 skeptical hockey players to the city they would call home.

"We were all in convertibles and there was no one at the parade except us," Flyers founding father Ed Snider said. "People were looking at us and saying, 'What is that?'"

"Nobody came," Angotti recalled. "And the ones who did didn't know who we were and what we were doing there."

"There were more people in the parade than there were watching," Watson said. "The mayor (James Tate) didn't even show up for the darn thing. One guy gave us the finger and yelled, 'You'll be in Baltimore or Washington in a year!'"

SINGING THE BLUES

If not for the Plager brothers and the bigger and badder St. Louis Blues, the Flyers may have never gained their reputation as the Broad Street Bullies.

During the 1967 expansion draft, the Flyers built a team of youth and speed. The Blues built a team of size, strength and brass knuckles. Barclay and Bob Plager, along with Noel Picard, were the ring leaders and it wasn't long before they flexed their significant muscle against the Flyers.

During the Flyers' maiden season, Bob Plager got into a scrap with Flyers rookie Gary Dornhoefer and finished off the willing but undersized winger by kicking him in the back of the leg and breaking it.

Later that same season Picard grabbed a hold of 5-foot-8 forward Claude LaForge and beat him like a rag doll.

"Poor Claude got his jaw broke and had nine teeth knocked out in one fight," Watson said. "It got to a point where some of our guys weren't willing to get the puck. They had such big defensemen and we had small forwards."

The Blues knocked the Flyers out of the 1968 playoffs in seven games and the beatings worsened the following season. Red Berenson scored six goals against the Flyers in an 8-0 loss at the Spectrum and when the Blues outscored the Flyers 17-3 in a first-round playoff sweep in 1969, a young but determined Snider had seen enough.

"This will never happen to the Philadelphia Flyers again," the 36-year-old owner promised.

Two months later the Flyers drafted Bobby Clarke, Dave Schultz and Don Saleski and the embryonic stages of the Bullies were in place.

Joe Watson and the Flyers took their share of beatings early on.

GOD BLESS KATE

Kate Smith is so revered in Philadelphia that for more than a decade a larger than life bronzed statue of her likeness greeted fans as they arrived at the Spectrum. But did you know it was political unrest that led to the first recording of her "God Bless America" before a Flyers game?

It was midway through the 1969-70 season that Flyers vice-president Lou Scheinfeld noticed a growing number of fans, in protest of the Vietnam War, refusing to stand for the national anthem.

"There was a lot of turmoil in the country," Snider recalled. "So, one day Lou decided to play 'God Bless America' and we won the game. After that I never wanted to know when she was going to be played. I was superstitious. Lou decided when we were going to do it and our record was fantastic."

Smith was 66 years old when the Flyers paid her $5,000 for her first live performance at the Spectrum before the 1973-74 season opener. When the Flyers defeated the Toronto Maple Leafs 2-0, it began a stretch of 18 straight wins over three seasons when her "God Bless America" was played before a game.

"She was an amazing woman and at her age she could belt out that song beautifully," Snider said.

When Smith passed away in 1986 at the age of 79, Snider served as a pall bearer for her funeral. Sixteen months later, a bronzed statue of her was erected in front of the Spectrum.

At last count the Flyers owned a record of 77-21-4 when "God Bless America" was played prior to their games.

Kate Smith was paid $5,000 for her first live performance at the Spectrum.

COLLAPSE OF 1970

After winning 31 games in their inaugural season and 21 the following year, the Flyers reached an all-time low with just 17 wins in 1969-70. But with an NHL record 24 ties, a feat that will never be broken with the advent of shootouts, the Flyers looked like a shoo-in for the Stanley Cup playoffs.

With six games to play they needed just one win. All six of the Flyers' remaining games were against expansion teams like themselves, five of them against teams with records worse than their own.

But like stones in an avalanche, the losses mounted in furious succession. One-goal losses in Oakland and Los Angeles were followed by back-to-back losses to the Penguins and a one-goal loss to the hated Blues.

The Flyers' playoff chances had been whittled down to one game. Flyers vs. North Stars, Saturday afternoon, April 4, 1970, at the Spectrum.

The North Stars, trailing the Flyers by two points with two games to play, needed to beat the Flyers to ensure themselves a berth in the playoffs. The Flyers, playing in their final contest of the season, needed either a tie or a win to clinch.

Bernie Parent, a 25-year-old future Hockey Hall of Famer, stood at one end of the rink. The legendary Lorne "Gump" Worsley, another future Hall of Famer who was one month shy of his 41st birthday, stood at the other.

There was brilliant sunshine outside the Spectrum as 14,606 patrons made their way to their seats.

For the next 47 minutes of action, Parent and Worsley matched each other save for save.

Then it happened.

With 7:48 gone in the third period, Minnesota defenseman Barry Gibbs wanted a line change. From about 80 feet, he lofted a high dump-in toward the Flyers net, then headed to his bench. Seconds later, he heard a groan like he had never heard before.

The puck had somehow eluded Parent, sailing over his right shoulder as he stood motionless in front of his goal.

"I was just trying to clear the puck into their end," Gibbs told reporters after netting just his third goal in 56 games. "I know he never saw it."

Parent agreed, but contrary to popular urban legend, he did not blame the goal on the ray of sunlight that shone through one of the open portals at the other end of the rink.

"No, I didn't see it," Parent said. "But it wasn't because of the sun. I saw it leave Gibbs' stick, then I think somebody stepped in front of him and I lost it."

The North Stars, who during one stretch in the season had won just once in 34 games, were in the playoffs.

The Flyers, victims of the most devastating 80-foot shot in their short history, were not.

"I don't remember if it was the most unusual goal scored against me," Parent said in a solemn Flyers dressing room. "I do know it was the worst."

THE HAZE BEFORE THE FOG

The Flyers went through two coaches, Keith Allen and Vic Stasiuk, in their first four seasons before hiring Fred Shero, a former boxer and World War II veteran, before the 1971-72 season.

In Shero's first season behind the Flyers bench, his team needed a tie against the Buffalo Sabres in the final game to reach the Stanley Cup playoffs.

The Flyers were four seconds away from accomplishing the feat when Gerry Meehan scored with four seconds remaining to give the Sabres a 3-2 win and leave the Flyers on the outside looking in with a 26-38-14 record.

"I feel as though I just lost a member of the family," Shero said.

Snider had a different feeling in the pit of his stomach, boldly predicting the Flyers would win the Stanley Cup within five years.

"Everyone thought I was crazy," Snider recalled.

To Shero, the Flyers had become family and he made it his business to know everydetail of his players' lives.

"In the first year, I know more about my players than their wives do," Shero once said. "And what's more important, I know who's willing to do what it takes to win."

Shero is credited with the most famous quote in Flyers history (more on that ahead), but he also authored these Sheroisms:

"Success is not the result of spontaneous combustion. You must first set yourself on fire."

"I'm like a duck: calm above the water, and paddling like hell underneath."

"There are no heroic tales without heroic tails."

Shero's quirky behavior – some say he would think nothing of sleeping in his office in the bowels of the Spectrum — baffled many of his players. Like the time he asked his defensemen to play with their sticks upside-down so that they could learn the art of body positioning.

"You know how hard it is to pass the puck with the butt end of your stick?" Watson said.

In 1972 , Ed Snider predicted the Flyers would win a Stanley Cup within five years.

Simon Nolet said Shero would conduct a variety of contests during practice.

"He used to call us the Black Aces," Nolet said. "There were five or six of us who would bet against each other. We'd drop pucks all over the ice. If you scored, you kept going; if you missed, you had to do pushups. I made a little bit of money off those games."

Shero began implementing his aggressive forechecking system right away, but it was not until his second season that players began playing it more consistently.

As winger Bob Kelly recalls, Shero instituted the KISS philosophy — Keep It Simple, Stupid — and the Flyers played it to perfection.

Fred Shero claims he knew more about his players than their wives.

"We all had roles and we were expected to play those roles," Kelly said. "That was the beauty of our team. No one wanted to be anything more than what Freddy wanted us to be."

In Shero's first three seasons as coach, the Flyers' win totals jumped from 26 to 37 to 50. And by the end of the 1973-74 regular season, the players knew they had what it took to contend for the Stanley Cup.

"With Freddy, it was always us against the world," Clarke said. "They're trying to screw us, guys. We'll show them. He took us from not being very good to the top, so we trusted him all the way."

PHILADELPHIA? FORGET IT!

While original Flyers Joe Watson, Ed Van Impe and Gary Dornhoefer were integrating newcomers Bobby Clarke, Bob Kelly and Bill Clement into the Flyers community, other new arrivals were less than enthusiastic about the prospects of playing in Philadelphia.

When Ross Lonsberry was shipped from Los Angeles to Philadelphia in a 1972 trade that included Bill Flett, Jean Potvin and Ed Joyal, Joyal refused to report to the Flyers. Lonsberry wished he hadn't.

"I flew in there in the dead of winter and the first thing I saw was that scrap heap (you know, the one beneath the Penrose Avenue Bridge)," Lonsberry said. "I thought, 'What am I doing here?' I was in a state of depression."

Lonsberry said he attended his first practice with the Flyers in Philadelphia, visited Rexy's Bar and Restaurant in West Collingswood Heights with a few teammates, got into his car, drove back to Philadelphia International Airport, and caught a flight back to Los Angeles.

"I went AWOL," he said.

The next day, Flyers general manager Keith Allen phoned Lonsberry in L.A.

"He said, 'Where the hell are you?'" Lonsberry said. "He convinced me Philly wasn't that bad and I came back."

COAL MINER'S SON

While the Flyers were scuffling through five straight losing seasons, a gap-toothed kid from Manitoba was emerging as their unlikely savior. Bobby Clarke grew up in the working-class town of Flin Flon, where his father, Cliff, worked the mines.

As a teenager Clarke spent three years in those mines, working full shifts in the summers and 8 a.m. until noon in the winters, allowing him to play hockey in the afternoons and evenings.

"We got paid for eight hours in the winter," he said with a grin. "I loved it."

Because he was well under 180 pounds, Clarke was not permitted to work underground like his father, so he operated a stone crusher in the mill and earned extra money shoveling sidewalks and cutting grass "for the big shots."

Centering a line with future teammate Reggie Leach, Clarke led the Flin Flon Bombers in scoring two straight seasons, amassing 305 points. But when NHL teams shied away from him because of his diabetes, Bombers coach Pat Ginnell took Clarke to the Mayo Clinic in Minnesota and had a doctor sign a form stating that Clarke could play professional hockey if he kept his diabetes under control.

Still, Clarke was passed over 16 times in the 1969 draft, including once by the Flyers and three times by the Bruins, before Flyers scout Jerry Melnyk convinced the Flyers' scouting staff to take him 17th overall.

Melnyk had seen Clarke play and with the help of Snider and Keith Allen they talked general manager Bud Poile into selecting him.

Bobby Clarke after scoring his first of 358 goals.

"Ed Snider really wanted to get Bobby," Allen recalled. "He said to me, 'See if you can talk Bud into taking Clarkie.' Bud finally went along with it."

Clarke was invited to the Flyers' training camp that September but wasn't sure if he had the talent to play in the NHL since he'd seen only a handful of NHL games.

"I took a leave of absence from the mine because in those days I was making 8 or 9 grand a year," Clarke said. "Bud Poile offered me $7,500 to play in the NHL and I thought, 'Holy Geez! I didn't even know if I could play in the American League. I had no idea."

Clarke never spoke much about his diabetes, but when he passed out in a cab following one of his first practices with the Flyers during training camp in Quebec, players, coaches and management wondered if the team had made a mistake with the scrawny kid from Flin Flon.

Clarke said he and his roommate, Lew Morrison, overslept that morning and since Clarke didn't want to be late for practice he skipped breakfast. When he arrived at the rink his blood sugar level was dangerously low.

"It was a good learning experience for me," he said. "It had never happened to me before."

Clarke was first diagnosed with diabetes when he was 13 after he experienced rapid weight loss and blurred vision.

"I didn't know the seriousness of the disease," he said. "I just asked the doctor if I would still be able to play hockey and the doctor said, 'Sure.' In those days you only had one type of insulin and they had to measure your food. I was more careless than I should have been, but I also got way more exercise than most people, so it probably balanced itself out."

Watson, who was 25 when the Flyers drafted Clarke, said the kid made a believer out of him almost overnight.

"You looked at the guy and you just shook your head," Watson said. "He was a skinny little thing, a diabetic who had to shoot himself up every day. Holy Geez, that's got to be tough. He'd take that glucose during games. He'd put it in his mouth and on his tongue. My God, it was terrible."

To keep his blood sugar levels in balance, Clarke made a habit of drinking a Coke before games and fruit juice between periods. Teammates recall that Clarke would not only do anything to win; he'd do anything to simply play.

Said Watson, "He played with three cracked ribs and a flak jacket. He played in pain so much we thought we all should be able to do it. And he played with so much intensity that we all started thinking, 'If we all played like Bob Clarke, we'd never lose.'"

HUMBLE BEGINNINGS

Clarke didn't exactly take the NHL by storm. On his NHL shift against the Minnesota North Stars on Oct. 11, 1969, Bill Goldsworthy stripped him of the puck and scored.

"I thought, 'Oh man.' But (coach) Vic Stasiuk loved me and he played the crap out of me."

Clarke lacked size and strength but he seemed to carry a nastiness the Flyers needed against bigger and stronger opponents like the Blues.

"Eddie Van Impe didn't fight very good, but he was really crude," Clarke said. "Guys were scared of Eddie on the opposition. And I could use my stick a little bit. We could cause some damage, even though we weren't a tough team."

FIGHT NIGHTS IN THE STANDS

By Clarke's third season, the Flyers had gotten tougher with the addition of young rookies Bob Kelly and Don Saleski.

"All of a sudden we went from getting pushed around to getting even," Clarke said. "St. Louis and the Bruins bullied everybody before us. We were accused of starting it all, but we were the ones who got tired of getting beat up. When we got to the top we took full advantage of it. It felt pretty good, actually."

In the early days of the Broad Street Bullies, fights were not necessarily limited to the ice.

On Jan. 6, 1972, St. Louis Blues coach Al Arbour was arguing a call by a referee at the Spectrum after the second period when a fan emptied a beer on the already irate coach. Bob Plager was so incensed he climbed into the stands to find the perpetrator. Several teammates followed him, swinging their sticks at fans until police broke up the melee.

Arbour had his shirt torn during the ruckus and needed 10 stitches to close a cut on his head. He finished the game wearing a sport coat, undershirt and tie.

"It got a little vicious," Allen said with a chuckle.

"It was fun," Clarke added.

Even the docile Rick MacLeish enjoyed getting into scraps.

After the game, Arbour and three players were charged with disorderly conduct and assault and battery of policemen.

The Blues had so much fun climbing into the stands that year the Flyers figured they'd try the same thing the following season in Vancouver.

During a game against the Canucks, a young Bob Kelly was chucking knuckles with Jim Hargreaves when Don Saleski grabbed the Canucks' Barry Wilcox and put him in a headlock.

While Saleski was squeezing, a Vancouver fan who was later identified as a dentist, reached over the glass and grabbed a hold of Saleski's wiry hair.

Flyers backup goalie Bobby Taylor saw his buddy's loose afro getting yanked like a rag doll, so he jumped off the bench, climbed into the stands and began throwing punches. So did teammates Barry Ashbee, Ed Van Impe, Andre Dupont and Bill Flett.

Hockey sticks whirled like helicopters, but fans escaped serious injuries and the game resumed. Later, six Flyers were charged with assault and fined $500.

"We may have gone a little overboard there," Allen said.

"If you did that now they'd suspend you for life," Clarke said. "Fans liked it. It filled buildings."

The Flyers had quickly become the most feared team in the NHL and the sportswriters who covered the team began kicking around nicknames. Following that post-Christmas road trip, Jack Chevalier, who wrote for the Evening Bulletin at the time, referred to the team as the Mean Machine, the Bullies of Broad Street and Freddy's Philistines.

The next day, a headline in the Bulletin read: "Broad Street Bullies Muscle Atlanta."

The Flyers had themselves an identity.

CLARKE'S LEGEND GROWS

Clarke's reputation as a fiery competitor who would do anything to win a hockey game became legendary in Game 6 of the 1972 Summit Series between Team Canada and Team USSR on Sept. 24, 1972 in Moscow.

Billed as a battle for world hockey supremacy, Team USSR held a 3-1-1 record after five games of the eight-game tournament, which began in Montreal and moved to Toronto, Winnipeg and Vancouver before shifting to Moscow for the final four contests.

Valery Kharlamov had been Russia's best player throughout the tournament and according to John Ferguson, Sr., who at the time was an assistant coach of Team Canada, Clarke was asked to put him out of the series.

"I called Clarke over to the bench, looked over at Kharlamov and said, 'I think he needs a tap on the ankle.'" Ferguson Sr., was quoted as saying years later. Clarke says he never remembers those words, but it didn't stop him from taking a two-handed swipe at Kharlamov's left ankle early in the second period of Canada's 3-2 victory.

"We had a bit of a rile going on the ice," Clarke said of Kharlamov."He jabbed me and took off, so I chased him down the ice and gave him a whack across the ankle. It was that type of series. I didn't need to respond that way, but it seemed appropriate at the time."

Kharlamov sat out Game 7 and was ineffective in Game 8 as Team Canada rallied to win the series with a 4-3-1 record.

BRING BACK BERNIE

With the Broad Street Bullies intact, the Flyers fought their way to their first-ever playoff series victory in 1973 when they defeated the Minnesota North Stars in six games. The series is most remembered for Gary Dornhoefer's breakaway overtime goal against Cesare Maniago to give the Flyers a 3-2 win in Game 5.

The Flyers were eliminated by the Montreal Canadiens in the second round of those playoffs. They were missing something and Keith Allen knew exactly what it was.

Shortly after the play-off defeat Allen tried to correct an earlier mistake by bringing popular goal-tender Bernie Parent back to the Flyers.

Allen had traded Parent to the Toronto Maple Leafs in 1971, then used one of those assets, Mike Walton, to acquire Rick MacLeish from the Boston Bruins.

Allen's trade of Parent left Flyers fans feeling betrayed. One banner at the

Gary Dornhoefer soars over goaltender Cesare Maniago in 1973.

25

Spectrum showed their displeasure over the trade. It said, "Judas, Benedict Arnold and now Keith Allen."

"The damn thing hung there for months," Allen said.

Allen gave up a first-round pick and goalie Doug Favell to get Parent and a second-round pick that turned out to be Larry "Izzy" Goodenough.

CHAPTER 2

GOD BLESS THE FLYERS
(1973–1976)

Never-told stories about the Flyers' rise to greatness,
their quirky head coach, and the record-setting
Stanley Cup victory parades.

A LEADER OF MEN

TO MOST FANS, BOBBY CLARKE WAS A TIRELESS HOCKEY
player. But to his teammates he was like an army general leading his team to battle
78 times a year.

To his teammates, Bobby Clarke
was the ultimate hockey warrior.

"Clarkie, to me, was as much like Robert E. Lee as anybody I can imagine," said former teammate and current television analyst Bill Clement. "When Robert E. Lee tried to lead his troops into battle at the head of the front, his troops would silently gather around his horse, shoulder him and escort him to the back of the lines because they didn't want him hurt.

"A lot of teams thought that Bobby never fought his own battles. Bobby Clarke fought his battles long before Dave Schultz ever played with him. If anybody did anything to Bobby, it was absolutely instinctive – because of what he meant to our team — for guys to back him up and protect him.

"He was our leader. He never said, 'Hey, will you help me and step in here?' Had nobody stepped in, Clarke would have fought to the death, I'll guarantee you that. He epitomized what a leader was."

How does Clarke remember himself? As the greatest Flyer who ever lived? "I just played as hard as I could every night," he said. "That's it."

By doing so, Clarke set the standards of an organization.

"If it wasn't for Bob Clarke," said Ed Snider, "I wouldn't be flying around in a private jet."

READY FOR PRIME TIME

Before the afternoon of May 19, 1974, Philadelphia had long been regarded, even by its own residents, as the City of Losers. For months, the Flyers fought to change that perception, even if it meant locking horns with league executives on a daily basis.

"My phone would ring late in the afternoon and it was always (NHL commissioner) Clarence Campbell," Keith Allen recalls. The conversations would start out with a pleasant, 'Hi, Clarence."

"But five minutes later we were swearing at each other," Allen said. "He wasn't too popular in my house."

Allen said the entire NHL hated what the Flyers were doing to hockey, but loved the results.

"We filled up every damn building in the world," Allen said.

By the end of the 1973-74 regular season the Flyers had fashioned a 50-16-12 record and had sold out 68 of their 78 games, including all 39 in the Spectrum.

They swept the Atlanta Flames four games to none in the Stanley Cup Quarterfinals, then survived a seven-game war with the New York Rangers. Next up were the Stanley Cup Finals and the Big Bad Bruins, a team the Flyers had not beaten in Boston Garden in more than six years

"We flew into Boston, where the Bruins had been waiting to play us for seven days (after beating Chicago 4-2 in the semifinals)," Joe Watson recalled. "I pick up the paper and Freddy's saying how we just beat the best team in the league. I said, 'Holy Geez, Freddy! Are you trying to get us killed?'"

"No, Joe," Shero replied. "Just a little reverse psychology."

"And you know what?" Watson said. "It worked."

Clarke still believes the Bruins had better players, but the Flyers had a better coach, a better goaltender and a better team.

"Even though they were the favorites, we had all the elements to beat them," he said. "We were way more dedicated. During the Finals, when they came to Philly they'd got to the (race) track and we'd go to the rink."

BEAT UP ON ORR

Shero's game plan against the Bruins deviated from most coaches. Instead of denying Hall of Fame defenseman Bobby Orr the puck, Shero told his players to let him have it — literally. He instructed his players to drill Orr every chance they could. By the end of the series, Orr was worn down.

"The golden rule was never shoot the puck in Orr's corner, give it to somebody else to handle," recalled Watson. "But Freddy said, 'We're going to shoot the puck in his corner and make him go back and get it.'

"Every time he went to get it, we'd take the body, get in his way and make him exert some energy because the buildings were so hot."

The Flyers lost their first game in Boston Garden by a 3-2 score, then won Game 2 on a momentous overtime goal by Clarke.

"I remember sitting on the bus as we were leaving Boston that night," said Flyers center Terry Crisp, "and saying, 'They know we're for real now. We can really win this series.'"

The physical style employed by Shero took its toll on his own players as well.

Many believe Clarke's overtime goal in Boston turned the series in the Flyers' favor.

"Before the third game I was in the whirl pool because I had torn knee ligaments and I couldn't even walk," Clement said. "Clarkie came up to me and said, "We've got two guys up from the minors who can't do the job you do, even if you're just killing penalties.' I warmed up on one leg and I played the last four games of that series. By the end, my leg was raw meat. But it felt great."

WIN TOGETHER NOW ...

The Flyers returned to the Spectrum, where they won the third and fourth games of the series to take a 3-1 lead.

It was after winning Game 3 that Shero scribbled on the dressing room chalkboard a mantra that has become a staple of the Flyers' philosophy: "Win together now and we will walk together forever."

"Everybody has clichés and everybody uses phrases," Crisp said. "But that is one that has really stuck with me wherever I go. Freddy said, 'You know what fellas? You won't realize what you've done as a team until 10, 12, 15 years down the road. He was dead-on right."

When the Flyers returned to Boston for Game 5 they were handed a 5-1 beating. Orr dominated early, setting up the Bruins' first goal and scoring their second.

It was the worst defeat of the playoffs for the Flyers, but they were returning to the Spectrum, where they had lost just six games all season, for the pivotal Game 6.

"We knew we weren't going back to Boston, so it didn't matter," said Flyers center Rick MacLeish.

Game 6 began on a brilliantly sunny afternoon in Philadelphia in front of a national television audience. But before the game, Flyers goaltender Bernie Parent was trapped in a smoke-filled room.

"I smoked a pack of cigarettes this morning, and I'm not a smoker," Parent would say hours later.

Prior to Game 6, the Flyers had quietly arranged for Kate Smith to make her second live appearance at the Spectrum and as she stepped onto a red carpet, Bobby Orr and Phil Esposito greeted her with a bouquet of flowers in an obvious attempt to change the course of history.

"They wanted to break the curse," recalled Snider. "It didn't work."

With Boston's Terry O'Reilly in the penalty box for hooking Bill Barber at the 13:58 mark of the first period, the Flyers scored the most memorable goal in their history. Fifty seconds after O'Reilly's penalty, MacLeish won a faceoff in the offensive right circle, dropped a pass back to defenseman Andre Dupont and broke for the net.

"I tried to time it so that I was in front of the net when Moose shot it," MacLeish said. "He took a low wrist shot — about a foot off the ice – and I got my blade on it."

The puck caromed behind Bruins goaltender Gilles Gilbert for a power-play goal and a 1-0 Flyers lead. With 20 minutes separating the Flyers from becoming the first NHL expansion team to win the Stanley Cup, the game became a tight-checking war.

Looking tired and frustrated, the Bruins took two penalties with less than five minutes remaining in the game. When a dejected and exhausted Orr went off for holding with just 2:12 remaining, the Flyers knew the Cup would be theirs.

"It paid off," Watson said of Shero's game plan against the Bruins' Hall of Fame defenseman. "Orr was dominating in the first five games of the series, but in the last game, he was tired. He took that penalty because he was tired."

The Spectrum was so loud at the end of the Flyers' Cup–clinching victory that defenseman Joe Watson could not hear the final horn.

Clarke said the Flyers' victory lap in Philadelphia was ruined by the fans.

As Orr's penalty expired and the clock ticked toward 0:00, Watson found himself standing over the puck behind the Flyers net.

"There was still two or three seconds left, but I didn't want to touch the puck because it would have been an icing call," Watson said. "Wayne Cashman came toward me, so I touched the puck. But the crowd was so loud, the timekeeper never heard the whistle."

With Watson still wondering what to do, fans streamed onto the ice and Parent, the Conn Smythe Trophy winner as playoff MVP, was mobbed by his teammates. Parent and Clarke were awarded the Stanley Cup and one of the most congested victory laps in Stanley Cup history took place on the Spectrum ice.

"It got ruined, I think, because so many fans got on the ice," Clarke said. "There was no real way to celebrate on the ice."

"That was mayhem," Clement said. "We were robbed of what we all dreamed about, skating around the ice with the Stanley Cup. Instead, players were punching people and pulling them off the Cup."

Afterward, in a champagne- and beer-soaked Flyers dressing room, a respectful Orr made his way through the crowd to congratulate Watson. Five years earlier, Orr had served as Watson's best man in his wedding.

Watson, holding a bottle of champagne, asked Orr if he'd like a little drink.

"No thanks," Orr replied.

"Why not?" insisted Watson.

"I don't deserve it," Orr said.

PARTY TIME

While the Flyers were celebrating their championship inside the locker room, fans from Wilmington, Delaware to Mount Holly, New Jersey were whooping it up.

"The celebration started instantly," Clarke said. "It was a three-day party that, for some of us, lasted three months."

Horns hocked through the night, as did drunken renditions of "God Bless America."

"There were parties all over," Clarke said.

The Flyers normally celebrated post-game victories at Rexy's, just over the Walt Whitman Bridge. But a mob scene at Rexy's prevented players from getting close to the bar and all the players made their way to Compton's in nearby Haddon Township.

"It actually worked out for the best," Clarke said. "We would have never been able to get through that crowd at Rexy's. We had a chance to celebrate together and nobody knew where we were."

Fred Shero enjoys the sweet taste of success.

Gene Hart leads the caravan of convertibles.

The next day Philadelphia organized a victory parade and expected a few hundred thousand spectators. An estimated 2 million showed up. It took three hours for the motorcade to make its way from the Spectrum to City Hall.

"It was a disaster," Clement said. "People were jumping all over the cars, trying to climb in through the sunroof. I was a smoker back then and I was burning people's hands with my cigarette to get them off the car."

Clement said police horses were used to thrust spectators away from the cars so the parade could continue.

"Scary cannot be considered enjoyable," Clement said. "We were afraid."

When the motorcade finally arrived at City Hall, Clarke was nowhere to be found. He had shared a Cadillac convertible car with his wife, Sandy, and when spectators threw everything imaginable at and into the car, Clarke asked his driver to turn off Broad Street and head in the other direction.

"It was his own personal car and it was beautiful, but people were throwing cans of beer and it just got filled with junk," Clarke said. "We couldn't get through and I finally said to the guy, 'Let's get back to the Spectrum.' He was relieved because his car was getting beat up.'"

Saleski said the car he rode in stalled outside the Spectrum and five guys pushed it all the way to City Hall.

"I wore one of those short-sleeved suits that were popular then," Saleski recalled. "And by the end of the parade, the sleeve was torn off. It was amazing."

"It was the first championship in God knows how long," said Terry Crisp. "They didn't care if it was ping pong or tiddly winks. They wanted a championship and we gave it to them."

More than 2 million people attended the first victory parade.

Don Saleski said he had his shirt sleeves torn off in the first parade.

Clarke said he couldn't understand how a bunch of Canadians could have such an impact on a city.

"How does that happen?" Clarke said. "How do two million people come out to see guys riding in convertibles? It was a big party."

When it was time for Shero to give his words of wisdom at the microphone in front of City Hall, the coach told fans they had the greatest team in hockey, then boldly predicted, "and you're going to win the Cup again next year."

ASHBEE CALLS IT A CAREER

While the rest of the Flyers basked in the glory of a championship, Barry Ashbee was contemplating life without hockey. Ashbee's brief but distinguished career with the Flyers included his selection to the NHL All-Star Team in his final season, one which ended with him on the sidelines and the Flyers with their first Stanley Cup.

It was one of the most painful victory celebrations a winning player could ever experience. Ashbee was playing the most intense hockey of his career just two weeks earlier when, in Game 4 of the Stanley Cup semifinals, he was struck in the left eye by a slapshot off the stick of New York Rangers forward Dale Rolfe. A hush swept across Madison Square Garden as Ashbee was carted off the ice, never to return.

Barry Ashbee's career was ended when a puck struck his left eye.

"That was very emotional for me because the puck went off me and hit him," recalled Bill Flett, who in 1999 died of liver failure "Seeing him with all that blood was tough to take. I think it drove us that much harder to win the Cup."

Partially blinded by the tragic incident, Ashbee's announced his retirement on June 4, 1974, just weeks after being escorted down Broad Street in a wild ticker-tape victory parade.

A slow-footed career minor leaguer before joining the Flyers at the age of 31, Ashbee spent much of his Flyers career troubled by a cracked vertebra but is credited with molding a young defense into one of the NHL's best.

"He was a tough son-of-a-gun," Joe Watson said. "And he was always in great shape. He did cement work over the summers when he played in Hershey and I'll tell you, people paid the price when he hit them."

"I was just a kid when I met him," said Tom Bladon, a defenseman who joined the Flyers at the age of 18. "I'd never seen a guy like him. I sat beside the man for two years and saw his pain. I'd whack him on the back, forgetting he had a cracked vertebra, and he'd collapse to his knees in pain. The next period he'd be out slamming somebody against the boards."

Bladon said Ashbee's greatest characteristic, however, was his honesty.

"He was just straight forward, no frills, pick up the lunch pail and do the job," said Bladon. "If you wanted to bitch and complain he'd tell you to go do it by yourself; he didn't want to hear it."

Ashbee died of cancer at the age of 38, leaving behind a wife and two children.

Ashbee accepted an assistant coaching role under Fred Shero before the 1974-75 season, and in an emotional ceremony following that season, his No. 4 became the first Flyers jersey to be retired and a banner bearing that number was hung from the rafters of the Spectrum.

Two years later it was discovered that Ashbee had leukemia. Like everything else he faced, Ashbee took the disease head-on.

"I'll never forget the day he told us he was sick," said Watson, the recipient of the first Barry Ashbee Award, presented each season to the Flyers' top defenseman. "He said to us, 'If I'm going to die, I want to die a man.' I will never forget that."

Ashbee's battle with cancer lasted less than a month. He passed away on May 12, 1977 at the age of 38, leaving behind his wife, Donna, and two children, Heather and Danny.

Bonded by her ties with the Flyers family and concerned with the well-being of her children, Donna Ashbee, a native of Toronto, decided to remain in the Philadelphia area and has remained there ever since.

"The support the Flyers gave our family was unbelievable," Donna said. "They've been a class act from Day One."

To those who knew him well, Barry Ashbee was the picture of courage; fearless and forthright. To those he never met, he remains a beacon of hope, a symbol of promise.

If there has ever been a player who transcended time and place it is Ashbee. Through his inspiration and the Flyers' Wives Fight For Lives Carnivals, more than $20 million has been raised for the research and treatment of cancer and blood diseases.

Ashbee, who played just four seasons with the Flyers from 1970-74, remains a permanent part of the Philadelphia community, where a laboratory wing of Hahnemann University Hospital bears his name.

COWBOY BILL RIDES INTO SUNSET

Eight days after the Flyers won their first Stanley Cup, Flett became the first prominent player to be sent packing when the 31-year-old winger was shipped to Toronto in an ill-fated trade for Dave Fortier and Randy Osburn.

"I was on vacation in Puerto Rico when I found out," Flett said years later. "I was disappointed. I really liked those guys.'"

Flett played one season in Toronto, three more in Atlanta and two more in Edmonton before retiring at the age of 37 in 1980.

But before he could ease his way into retirement, Flett was forced to deal with the most horrifying experience of his life.

The father of three young sons, Flett was in his first year with the Oilers when he and his oldest son, Cody, were involved in a serious auto accident.

"It was about 2 in the afternoon and I was going westbound," Flett said. "I don't know how it happened but the car went over a half ton truck and through its tailgate. We flipped over and slid along the road before we stopped."

In a fit of rage and adrenaline, Flett said he flipped the car back on its side, crawled in and pulled his 12-year-old son out of the wreckage.

"I was so emotional," said Flett, who escaped serious injury. "I knocked out a couple cops because I wouldn't let them put me in an ambulance."

Cody had no choice. He was unconscious after the accident and remained that way for eight weeks. When he finally regained consciousness, his mental capabilities were limited, his leg needed to be re-broken and he needed a skin graft from the burns he suffered as a result of the car sliding on its roof.

Bill Flett was the first player traded from the first Cup team.

More than a year after the accident, Cody Flett was released from the hospital and years later competed in slalom skiing in Special Olympics.

Bill Flett walked away from hockey in 1980, taking a consulting job with an Edmonton company that rented machinery for work in the oil fields. He remained in that position until a second car accident nearly took his life.

"I got hit head-on by a person going 110 (mph) on cruise control," Flett said. "I shouldn't have lived. The motor of my car was sitting beside me."

Flett suffered a fractured sternum from the accident and needed doctors to "sew my left eye back in." A week later, Flett was on the golf course for a charity tournament sponsored by former Oilers teammates Wayne Gretzky and Mark Messier.

"I guess God didn't want me up there, or down there," he said. "Who knows?"

Flett said neither car accident involved alcohol but acknowledged that when he was diagnosed with a bleeding ulcer in 1993 it scared him sober.

"The doctor told me I needed to stop drinking," Flett said. "I had been drinking every day, but I was never falling-down drunk."

With the assistance of the Flyers' Alumni and longtime friend and former teammate Glen Sather, Flett entered the Betty Ford Clinic in Palm Springs, California.

"I can't say enough about the Flyers Alumni," Flett said. "Bob Kelly talked to me the most and he told me they were all supportive."

Flett spent a month in the clinic, where he participated in counseling sessions and was given strategies to combat his illness.

"You've got to realize it's a disease and live one day at a time," he said. "It can come up and grab you in a hurry."

Flett passed away of liver failure on July 13, 1999, leaving behind his wife, Doreen, and three sons: Cody, Dean and Shane.

TWICE AS NICE

On paper, there were very few changes from the Flyers' first Stanley Cup team to their second.

Thirty-eight-year-old veteran Ted Harris replaced Ashbee on defense and sniper Reggie Leach, who was acquired from the California Seals for Al MacAdam, replaced Flett on right wing. Defenseman Larry Goodenough and goaltender Wayne Stephenson took the other two roster spots vacated by forwards Bruce Cowick and Simon Nolet.

The Flyers finished the 1974-75 regular season with one more win (51) and one more point (113) than the previous season and led the NHL in penalty minutes with 1,969.

The Flyers had become as defiant as they were intimidating. In a game against the Oakland Seals early that season, Bob Kelly and Don Saleski each were suspended six games for a bench-clearing brawl in which Seals defenseman Mike Christie was held by Orest Kindrachuk while Kelly and Saleski took turns punching him.

Years later, Saleski admitted regretting the incident.

Despite their transgressions there was no denying the resolve of the Flyers, who seemed destined to back up Shero's City Hall prediction.

To get to each of their first two Stanley Cup Finals, the Flyers had to beat a New York team in a pivotal Game 7 at the Spectrum. In 1974 they beat the Rangers 4-3 to reach the finals, and in 1975, after blowing a three-game lead in the series, they beat the Islanders 4-1 after a rousing rendition of "God Bless America" by Kate Smith.

Islanders goalie Chico Resch was no fan of Kate Smith.

Smith's voice brought tears to the eyes of Watson, but Islanders goalie Chico Resch was seeing red over the pomp surrounding Smith's appearance.

"I should have skated over her wires," Resch said after the game.

REXY'S BURNS DOWN

The Flyers were still standing after that thrilling seven-game series with the Islanders, but their favorite watering hole was not.

While the Flyers were on Long Island for Game 6 of the Semifinals, Rexy's, which one year earlier was a mob scene after the Flyers won the Stanley Cup, was filled to the gills with fans watching the Mother's Day game.

It was a warm afternoon and the place was so crowded no one knew a circuit had shorted in the basement and a smoldering fire had turned into a raging inferno. When the manager of the restaurant opened the door to the basement, the combustion blew him from one room to the other.

The Flyers game was well into the third period when fire fighters and rescue workers began forcing everyone out of the restaurant, but one female patron refused to leave her bar stool.

"There was one minute left in the game and she would not go," said Kim Gaston, the daughter of long-time owner Pat Fietto. "The fire fighters literally had to pick up her up from her bar stool and carry her out."

The next day, the Flyers showed up at practice wearing black arm bands in memory of Rexy's, which reopened to the delight of their loyal patrons the following December. The restaurant remained a family-owned business for 66 years until Fietto sold it on June 24, 2009.

MACLEISH GOES BATTY

In the Stanley Cup Finals, the Flyers jumped out to back-to-back home wins against the Sabres but played as if they were in a fog in Buffalo, where the Sabres tied the series at two wins apiece.

Game 3 was as ominous as the opening scene of an Alfred Hitchcock movie as a bat swooped down to the ice level and was chopped out of the air by Sabres forward Jim Lorentz. To this day, several Flyers believe it was Rick MacLeish who swatted the bat to the ice. MacLeish says no.

"Lorentz killed it," MacLeish said. "All I did was pick the thing up." "He picked it up with his bare hand and skated it over to the penalty box," Watson recalled. "I said, 'Rick, you can get rabies off a bat.' He said, 'What are rabies?'"

Bill Clement said he knew it was Lorentz who killed the bat because Lorentz later told him he received hate mail from animal rights activists for months after the incident.

Keeping an eerie theme throughout the series, the Buffalo Auditorium turned into a house of horror for the Flyers as the humidity in the arena created a dense fog for Games 3 and 4.

Rick MacLeish says Sabres forward Jim Lorentz killed the bat, not him.

Twelve times Game 3 was stopped and players were asked to skate around in circles to lift the clouds.

"It was hotter than hell," Watson recalled. "Hotter than any building I've ever played in."

The Sabres took advantage of the conditions when Rene Robert, a member of the famed French Connection line with Gilbert Perreault and Rick Martin, ripped a long-range shot through the pads of Bernie Parent for a 5-4 win in overtime.

"Bernie said he never saw it," Clement said. "He felt it hit one of his pads and then he skated off the ice."

In Game 4, arena workers tied bed sheets to bamboo sticks and skated around the ice to dissipate the fog. The Sabres won the game 4-2 to knot the series and send it back to Philadelphia.

Clarke was upset with the effort his team gave in Buffalo and tore into many of them after the Game 4 loss.

"A lot of the wives and family were invited to Buffalo and there were some parties at the hotel," Clarke said. "I think some of the guys needed to know we were there to play hockey."

TAKING CARE OF BUSINESS

The Flyers took care of business in Games 5 and 6, getting two goals from Schultz in a 5-1 win at the Spectrum, then getting third-period goals from Bob Kelly and Clement in the 2-0 clincher in Buffalo for their second consecutive Stanley Cup.

"The difference between winning the first Cup and the second Cup," recalled Joe Watson, "was that we were hoping to win the first one and we knew we were winning the second. And you know what? We revolutionized the game."

The celebration in Buffalo was far different than the one in Philadelphia a year earlier when fans mobbed the ice and the players had no room for a victory lap.

"I don't know if Schultzie had as much fun the second time," MacLeish said. "He had nobody to hit."

Clarke said the second celebration was far more enjoyable because the players had the chance to bond on the plane ride home.

"Because we were in Buffalo it was just us celebrating," Clarke said. "It was nice."

Ed Van Impe, a rock steady defenseman on both teams, decided to refrain from alcohol after the second Cup, saying he wanted to savor every moment. He was in the minority.

The Flyers partied on the 50-minute plane ride home and when they landed in

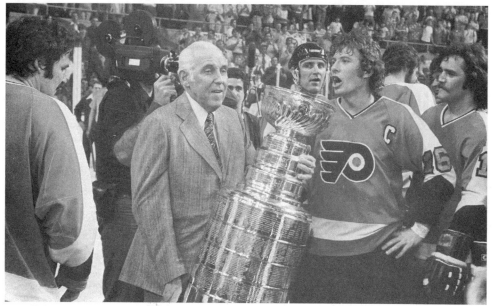

In Buffalo, Clarke and the Flyers had room to celebrate their second Cup.

Philadelphia, Clarke and Parent insisted that Shero carry the Cup down the steps of the plane.

"I'm happier this year than I was last year," Shero said at the time. "We proved it wasn't a fluke."

After being greeted by thousands of fans at the airport, the Flyers had a private party at the Blueline Club at the Spectrum, where players celebrated from 2:30 a.m. until 4:30.

The victory parade began at 11 a.m. the next day and was attended by an estimated 2.3 million spectators.

To this day, Snider says those championship celebrations are the most amazing sights he's ever seen.

"After the first parade, people said, 'Well, it's an anomaly, They only have about 17,000 fans and everybody in the city was celebrating.'

"People have always underestimated the number of hockey fans that are in this city. I mean, this city is a hockey town. We have hundreds and hundreds of thousands of fans. Our fans love the Flyers and we love them and we're very, very fortunate to have this fan base.

"Those were parades I've never seen the likes of before or since in any city."

Several Flyers said the second parade, made up of flatbed trucks, was far more organized than the first, in which each player rode in either a convertible or a car with a sunroof.

Clarke shares some bubbly with Keith Allen, Marcel Pelletier and Ed Snider.

In the second parade, players were placed on three flatbeds, the first holding team executives and Clarke and Parent, and the second two holding the rest of the players.

"The second parade was more organized, but it was pretty crazy, too," recalled MacLeish. "There were people nude clinging to telephone poles."

At one point, a Philadelphia police officer asked Shero to stop leaning over to shake hands with fans, to which he replied, "They supported us all year and what are they asking in return? Just a handshake or a chance to touch one of us. I don't think they should be denied that."

Before approaching JFK Stadium for a pep rally attended by more than 100,000, the lead float stopped at the 1500 block of South Broad St. to allow Parent the use of a bathroom in someone's rowhouse.

"I couldn't hold it in anymore," Parent recalled. "Later, I found out the people who lived there put the bowl up on their wall with a note that said, 'Bernie Parent Peed Here.'"

Terry Crisp says there is more to that story.

"Two young ladies are yelling, 'Bernie Bernie!'" Crisp recalled. "He says, 'You got a bathroom up there?' And they say, 'Yeah, yeah, come on up, Bernie!'

"Two days later in the paper there's a picture of the toilet seat bronzed. That could only happen to Bernie Parent."

Clement said he didn't get the same royal treatment as his popular netminder.

"I saw a service station, so I jumped off the float and pushed through the crowd to get a key for the men's room," Clement said. "When I got out, the flatbed was two blocks away. Fortunately, two cops recognized me. They grabbed onto my belt, put their billy clubs in front of them to form a 'V,' and pushed me through the crowd back to the flatbed."

Before the end of the parade route, at least one anonymous Flyer didn't wait to use a rest room.

"Somebody took a leak at the front of the flatbed and it rolled all the way to the back," Clarke said. "I think it was Parent, but he denies it."

Joe Watson said there was a good reason for players needing to use the rest rooms.

Reggie Leach poses with Lord Stanley, Clarke and his father.

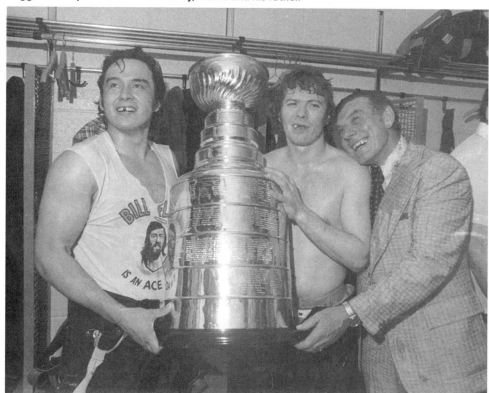

An estimated 2.3 million people attended the second Cup parade.

Bernie Parent was a welcome guest in one South Philadelphia row home.

"It had to be 90 degrees," he said. "And people were handing us drinks — whiskey, beer, water, everything."

Parent said he was overwhelmed by the joy in people's faces that day, but remembers the concern expressed by Philadelphia Mayor Frank Rizzo, who sat next to Parent on the lead float.

"He kept looking at the tops of the buildings and I said, 'Frank, what are you looking at?'" Parent said. "He said, 'Snipers.' And I said, 'Frank, the season is over. I'm not making any more saves.'"

The Flyers did not realize it at the time, but their back-to-back titles would be a harbinger of the greatest era in Philadelphia sports history. Five years later the Phillies won their first World Series and the Eagles played in their first Super Bowl. Before 10 years had passed the 76ers also won an NBA title.

"We brought a lot of happiness to the area at a time when it needed it," Watson recalled. "The Vietnam War was just getting over at that time and there was a lot of unemployment in Philadelphia. We came along at the right time and gave the area a boost."

ONE–HIT WONDER

Dave Schultz recorded an NHL record 472 penalty minutes in 1974-75, leaving an indelible mark as one of the game's most feared bullies. Standing 6-foot-1 and weighing 185 pounds, small by today's enforcer standards, Schultz was required to fight so often that when he injured his wrist in a fight, he wrapped his hands with tape for protection.

"There were times after games that I'd put my hands in buckets filled with ice and I wasn't even hitting helmets the way they are today," Schultz said.

The NHL responded with what was dubbed the "Schultz Rule," banning hand wraps. Schultz said the scariest injury he ever suffered actually came after a fight with Bruins grappler Terry O'Reilly when he smacked his head on the ice after being thrown down by O'Reilly.

"My head hit the ice and I almost got killed," Schultz said. "I really couldn't function for a week."

Schultz' greatest hits were not confined to the ice.

Two weeks after the Flyers won their second Stanley Cup, Schultz released his first and only record with a song entitled "Penalty Box." It climbed to third on WFIL's Top 40 list of popular songs:

Dave Schultz was a hit in the record stores as well.

1. I Write The Songs (Barry Manilow)
2. That's The Way I Like It (KC And The Sunshine Band)
3. Penalty Box (Dave Schultz)
4. Saturday Night (Bay City Rollers)
5. Fly, Robin, Fly (Silver Connection)
6. I Love Music (The O'Jays)
7. Sky High (Jigsaw)
8. Island Girl (Elton John)
9. Paloma Blanca (George Baker Selection)
10. Miracles (Jefferson Starship)

The "Penalty Box" chorus went something like this:

> "Baby, how long will you keep me in the penalty box?
>
> Baby, how long — it's lonely in the penalty box.
>
> You know I broke the rules, but rules are broken by fools.
>
> Baby, how long will you keep me in the penalty box?"

In just four years with the Flyers Schultz racked up 1,386 penalty minutes and his record 472 penalty minutes in 1974-75 still stands today.

Clarke and Soviet captain Boris Mikhailov were all smiles before the game.

FLYERS VS. THE WORLD

The Flyers' 1975-76 season is best remembered for a game that was meaningless in the NHL standings yet carried more national significance than perhaps any game that winter.

The Russian Hockey Federation had agreed to play an exhibition series with the NHL, pitting its top two teams against the NHL's elite. Entering its final stop on the tour, the powerful Central Red Army team had gone unbeaten against the NHL when it arrived in Philadelphia for a Jan. 11, 1976 contest at the Spectrum.

The Flyers, who at the time were the scourge of the NHL, were suddenly torch bearers for the rest of the league.

"We were the last stand," Clarke said. "The Russians had beaten the other NHL teams, but we were ready for them."

The Flyers didn't need much motivation for the game. Their hatred for the

Russians was deep-seeded. Owner Ed Snider strongly opposed the Soviets' treatment of Russian Jews and center Orest Kindrachuk had been told by his Ukraine-born grandparents about the Soviets' mistreatment of his ancestors.

As for Clarke, he was already vilified by the Russians for breaking the ankle of Kharlamov in the 1972 Summit Series.

From the opening face-off the Flyers hit the Russians at every turn, with Moose Dupont and

Ed Van Impe said he's hit several players harder than Valery Kharlamov.

Bill Barber leading the charge. With 8:39 remaining in the first period and the score tied at 0-0, Ed Van Impe busted out of the penalty box and made a bee-line toward Kharlamov, dropping him with a blind-sided elbow to the head. Kharlamov crumbled to the ice and remained there, face down, until a whistle blew to stop play.

"I've hit guys a lot harder than I hit Kharlamov," Van Impe said years later. "He wasn't hurt at all. I think they were scared to play the rest of the game because they knew we were going to keep hitting them."

The Red Army bench was incensed at the Flyers' physical tactics and after arguing with the game officials, coach Konstantin Loktev instructed his team to leave the ice and retreat back to the visiting dressing room.

Ed Snider, watching from his owner's box, immediately raced downstairs to meet with NHL president Clarence Campbell and NHL Players' Association executive director Alan Eagleson.

"They went down to their locker room ready to take off their uniforms and just leave," Snider recalled. "I asked through an interpreter what was happening and was told they were leaving."

Snider asked Eagleson if the Russian players had been paid.

"Well, they haven't been paid for this game and they haven't been paid for the entire series," Eagleson said.

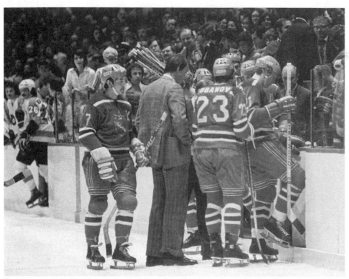
Soviet coach Konstantin Loktev leads his team off the Spectrum ice.

"We were the eighth game of the tournament and they were getting $25,000 a game — big money in those days," Snider said. "So I said, 'Why don't we tell them we're not going to pay them?' They went back to the interpreters, told them that, and they huddled together talking in their language and came back and said, 'We'll play!' They wanted American dollars."

The Russians said they would return to the ice only if the game officials agreed to rescind their impending delay of game bench penalty. The officials refused and after some more deliberating Snider's "no play, no pay" tactic prevailed and the Russians returned to the ice.

The Soviets' retreat actually backfired because when they returned the ice they found the Flyers even more resolute than before. Reggie Leach, Rick MacLeish, Joe Watson and Larry Goodenough scored in the 4-1 victory as the Flyers outshot the Russians by an overwhelming 49-13 margin.

"They just quit," Clarke said years later, still with a sneer.

"It was important that we upheld the prestige of hockey in North America," Joe Watson said. "We wanted to prove that we were the best team in hockey. We played with a lot of emotion and it showed throughout the entire game. Our intensity never let up and we were very proud of our accomplishment."

Snider's eyes still light up when he talks about that monumental victory. In fact, he still has the front page of a Soviet newspaper from the following day.

"It shows big behemoths with Flyers logos beating the Russian players with big clubs," Snider said. "I can't tell you how much I love that cartoon."

The Flyers' conquest of the Soviets left a lasting impression on a 17-year-old forward from Timmins, Ontario as well.

"The Flyers managed to chase a whole political system out of the building that day, not just a team," Dave Poulin said. "They chased Communism out of the Spectrum."

A TEAM WITH HART

Play–by–play voice Gene Hart was one of the Flyers' best storytellers.

One of the best storytellers in Flyers history was their robust television play-by-play man, Gene Hart. His ability to colorfully describe hockey to an uneducated region was second only to his ability to spin a tale.

"He was as much a part of the team as me or Bob Kelly or any other guy who played," Bill Barber said. "I think us winning and his voice kind of blended in together."

One of Hart's favorite tales goes something like this:

On one of the Flyers' long bus rides after a tough road loss, Fred Shero ordered the team's bus driver to stop at a roadside bar. Shero told his players to remain on the bus as he slipped into the bar.

Moments later, he emerged with several cases of beer and the bus erupted in cheers. As the cold beverages were distributed from the front of the bus to the back, loud-mouthed defenseman Joe Watson realized the bottles did not have twist-off caps. Elation quickly turned to frustration.

Shero, waiting until every player was aware of the crisis, rose from his seat, reached into his coat pocket, and pulled out a bottle opener to a round of cheers.

Here's another one of Hart's favorites:

Midway through the 1972-73 season the Flyers were celebrating a 10-5 victory in Vancouver over the Canucks. Days earlier, several Flyers were warned about being jailed for the fisticuffs they caused on the ice and in the stands in their last visit to Vancouver.

According to Hart, Moose Dupont, who had just joined the Flyers and was wearing nothing but a helmet, summed up the evening's events by saying in a thick French accent: "Great trip for us. We don't go to jail. We beat up dere chicken forwards. We score 10 goal. We win. An' now de Moose drink beer."

CHAPTER 3

BREAKING UP IS HARD TO DO

(1976–1979)

A look at the hard and unusual roads the Flyers legends took after hanging up their skates.

FROM BANKRUPTCY TO BROADCASTING

LIFE AFTER STANLEY CUP GLORY WAS NOT ALL PEACHES and cream for several members of those Stanley Cup teams.

Bill Clement lost two marriages, filed personal and corporate bankruptcy and suffered painful bouts of depression before discovering what he calls his "innermost self."

We'll pick up his story seven days after the Flyers won their second Stanley Cup. The date was June 4, 1975.

Clement had just completed his first 20-goal season in the NHL and, at the age of 25, was considered a valuable commodity around the league. The Flyers were looking to upgrade their position in the upcoming amateur draft and decided to send Clement and their first-round draft choice to the Washington Capitals for their number one pick overall (Mel Bridgman).

The deal gave Clement the dubious distinction of being the first Flyer traded from the Stanley Cup teams and sent him to a franchise that was coming off an embarrassing 8-67-5 record the previous season.

"My wife knocked on the bedroom door and said, 'Keith Allen's on the phone,'" Clement said. "And I remember sitting right up in bed and saying out loud, 'Uh-oh.' I went from the best team in the world to the worst professional team in the history of the globe."

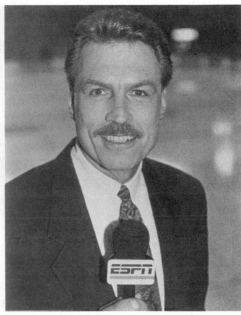

Bill Clement's first game after he was traded was against the Flyers.

The trade stunned Clement and left him groping for a way to justify it.

"I felt an overwhelming sense of having lost my life support system," he said. "The team was, and still is, everything to me. I felt absolutely isolated and lost."

What bothered Clement most was seeing the Flyers go on without him.

"The loss was all mine," he said. "They still had one another."

Ironically, Clement's first game as a former Flyer was against them in both teams' season opener the following season at the Spectrum. When he was introduced as the Capitals' captain, he received a standing ovation. Another came when he represented the Capitals in the 1976 All-Star Game in Philadelphia.

Other than that, he was treated like every other common criminal that entered the Spectrum.

"Mel Bridgman told me, 'Boy, did I ever make a mistake when I took number 10,'" Clement said with a laugh. "He said people were leaning over the glass screaming at him all the time."

Clement lasted only 52 games in Washington and was traded the day after that All-Star Game, becoming the first player in NHL history to play for three different teams (the Capitals, the Campbell Conference All-Stars and the Atlanta Flames), in three different cities on three consecutive nights.

Clement said Capitals general manager Max McNab traded him between bites of a hamburger.

"He said, 'Good game last night.'" Clement recalled. "I said, 'Yeah, I thought we had 'em.' He took a bite of his burger and said (muffling his voice) 'We had to make some changes and it's a good one for you.' He had (Atlanta general manager) Cliff Fletcher on hold and he handed the phone to me. What a way to go."

Clement finished his NHL career with the Flames, playing in Atlanta, then Calgary, from 1976-82.

Fletcher was almost as compassionate as McNab when he told Clement that the club was releasing him in the summer of 1982.

"To break the ice with Cliff, I said, jokingly, 'Well, Cliff, am I still part of the organization?' And he looked at me and said, 'No, you're not. We're fazing you out.'"

Just like that, Clement's 11-year NHL career was over.

"If I had it to do over again," Clement said, "I would have played until I couldn't walk."

NO HAT TRICK IN '76

The Flyers were literally on top of the hockey world after beating the Russians on Jan. 11, 1976 and the LCB Line of Reggie Leach, Bobby Clarke and Bill Barber was destined to become one of the greatest forward lines in hockey history.

Leach went on to become just the second player in NHL history to score 60 or more goals (Phil Esposito was the other) and Clarke netted a club record 119 points as the line combined for an NHL record 141 goals.

"That was my Roger Maris year," Leach said, referring to his career-high 61-goal outburst. "Everything I shot went into the net. Clarkie knew that if I wanted to play, I could be one of the top players in the world. He's the one who pushed me and pushed me and pushed me."

Leach's prolific regular season flowed right into the playoffs when he scored 19 goals in 16 games and became the third player in NHL history to win a Conn Smythe Trophy for a losing team.

Five of those goals came in a series-clinching 6-3 win over the Bruins in Game 5 of the Stanley Cup Semifinals, after Leach had been found passed out in his basement earlier in the day.

"Everybody in the league drank in those days, and drank a lot," said Leach, a recovering alcoholic who has been sober since 1982. "I bet 15 guys from those teams I played on had problems. That's the way hockey was back then. It was a big party."

The Flyers' hopes of a three-peat were dealt a serious blow in the spring of 1976 when injuries to Bernie Parent and Rick MacLeish sidelined them for the Finals against the bigger, faster and more skilled Montreal Canadiens.

The LCB Line combined for 141 goals in 1975–76.

Led by Guy Lafleur, Ken Dryden, Larry Robinson, Bob Gainey and Doug Jarvis, the Canadiens swept the Flyers in four games and issued in a new era of hockey in the NHL. The days of intimidating players with fists were over, replaced by size, speed and skill.

"That was one of the best teams I've ever seen," Leach said of the 1976 Canadiens, who went on to win four straight Stanley Cups. "Those guys were just hitting their peak when we played them."

Clarke agrees.

"It would have been a longer series if Parent and MacLeish played, but at that stage they were young and big and strong," said Clarke, who won his third Hart Trophy as the league's Most Valuable Player that season. "They built that team really good. Every team in the league had to change."

HOMER'S ODYSSEY

It was late in the 1975-76 season that a young and very willing left wing named Paul Holmgren began his NHL career by playing one game with the Flyers.

It was almost his first and last game in the NHL.

A few days before being recalled by the Flyers, the hulking 6-foot-3, 210-pounder from St. Paul, Minn., was cut in the eye by a skate blade when he was at the bottom of a pile of players in a game with the Richmond (Virginia) Robins of the American Hockey League.

Holmgren didn't pay much attention to the injury and played his first NHL game against the New York Rangers on March 25, dropping Phil Esposito with a menacing shoulder check.

The next night, Holmgren showed up for a 10 p.m. team meeting in Boston sporting an ugly, swollen eye and teammates Barry Ashbee and Bobby Clarke convinced him to go to the Massachusetts Eye and Ear Infirmary.

Holmgren was told he had a puncture wound that required immediate surgery.

During the surgery, Holmgren went into convulsions, apparently suffering a reaction to the anesthetic.

"They told me my heart stopped beating," Holmgren said. "But I don't remember seeing a white light or anything."

ST. PAUL VS. HAMMER

Holmgren had a full recovery from his surgery, but did not play again until the following season. On Oct. 10, 1976 he had the good fortune of becoming the first Flyer to face Dave Schultz in a fight in a home game against the Los Angeles Kings.

In his first few shifts Schultz dropped MacLeish with a cross-check and slashed Dupont, creating a stir on the Flyers bench.

"The fans gave Schultzie a nice ovation and then he starts running around hitting everyone on our team," Kelly recalled. "I said to him, 'Listen, if you keep running around like an idiot, we're going to have to go.' He didn't listen and Homer let him have it."

Holmgren removed his visor and hammered Schultz with a flurry of right fists before throwing Schultz to the ice.

But that wasn't the last time Holmgren had to take on a former Flyers legend.

Four years later, Kelly's first fight against the Flyers was against Holmgren.

Dave Schultz' first fight against the Flyers came against Paul Holmgren.

"He was a tough kid and he went after all the heavy-weights," said Kelly, who was a Washington Capital in 1980. "I knew it was coming. He let me live."

Holmgren went on to lead the Flyers in career penalty minutes with an even 1,600 in 500 games before a player built in his likeness, Rick Tocchet, surpassed him with 1,817 penalty minutes in orange and black.

Holmgren left an unusual legacy as a Flyer. During a 1977 preseason game against the Bruins at the Spectrum, Holmgren and Wayne Cashman got into a fight on the ice and were ejected from the game. As the two left the ice they continued jawing at each other until Cashman stepped into the visiting dressing room and grabbed a stick and began swinging at Holmgren.

"The next thing I knew a bunch of us were underneath the stands throwing punches," Holmgren said.

As a result of the fracas, 16 game misconducts were handed out, leaving just eight Bruins and nine Flyers to finish the game.

After the incident, workers installed an iron gate that separates the visiting locker room from the home locker room. Many still refer to it as the Holmgren-Cashman gate.

END OF AN ERA

The slow and deliberate dismantling of the Flyers continued after the 1976 Finals sweep against Montreal. Bobby Taylor and Ed Van Impe were traded to Pittsburgh and a few months later Dave Schultz was sent to the Los Angeles Kings before the start of the 1976-77 season.

Clarke said some of the camaraderie that bonded the Flyers began to wear off and it affected the play on the ice.

Shero's seven seasons with the Flyers are the longest of any coach.

"In the beginning, everybody went out after games, our wives and girlfriends, too," he said. "I think it brought us together. We liked each other. If you're on a team you're spending hours and hours together and if you don't like each other, that's what normally breaks teams up.

"After four or five years, guys start getting jealous of each other and not liking each other as much and finding different friends. It's hard to keep a good team together for a long time."

No one recognized this more than Fred Shero and after the Flyers were eliminated by the Boston Bruins in five games in the 1978 Semifinals, the well-respected coach submitted his resignation in a letter to Keith Allen.

"Freddy was a great coach and when he decided to leave I think it took us all by surprise," Allen recalled.

What took the Flyers by even greater surprise was the fact Shero was negotiating a return to the rival New York Rangers, where he began his career and would return as coach and general manager.

Shero still had another year left on his contract with the Flyers when he began talking to the Rangers. As a result, Snider refused to accept Shero's resignation and demanded compensation from the Rangers before he would release Shero from his contract.

The Rangers complied, giving the Flyers their first pick (seventh overall) of the 1978 draft and $50,000 in cash.

Hockey purists still argue that the Flyers' bully tactics under Shero left a black eye on the sport. Shero never apologized for his players' actions on the ice or off. To him, a team was like family, always defending itself against those who tried to tear it apart.

"If it comes to a confrontation between management and the players," Shero said, "I want the players to know that I'm on their side."

Shero fashioned a record of 308-151-95 with the Flyers and remains the team's all-time leader in seasons behind the bench (seven), wins (308) and winning percentage (.642).

His winning percentage was rivaled only by Mike Keenan (.638 over four seasons), Pat Quinn (.630 over four seasons) and Terry Murray (.627 over three seasons).

In New York, Shero never attained the prominence he gained with the Flyers. He was inducted into the Flyers Hall of Fame in March of 1990 after retiring from the game. Eight months later he died after a long battle with kidney disease. His legacy not only will be the back-to-back championships he brought to Philadelphia, but the indelible words he left behind.

"Every one of us loved Freddy," Leach said. "He was very innovative and we all thought he was smarter than the other coaches. He probably was."

BAD BREAK FOR THUNDERMOUTH

It was during the 1977-78 season that Watson realized his days in Philadelphia were numbered. Young defensemen Behn Wilson and Rick Lapointe were ready to become solid NHL blue liners and it had become apparent that Watson, at the age of 35, had reached the twilight of his career.

"Keith Allen called me and asked me if I'd be willing to play 30-35 games here in Philadelphia, or play an 80-game schedule somewhere else," Watson recalled. "I felt I could play a full schedule. He asked where I'd like to go and I said I'd prefer Colorado because I enjoy skiing. He phoned Colorado and a deal was made in three weeks."

Watson was sent to the Rockies for a third-round draft pick in the summer of 1978, but a gruesome knee injury on Nov. 11 prevented him from ever reaching the slopes. It also ended his playing career.

"I was going back to our zone to get the puck and the goalie went behind the net

A badly broken right leg ended Joe Watson's career.

and stopped it for me," Watson said. "I went to reach for it and (St. Louis Blues forward) Wayne Babych pushed my lower back and I just exploded into the boards.

"My leg was at a 90-degree angle and the bone was sticking out. Right then I realized my career was over."

Earlier that day, Watson had been informed that his uncle had been killed in a tragic train accident.

"He was very dear to me," Watson said. "He worked for CN Railroad up in British Columbia and it had rained for four days. He was an engineer and he came around a corner with no track and dropped 200 feet into a river. They never found the four people or the engine."

Compounding the news of his uncle's death was the discovery that Watson had broken his right leg in 13 places and there was fear he might never walk again. Watson spent six weeks in a St. Louis hospital, where he underwent three operations before returning to Philadelphia. When the bone failed to heal properly, Watson was admitted into University of Pennsylvania Hospital.

Over the course of a year and a half, Watson underwent a total of six operations to correct his damaged right leg, which is now 2½ inches shorter than his left.

"They had to take a bunch of bone out of my hip and put it in my leg," he said. "Then they took two wires and gave me electric shock every four hours so the bone would heal."

THE HOUND AND THE GOOSE

While many of the Flyers' Stanley Cup heroes were packing their bags for other NHL cities, a handful remained to keep things interesting around the locker room and in hotel rooms across North America.

One of the team's greatest pranksters was Bob Kelly.

After a team sinner during the 1978 Stanley Cup Semifinals in Boston a few players walked back to the hotel and sabotaged a few unassuming geese. To protect the guilty, we'll just call them the Boston stranglers.

One of those geese ended up in Bobby Clarke's hotel room, neatly nestled in his bed, head on a pillow and cigar in its bill.

"I came into the room," said Paul Holmgren, who was often paired with Clarke as a road roommate, "and Clarkie was lying on the bed and he said, 'What's that smell?'

"He pulled the cover down and there's a dead goose on his pillow."

Clarke wasn't the only player stunned to find a goose in an unusual place. One was found in a hotel ice machine.

Bob Kelly was one of the Bullies' best pranksters.

Clarke figured Kelly had to be the goose prankster and got him back by stuffing the fowl-smelling bird in Kelly's leather duffle bag.

Two days later Kelly went to pack for the team's return trip to Philadelphia.

"Let's just say goose feathers and leather didn't go well together," he said. "I had to throw both of them away."

Kelly was behind many of the pranks pulled by the Flyers in the 1970s. He remembers an obnoxious pair of cowboy boots worn by goaltender Wayne Stephenson.

"They were bad ugly and we told him, 'Just don't wear those things around us,'" Kelly said.

When Stephenson showed up at the University of Penn Class of '23 practice rink wearing the boots, Kelly waited until he got on the ice, cut the toes off the boots and glued them to the ceiling above Stephenson's locker.

"If you didn't do it to somebody else, they'd do it to you," Kelly said. "We flew commercial, so if you were late getting to the luggage carousel, your clothes were everywhere. Clarkie was the only one who didn't care what we did to his clothes because he did those silly Jack Lang commercials and got all his clothes for free."

Of course, dishing out pranks comes with its own perils.

Kelly remembers packing one pair of dress pants for an overnight road trip to Minnesota and coming home with one of his pant legs cut off.

"It was pretty embarrassing walking through the airport," he said.

BERNIE MAKES HIS FINAL SAVE

The night of Feb. 17, 1979 was not unlike any of the other 607 games Bernie Parent had played in his professional career.

Moving gracefully from one side of his net to the other, the Flyers' goaltender thwarted shot after shot as the Flyers and New York Rangers engaged in another of their heated battles.

But, in the blink of an eye, it ended.

Late in the first period, a shot from the point headed toward Parent. His defenseman, Jimmy Watson, became entangled with Rangers forward Don Maloney and with one swift motion, the blade of Watson's stick entered the eye hole of Parent's goaltender's mask, an opening no larger than the size of a half dollar.

Parent instinctively grabbed his face and rushed to the Flyers' bench. Hours later he was told he'd suffered two small conjunctional tears in his right eye. His depth perception would never be the same and just like that his life as a professional athlete was over at the age of 33.

"It was like hitting a brick wall like this," Parent said, slapping his hand against a cinder block wall inside the Spectrum, "because you're not prepared."

From the time he could tie his own skate laces as a young boy in Montreal until his final frightening moments as a Flyer, Parent was consumed with the sport of ice hockey. Thirteen years in the NHL had not prepared him for the day he'd retire.

"It was scary because one day you're playing in the National Hockey League, the next day you're wondering what the heck you're going to do with your life," he said.

"It's not the same kind of situation like today's athletes. With the amount of

Bernie Parent speaks with reporter Bill Fleischman after a game.

money they're making, it's not a faze they have to worry about."

Parent's biggest concern was his lack of skills outside the world of hockey. In a matter of days, he had gone from the top of one profession to the bottom of another.

"It's scary because within yourself, you know you don't have any training to do anything else. I had no self worth, that's what was missing in me."

Desperate to fill the void in his life, Parent turned to alcohol.

"I can only speak for my own situation, but it wasn't fulfilling whatever my needs were," he said.

With the Flyers' support, Parent went back to school, taking courses in business, marketing and public relations. Those courses gave him enough confidence to experiment with the business side of hockey.

The Flyers gave Parent his first job in public relations in 1980, then appointed him as the first goaltending coach in the team's history a year later.

"I knew there was something out there I could do besides playing hockey, but I wasn't sure what it was," Parent said. "It took me years before I finally found my niche."

Now, Parent is happily semi-retired, splitting time between the Jersey shore and special appearances for the Flyers throughout the Delaware Valley.

"I'm very, very happy," Parent said. "To get up in the morning and see the sun come up, it's just nature at its best. I really enjoy that. The water takes on a different life."

CHIEF'S NEW CAREER

Very seldom does a professional player achieve more fame after his playing career than during it. But to hockey fans in Philadelphia and Tampa Bay, Bobby Taylor's work in front of a camera has overshadowed his work inside the goal crease.

Shortly after being traded along with Ed Van Impe for Pittsburgh's Gary Inness on March 9, 1976, Taylor met with Penguins general manager Wren Blair to see where he fit into the organization.

"First he told me he wanted me in Hershey (Pittsburgh's AHL affiliate), then he said he wanted me in Pittsburgh, then he wanted me in Hershey again," Taylor recalled. "I started in the worst hockey league in the world (with the Eastern League's Jersey Devils) and I wasn't about to go backward."

Taylor, who was 31 at the time, said he refused to go back to riding buses and stormed out of Blair's office. Moments later, he realized he had just ended his playing career.

"I thought, 'Smart move, Indian. Now what are you going to do?'"

Bill Foody, a longtime neighbor of Taylor's in Medford Lakes, New Jersey, suggested he try broadcasting.

At the time, Flyers color analyst Don Earle had another year remaining on his television contract with Channel 48 and the Flyers were less than thrilled with Taylor's lack of experience behind a microphone.

Lou Scheinfeld was starting up PRISM at the time and was looking to hire his first broadcaster. Taylor, who had a marketing degree from Seattle University but no broadcasting experience, seemed like a good gamble. He teamed with Channel 10's Hugh Gannon as PRISM's first broadcasting duo.

"We did everything but baseball and basketball," Taylor said. "We did Marvin Hagler's first professional fight (he lost to Willie "The Worm" Monroe at the Spectrum). We did the Cowtown Rodeo. I interviewed Olga Korbut, Eammon Coughlin, Dwight Stones. I did more in my first year than most people do in a career."

But it wasn't enough to pay the bills.

"I was getting a hundred bucks an event," Taylor recalled, "and I might have had 55 events that year."

Taylor said he was forced to become PRISM's second half of a two-man marketing team (former Phillies infielder Terry Harmon was the other half). In his first year with PRISM, he put 30,000 miles on his car trying to sell potential subscribers on the concept of cable television.

"I'd go door-to-door, I'd do advertising over the phone, I even cut and pasted the newspaper ads," he said. "It wasn't unusual for me to try to sell PRISM to a cable company in Allentown, then drive to Atlantic City and do a fight the same night."

When Earle finished out his contract with the Flyers in 1977, Taylor was hired as Gene Hart's partner and became one of hockey's first ex-jocks in the television booth.

"I think Gene might have resented the fact that I came right out of hockey," Taylor said. "He paid his dues. He did high school football games in bad weather and worked his way on up. It took a couple years before we were comfortable with each other."

Taylor said the most difficult adjustment for him as an announcer was knowing when to speak and what to say.

"You never realize how bad you are at English until you hear yourself on the air," he said. "I had to remind myself to get out of that locker room talk and begin analyzing the game."

Bob Taylor interviews Lou Nolan for Prism.

Taylor said the most important lesson he learned from Hart was the value of game preparation.

"I learned a hell of a lot from Gene," he said. "People think color guys just (talk) about the game. I'd spend two or three hours going over each guy in the lineup and I might get to use two minutes of that on the air. There is so much research you never use."

But there was a significant flaw in his approach to broadcasting and Taylor knew what it was.

"It took a long time for me to be able to criticize a player," he said. "Most of those guys I went through wars with. I didn't think I had a right to criticize them."

It was former Boston Bruins great Ed Westfall who helped influence Taylor's change of heart.

"Eddie told me that if you're constantly praising these guys, people will stop believing you," Taylor said."To have any credibility, you have to praise and criticize. You can't just say what happened, people want to know why."

When Taylor's 15-year career as a Flyers announcer ended in 1993, he was hired as a color analyst by Lightning president and general manager Phil Esposito and has been there ever since.

Taylor said the Flyers kept him on their payroll during his four months between broadcast jobs.

"That's the way they treat people," he said. "That's one reason I'll always respect the Flyers."

BIG BIRD FLIES THE COOP

When Don Saleski saw his playing time reduced under new coach Bob McCammon in the 1978-79 season, he asked to be traded. Keith Allen obliged, sending him to the Colorado Rockies for future considerations.

"I still don't know who they were" Saleski said of the players, if any, the Flyers received in return.

Don Saleski couldn't find the same success in Colorado that he enjoyed in Philadelphia.

Saleski and his family moved to Colorado but found themselves back in Philadelphia two years later. Saleski said it wasn't until he played in another city that he truly understood what it meant to be part of a championship team.

"As a group, we peaked pretty early," Saleski said of the Stanley Cup teams. "And when each of us was traded to other teams, there was an aura that surrounded us. The expectations people had for us were greater than we were able to meet.

"Teams would make us captains and expect us to be their leaders. We all weren't leaders in Philadelphia. We had very defined roles, and when we were pulled away from each other, none of us produced the same results."

In fact, of the 27 players who were on one or both of the Flyers' Stanley Cup teams in 1974 and 1975, none went on to win another Stanley Cup in another NHL city.

CHAPTER 4

THE STREAKERS AND THE SMURFS

(1979–1984)

The people and stories behind the longest unbeaten streak in professional sports history, followed by three seasons of playoff futility and the retirement of Bobby Clarke.

BOB WHO?

THE FLYERS' SEARCH FOR A REPLACEMENT FOR THE legendary Fred Shero led them to Bob McCammon, a little-known 37-year-old coach who had coached the Port Huron Flags of the International League and the Maine Mariners of American League, but had never managed an NHL bench.

Despite a record of 87–51–20, Bob McCammon could not get the Flyers past the first round of the playoffs.

Suffice it to say not every Flyer took an immediate liking to McCammon.

"Bob McCammon? Who was he?" Reggie Leach remarked recently. "He couldn't coach his way out of a wet paper bag. We clashed all the time. He picked on me every chance he could."

McCammon lasted just 50 games and was replaced by Pat Quinn, a mountain of a man who could make players shake in their skates simply by shooting them a stare.

"To be honest, I was kind of intimidated by Pat," said Holmgren, one of the organization's most intimidating players. "He had this presence. He was a big man and people snapped to attention when he walked in a room."

As fate would have it, Shero's Rangers faced Quinn's Flyers in the second round of the 1979 playoffs and after an overtime victory in Game 1, the Flyers got smoked in four straight, getting outscored 26-5 in the defeats.

Clearly, it was time for a change.

QUINN TAKES ACTION

The Flyers began the 1979-80 season caught between the past and the future but they played like there was no tomorrow.

A big reason was Quinn's big gamble. With young speedsters Kenny Linseman, Brian Propp, Al Hill and Tom Gorence joining forces with veterans Bill Barber,

Pat Quinn's intricate breakout systems confused his players as much as they did opposing defenses.

Bobby Clarke, Rick MacLeish and Reggie Leach, Quinn decided to employ a new offensive system that encouraged wingers to leave the boards and weave in and out of center ice.

"Up until then, the NHL went north and south," Clarke said. "It was a stop-and-go game. Pat's system put everybody in motion."

"It not only confused other teams," Holmgren said, "it confused us."

Quinn's system worked to perfection in a season-opening 5-2 win over the upstart Islanders, but a 9-2 loss the next night in Atlanta had Quinn wondering if it was time to forget the whole thing.

"To get beat by that score was startling," Quinn said. "I

couldn't yell at the guys. I was too busy trying to establish my style."

Pete Peeters, an unassuming 22-year-old rookie on that 1979-80 team, didn't spend too much time dwelling on the 9-2 loss.

"I don't think many people expected much from us," he said. "We weren't even picked to make the playoffs."

COURT MARSHAL HIM!

One night after getting blitzed by the Flames, the Flyers were clinging to a 4-3 lead against the Maple Leafs when back-to-back penalties put them down two men for the remainder of the game.

That's when Bob Kelly hatched a plan.

Figuring another penalty would not change the number of players on the ice – teams can play with no less than three skaters at any given time – Kelly hopped over the boards on a line change to give the Flyers a fourth skater.

Kelly was hit with a "too many men on the ice" penalty and the referee awarded Darryl Sittler a penalty shot.

"I should have court marshaled him!" Quinn said.

Peeters stopped Sittler on the free shot, Clarke won a key defensive faceoff in the closing seconds and – lo and behold – the first victory of The Streak was in the books.

It would be 84 days before the Flyers lost another game.

FOR PETE'S SAKE

The Flyers began the 1979-80 season without a true No. 1 goalie. Pete Peeters was a promising rookie and Phil Myre, who was added in a trade over the summer, was a well-traveled veteran.

Six games into the season, with the club on a modest three-game win streak, Quinn decided to give his rookie goalie his first start in the Montreal Forum.

Maybe Peeters was still in shock from paying the dinner bill the night before in Detroit – "I thought I was paying for my own meal and when I saw the liquor bill I almost fell off my chair!" – because during the morning skate in Montreal, Peeters could feel the ghosts of the Forum – Howie Morentz, Rocket Richard, Boom Boom Geoffrion – skating by him and whispering in his ears.

"It was alive," he said, "even when nobody was in there."

Hours later, Peeters must have felt like the Ghost from Christmas Past because he gift-wrapped three quick goals and was yanked in favor of Myre.

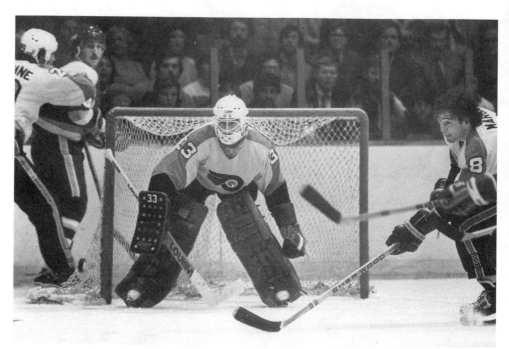

Pete Peeters went 29-5-5 with a 2.73 goals-against average in his rookie season with the Flyers.

"Here I was playing against the Canadiens in the Forum," Peeters said. "I'm in the net and I'm thinking, 'Holy Smokes! There goes Guy Lafleur!' 'Hey, that's Bob Gainey and Steve Shutt and Larry Robinson!' I thought I was watching Hockey Night in Canada on TV and the next thing you know I'm sitting on the bench."

The Flyers rallied back for a 6-6 tie and with their unbeaten streak at four games, their confidence began to build.

"We kind of stumbled our way along, but 10 games became 15 and then 20 and it was like – Holy Mackerel! - let's see how long this can go," said Clarke. "Everybody wanted to beat us."

COMEBACK STREAKERS

The Flyers' 35-game unbeaten streak – still the longest by a professional team in North America — lasted from Oct. 14 until Jan. 7. During that time they stormed back from a three-goal deficit one time, erased a two-goal deficit eight times and rallied to either win or tie a game in the third period six times.

"We knew that if we were one or two goals down we were going to tie it," Leach said. "If we were down, Clarkie would come up to me and Billy (Barber) and say, 'It's time to go to work.'"

There were some hairy moments when the streak was in peril. On Dec. 6, with the streak at 21 games, the Flyers stormed back from a 3-0 deficit to beat the Los Angeles Kings at home, 9-4.

On Dec. 13, with the streak at 24 games, they trailed the Quebec Nordiques 3-1 early in the third period, then scored five times to win 6-4.

And on Dec. 20 in Pittsburgh, with the Flyers attempting to tie the Bruins for the NHL's all-time unbeaten streak at 28 games, they were trailing 1-0 when referee Dave Newell whistled Penguins defenseman Bob Stewart for tripping and Behn Wilson scored on the power play 31 seconds later to give the Flyers a 1-1 tie.

Fittingly, the Flyers broke the Bruins' record of 22 straight games without a loss with a dominant 5-2 win in Boston Garden. That win spurred a 6-1-0 run that extended the streak to an amazing 35 games.

"It was a group effort," said Hill, a center on that team and now a scout with the Flyers. "We never counted on one guy."

Leach led the Flyers that season with 50 goals, but he was not alone. Hill was one of nine Flyers to score 15 or more goals that season. That team also had eight players with 100 or more penalty minutes, led by Paul Holmgren's 267.

"We were a real tough team," Hill said. "Nobody screwed around with us. But we had some luck, too."

The Flyers' streak came to a crashing halt on Jan. 7 in Minnesota when Phil Myre was blitzed in a 7-1 defeat. But after splitting the next two games, the Flyers went on an 8-0-3 run to give them a record of 34-3-13 after 50 games.

Peters didn't lose a game until Feb. 19, 1980, sporting a personal unbeaten streak of 27 games (22-0-5).

Since that remarkable run of invincibility, no professional team on the continent has come close to challenging the Flyers' 35-game unbeaten streak.

The institution of sudden-death overtime in 1999-2000 all but assures the streak's place in NHL history.

"That team had an indominatable spirit," Quinn said.

Peeters made believers out of the Flyers and their fans, including "Sign Man" Dave Leonardi.

Joe Watson, an assistant coach under Quinn on that team, said there was more than just luck that played into the Flyers' streak.

The NHL added four expansion teams — the Edmonton Oilers, Hartford Whalers, Quebec Nordiques and Winnipeg Jets — that went a combined 100-166-54. During the streak, the Flyers went a combined 6-0-2 against the four expansion teams.

"When we played expansion teams they'd get blown out for the first three or four years," Watson recalled. "Now, an expansion team comes in and in two years they're parallel with the other teams."

"But no matter what happens, that record will never be matched in pro sports," Watson said.

"Never."

THE RAT AND THE OWNER'S DAUGHTER

One of the most colorful players of that streak team was Kenny Linseman, a short, hairy fella whom Clarke nicknamed "The Rat" because, in Clarke's words, he looked like one.

When Linseman was a 20-year-old rookie with the Flyers, he committed the mortal sin of dating Ed Snider's daughter, 19-year-old Lindy.

"She was working at the Art Museum and I went to see her one day and we took it from there," Linseman said. "I guess I was crazy enough at that age not to consider the circumstances."

Linseman said he never tried to hide his relationship with the team owner's daughter but recognized right away what he was up against.

"We went out one night and her curfew was 11 p.m.," Linseman said. "I brought her home at midnight and the first thing he said to me was, 'I'm her father first – not the owner.'"

Twice a Flyer, Ken Linseman was traded after dating Ed Snider's daughter, Lindy. The two remain friends.

Linseman, who was the centerpiece of the 1982 trade that brought defenseman Mark Howe to the Flyers, won a Stanley Cup with the Edmonton Oilers in 1984 and is now living in New Hampshire.

"The trade had nothing to do with Lindy," Linseman said. "I was very respectful of her and thirty years later we're still friends."

'MR. SNIDER' LIKE A FATHER

Considered by many as a hard and sometimes ruthless businessman, Snider was beloved by his players, most of whom still refer to him as "Mr. Snider."

"He did what other owners didn't in those days," Clarke said. "He cared about his players. It wasn't a toy for him. He invested the money he had in the team and he cared about players and their families and that hasn't changed.

"He paid for players' kids to be educated, got players jobs after they retired, and he was always there with the players shaking hands after games."

When Reggie Leach had trouble with alcohol addiction, he said Snider was the one who enrolled him into a rehabilitation program that eventually turned his life around.

Ed Snider's quiet acts of kindness have made him one of the most popular owners in professional sports.

The respect and class with which Snider treated his players – from chartered flights to accommodations in the finest hotels — was almost always reciprocated. There was, however, one brief, intended pause that poked fun of the Flyers owner in front of 17,000 fans.

During an on-ice ceremony before a home game in the early 1990s, former player and Flyers broadcaster Bill Clement introduced Snider to the Spectrum crowd as "Mr. Ed ... Snider."

It was, of course, a subtle and perfectly timed reference to television's famous talking horse.

DID LOU SAY THAT?

It was during the Flyers' 35-game unbeaten streak that public address announcer Lou Nolan experienced one of his more embarrassing moments.

The Flyers were beating one of their opponents by a lopsided score when Nolan's mind — and eyes — began to wander.

"I'm looking around the Spectrum and I see a really cute girl with a nice tan and a ski jacket on and I turn to the guy next to me and say, 'Boy, there's a good looking girl down in the first row,'" Nolan said. "My phone rings and the voice on the other end says, 'Lou, is she to the right or to the left?'

"I had left the mike on and the whole building heard me say it."

In all fairness, Nolan's mind wasn't always on other women. He is, after all, a happily married man. But during a game in the early 1980s a puck was deflected at center ice and struck Nolan in the middle of his forehead.

"I was conscious, but I couldn't talk, my tongue wouldn't work," Nolan recalled. "When my speech finally came back a guy is leaning over me asking if I'm OK. And I said, 'Honey, I'm fine.'"

Flyers public address announcer Lou Nolan occasionally allowed his eyes to wander into the Spectrum crowd.

SHORT END OF THE STICKLE

You could fill several penalty boxes with the most vilified opponents in Flyers history – Tiger Williams, Terry O'Reilly, Dale Hunter, Tie Domi, Rob Ray, Matthew Barnaby, Darcy Tucker, Sidney Crosby – the list goes on and on.

But no one's name provokes more angst and anger to old-time Flyers and their fans than the one belonging to linesman Leon Stickle.

Never before has one official been reviled so vehemently, so consistently, by one city for a call he never made.

The Flyers breezed through the first three rounds of the 1980 playoffs, defeating the Edmonton Oilers in three straight, the New York Rangers four games to one and the Minnesota North Stars four games to one.

But the upstart New York Islanders, who had finished a distant second behind the Flyers in the Patrick Division standings with 91 points, had lost just four times in their series victories over Los Angeles, Boston and Buffalo.

Just as the Flyers had done in Boston six years earlier, the Islanders gained a split in their first two games in Philadelphia, winning the opener 4-3 on an overtime goal by Denis Potvin then losing 8-3 in Game 2.

Pat Quinn, who has the memory of an elephant, said the Flyers should have carried a 2-0 lead into New York.

"There was a lame hooking penalty on Jimmy Watson in Game 1," Quinn recalled, "and I can tell you for a fact Potvin's overtime goal was offsides."

The Flyers, now needing at least one win in Nassau Coliseum to regain the home-ice advantage, dropped each of the next two games on Long Island, 6-2 and 5-2, and returned to the Spectrum for Game 5 one loss away from elimination.

A pair of goals by MacLeish helped the Flyers to a convincing 6-3 win at the Spectrum, forcing the series back to Long Island for Game 6.

A Saturday afternoon crowd of 14,995 packed Nassau Coliseum on May 24, hoping to see the Islanders become the first expansion team since the Flyers to win the Stanley Cup.

Unlike most Stanley Cup playoff games, this one was pock-marked with penalties. Referee Bob Myers handed out 33 infractions, four of them fighting majors.

Leach opened the scoring 7:21 into the game and Potvin tied it less than five minutes later when he batted in a shot with his stick raised at shoulder level.

The Flyers argued the goal, but not nearly as vociferously as they did just over two minutes later on what will forever be remembered as "The Offsides Goal."

Leach recalls it like this:

Brian Propp recorded 15 points in 19 playoff games in 1980, but is among the many who felt robbed by Leon Stickle.

"(Clark) Gillies was coming down the left side and I was right behind him chasing. He crossed over the blue line and dropped a pass for (Butch) Goring. Goring was a good 10 feet — I'm not kidding — he was 10 feet behind the line when he took the pass.

"Everybody kind of gave up on the play, waiting to hear the whistle (from Stickle). When there wasn't a call, Goring found (Brent) Sutter all alone in front of the goal and he scored."

Replays showed that Goring was clearly behind the blue line when he took Gillies' pass, but "only" by about two feet, not 10, as Leach recalls.

After reviewing television replays long after the game, Stickle sheepishly admitted he missed the call.

Even after the infamous non-call, there was more than two periods of hockey remaining and Propp tied the score at 2 with 1:22 left in the first period.

The Isles owned the second period, taking a 4-2 lead on goals by Mike Bossy and Bobby Nystrom, but the Flyers fought back to tie the score at 4 on goals by Bob Dailey and John Paddock.

"I hardly remember the game I was so drugged up," joked Dailey, whose injured right shoulder had been shot up with cortisone.

Dailey's goal came 1:47 into the third period and Paddock, who had scored just three goals all season, scored at the 6:02 mark to heighten an already intense game.

Kenny Linseman gave the Isles a power play when he was called for roughing midway through the final period, but Peeters held the Isles scoreless the entire third period and the game spilled into overtime.

Leach came within an inch of sending the series back to Philadelphia for a seventh and deciding game when his slap shot from the blue line beat goaltender

Billy Smith to the glove side, but the puck rang off the crossbar.

It all ended for the Flyers at the 7:11 mark of overtime when Nystrom slipped a shot under Peeters, giving him the title of Long Island's Mr. Overtime — and giving Stickle the title of ...

"I know Mr. Snider called him every name in the book," Leach said. "But once the game was over and we lost, there's nothing left in you. As time goes on, you get more and more (ticked) off about it, but at the time you're just deflated."

Quinn, who in 30 years as an NHL player and coach has never had his name inscribed on the Stanley Cup, said the hurt of that Game 6 defeat still resides deep inside him.

"I still have bad feelings from that series," he said. "Our boys deserved a better result."

BIG BEHN

One of the Flyers' most entertaining and perplexing players of the Pat Quinn era was defenseman Behn Wilson.

"He had an extra streak about him," Quinn recalled. "He wasn't just tough; he could be a real mean guy."

A hard-hitting, hard-skating 6-foot-3, 210-pound redhead, Wilson had just about everything a coach could want in a defenseman.

But it was his dark side that made him one of the most feared fighters in team history.

"I remember the Washington Capitals calling up a guy named Archie Henderson (in 1980-81)," recalled Quinn. "Behn wanted to play the game, but Henderson wanted to fight him. Behn beat him up pretty bad and Henderson came after him a second time.

"Behn beat him up again and Henderson wanted to fight him a third. I finally had to get him off the ice so he didn't hurt anyone."

Considered one of the toughest Flyers of all-time, Behn Wilson's diet consisted of chili con carne and SpaghettiOs.

Wilson's first impression as a Flyer was a lasting one. As a rookie in 1978-79, he took on Dave "Tiger" Williams in his first NHL fight and pummeled him with five straight punches that left Williams stunned.

"I played with him and against him my entire career," said Linseman, who was taken one pick behind Wilson (they were sixth and seventh) in the 1978 draft. "Once the switch went on, he went nuts. He was very intelligent and certainly one of the all-time heavyweights in my era, but he was also incredibly mean. A lot of tough guys didn't have that mean streak in them, but he did. And that's what made him so scary to play against."

Mel Bridgman lived in an apartment a few blocks away from Wilson in Philadelphia's Logan Square and after Bridgman invited Wilson to his place for a few pre-game meals Wilson insisted on repaying the favor.

"I walk into his kitchen," Bridgman said, "he opens up the cupboard and there's nothing but cans of chili con carne and SpaghettiOs."

Wilson's on-ice demeanor bore no resemblance at all to his off-ice interests. An astute fan of the arts he actually performed on stage in theatrical productions of Shakespeare's Othello and A Midsummer Night's Dream. He later played classical guitar and earned a teaching degree in speech and drama.

Wilson's flare for the dramatic on the ice made him a liability defensively and his indifference toward coaches eventually led to him being traded for Doug Crossman and a draft pick (Scott Mellanby) in 1983.

COACHING CAROUSSEL

Despite their run of success in 1980, the Flyers were a team in transition over the next two seasons and after a second-round playoff loss to the Calgary Flames in 1981, the ground began shifting beneath Quinn's feet as several players openly questioned his ability to motivate.

With just eight games remaining in the 1981-82 season and the Flyers sporting a 34-29-9 record, Quinn was fired as coach and replaced by, of all people, McCammon, who had done well behind the bench of the Maine Mariners the previous two seasons.

Quinn was upset at having the carpet pulled from under his feet so late in the season, but took the opportunity to pass his spring entrance exam for law school. With another year remaining on his Flyers contract Quinn used the income to pay his way through the Widener University School of Law.

"That's what provided my opportunity," Quinn said later, "and that's what sports was supposed to do for me anyway."

BELL BOTTOMED COOPERALLS

The Flyers became fashion trend-setters in 1981 when they unveiled a new clothing line.

Players hit the ice wearing long pants, leaving the old shorts and suspenders to the league's other old fogies.

Kenny Linseman, a big fan of leisure suits with big open collars, absolutely hated the form-fitting pants.

"I was already pretty close to the ice," said Linseman, who was probably an inch or two shorter than his advertised 5-foot-11. "So when I bent down to a crotch position, I felt like I couldn't move. Let's just say they were very restricting."

The Flyers (1981–82) and Hartford Whalers (1982–93) were the only NHL teams to wear Cooperalls.

The Flyers added an orange stripe to the long black pants the following season and the Hartford Whalers copied the idea with long green pants, but too many goaltenders complained they could not see the puck through the forest of black pants and the NHL forced the Flyers to go back to the shorts and socks look in 1983-84.

JIMMY WATSON BOWS OUT GRACEFULLY

Flyers historians may forever debate whether Jimmy Watson, Mark Howe or Eric Desjardins was the greatest defenseman to wear the orange and black.

Many who saw Watson in his prime believe it would have been a moot argument if persistent back pain had not limited his career to parts of nine seasons.

In the fall of 1982 Watson gracefully retired at the age of 30, seven years after first receiving treatments for back pain.

Watson was 17 years old and working for a British Columbia water company when he tried to lift a heavy water pipe and strained his lower back muscle.

"I was young and foolish, and I thought I could pick it up," he said. "It probably wasn't a very good idea."

A chiropractor jarred Watson's back into place and he remained pain-free until he was 23. Five agonizing years later, he underwent a spinal fusion in which bone from his hip was removed, ground into a sand-like substance and inserted into his lower spine.

The surgery improved Watson's condition, but only temporarily. He played one more season and decided the pain was too much to bear two weeks into the Flyers' 1982 training camp. A five-time NHL All-Star, he walked away from hockey with 38 goals and 186 points in 613 games, but with few regrets.

"I planned on playing another four or five years, but I was in agony the last three or four years, and it just wasn't worth it," Watson said. "It's like an engineer not being able to see properly. Whatever line of work you're in, if you're not capable of performing at the level you're used to, it's time to get out."

MOOSE GETS HIS DUE

One of the most humorously heated one-on-one battles of the early 80s pitted Flyers defenseman Moose Dupont against 5-foot-6, 166-pound Detroit Red Wings forward Dennis Polonich.

After one of their on-ice altercations, they had etreated to their respective penalty boxes when Polonich heard the phone ring at the scorer's table.

"Hey, Dupie!" Polonich shrieked in a high-pitched voice. "Answer the phone … the Flyers just traded you for me!"

THE RAT GETS A SHAVE

The locker room horseplay that was common in the 1970s continued through the early 80s when youngsters like Peeters, Linseman and Propp tried to find their places on a team with veteran pranksters like MacLeish, Kelly and Watson.

During one road trip, Linseman was held down by his teammates, who shaved him from head to toe.

"I got them back, though," he said with a snicker. "I put Nair in their shampoo bottles and saw clumps of their hair fall out in the shower.

"They never knew it was me."

Until now.

While Linseman dished it right back, guys like Peeters and Propp walked on eggshells in their first couple seasons in Philadelphia.

"Neither one said a word," Linseman said. "If you got two words out of Propp in one week it was a lot. Now, you need to put a muzzle on him to get him to stop talking."

As fate would have it, Propp went on to enjoy a successful career as a Flyers radio color commentator from 1999 through 2008.

SMURFS ATTACK MCCAMMON

Bob McCammon's second stint as coach of the Flyers was not much better than his first.

His teams were bounced from the playoffs by the hated New York Rangers in 1982 and 1983, the first time in four games and the second in a three-game sweep punctuated by a 9-3 loss that Clarke called the worst of his career.

McCammon had provided the Rangers with all the incentive they needed on March 14, 1983 when, after an 8-2 loss in Madison Square Garden, he said, "Nobody hit their smurfs all night."

McCammon was referring to smallish Rangers forwards Marc Pavelich, Reijo Ruotsalainen, Rob McClanahan and Robbie Ftorek.

Herb Brooks, who three years earlier coached the U.S. Olympic team to its Miracle on Ice gold medal, was coaching the Rangers at the time.

"I know he took it personally," Holmgren said.

So did the Rangers' faithful. Thousands of fans showed up at Madison Square Garden with stuffed Smurf dolls and joyfully hurled the purple imps onto the ice after the three-game sweep.

"If they don't learn from this," Ron Duguay said of the Flyers, "they never will."

JAY TAKES CHARGE

Following the 1982-83 season, Ed Snider's son, 25-year-old Jay Snider, replaced Bob Butera as Flyers president and was hit with the news that McCammon had been offered the dual role of coach and general manager of the Pittsburgh Penguins.

In 1983, at the age of 25, Jay Snider became the youngest president in the history of the NHL.

Ed Snider later said he should have let McCammon go, but instead they offered him the job of coach and general manager of the Flyers and McCammon accepted, replacing longtime general manager Keith Allen.

"At that time I wasn't ready to step upstairs," said Allen, who was 59 at the time. "And to be honest, I don't think McCammon was ready, either."

McCammon's one year as coach and general manager proved disastrous.

He upset the entire organization when he traded Holmgren to the Minnesota North Stars hours before a Feb. 23 game against the North Stars at the Spectrum.

"I didn't play the game that night and I left the building with five minutes to go because I was so (ticked)," Holmgren said. "When I turned on the radio on the way home, I heard I was traded to Minnesota."

McCammon waited until the next day to tell Holmgren that he was now a North Star.

CLARKIE TAKES A LONG VACATION

With Tim Kerr emerging as a 50-goal scorer and Brian Propp, Dave Poulin and Ron Sutter establishing themselves as the Flyers' new young core, Clarke and Barber saw their roles and their ice times reduced.

With about a month left in the 1983-84 season, McCammon decided to give

Clarke, Barber and veteran defenseman Miroslav Dvorak involuntary vacations. Clarke would take a five-game break to Florida, while Barber and Dvorak would take four-game breaks after Clarke returned.

Clarke, who was 34 at the time, didn't like the idea. He was on his way to a 17-goal, 43-assist season and had found his niche as a checking-line center. But he went along with the plan, even though in the back of his mind he knew the end of his career was coming.

"I was still good enough to play, but I noticed that if practice

Bob Clarke was torn between playing another season or taking the Flyers' offer to become general manager.

was at 10, I was here at 8:15 in the morning skating around and around. I never thought about retiring, but I must have known to absorb it all as best I could. I could tell it was coming."

Barber's forced exile essentially ended his career.

While doing leg squats in the Poconos, he felt a pop in his knee. Barber missed the playoffs that season, underwent reconstructive surgery that summer, took an entire season off to rehab and called it a career when the knee did not respond.

The Flyers were swept again in the 1984 playoffs, this time by the Washington Capitals, and when Jay Snider demanded that McCammon find a new coach, he refused and was fired from both positions as coach and general manager.

FROM THE LOCKER ROOM TO THE BOARD ROOM

If Bob Clarke could do it all over again, he probably would have played another year or two before trading in his hockey skates for wing-tipped shoes.

But when Jay Snider offered him the general manager's job, he saw an opportunity that might not come along a year or two later.

"Basically, they told him they wanted him to quit," Holmgren said of a summer meeting between Snider, assistant general manager Gary Darling and Clarke. "Bob still wanted to play. He was at a point in his life where he was at a real crossroads. We talked for a long time over the next few days and he finally decided to take the offer."

"I think I got everything I could out of my career," he said, referring to a 15-year journey that produced 358 goals, 852 assists, 1,210 points, 1,453 penalty minutes, three Hart Trophies and two Stanley Cups. "If you had your choice, you'd win the Cup more, but on a daily basis I feel I got everything I could out of whatever abilities I had."

Many of his former teammates still call Clarke the best captain they've ever played with. Watson and Clement called him the best leader in the history of sports.

But when asked if he ever considered himself a leader, Clarke grimaces.

"No, I was just a player," he said. "I never thought about those kinds of things. I just did what came naturally to me, that's all.

"There are really only a few natural captains. You've got to be able to confront a player face to face and demand that he play good, and to do that you have to play good yourself. "It's hard for people to do that. Every once in a while I would stick my nose in Ricky MacLeish's face and say, 'Listen, if you don't … play we're going to lose. So, you have to play.' He'd say OK, and he would. Generally, people don't like to do that to somebody else. You need to know when to do it."

CHAPTER 5

IRON MIKE'S ARMY

(1984-1988)

Follow the meteoric rise of Mike Keenan's band of no-names who twice went to the Stanley Cup Finals in three seasons, overcoming the tragic loss of the NHL's top goaltender.

GRILLING IN THE SUN

ON THE SAME DAY BOB CLARKE PHONED JAY SNIDER TO accept the position as Flyers general manager, he and his wife, Sandy, boarded a flight to the British Virgin Islands with Dave Poulin and his wife, Kim, and another couple.

Poulin was unaware that his teammate had just become his boss, so Clarke pulled him aside and informed him of his decision to hang up his skates and begin wearing a tie. Figuring he might need some informal training dealing with the tough Philadelphia media Poulin set up several mock press conferences during their vacation.

"The five of us figured if he was going to be the GM, we might as well start grilling him with questions," Poulin said. "Kim didn't hold back. She said, "What makes you think you're prepared to take on a management position with no former experience and no formal eduation?'

"It's a good thing Bob liked my wife," Poulin said with a laugh.

KEENAN TO THE RESCUE

Before Clarke said yes to Jay Snider's proposal, the young Flyers president had already scouted out a young and aggressive coach who led the AHL Rochester Americans and the University of Toronto to back-to-back titles.

Mike Keenan, who at 34 was nine weeks younger than Clarke, was about to take a family vacation in Florida when Jay Snider asked him to complete a questionnaire on how to turn the Flyers around.

Keenan returned a 19-page manuscript completed in his hotel room.

"It was like a small book," recalls Clarke. "It was really impressive. I didn't even know who Mike Keenan was. I knew he had won at the junior level and at the American League level and I heard he was very demanding and made everybody really accountable. But I didn't know he could coach."

Keenan's dissertation, which included phrases like "imbalance of predictability," "intrinsic enthusiasm" and "attitudinal methods," blew Snider away and made him the clear choice over Dave King, who was coach of the Canadian Olympic team, and junior coach Bill Laforge of the Kamloops Blazers.

Mike Keenan impressed Jay Snider with a 19–page report on how he would turn the Flyers into champions.

Once he was hired, Keenan's first order of business was meeting personally with each player. The first was Poulin, a second-year player whom Keenan later would dub the Flyers' next captain.

"He didn't even say hello," Poulin said. "The very first question he asked me was, 'Do we have a goaltender who can win the Stanley Cup? I immediately said yes."

With that, Keenan met with Swedish goaltender Pelle Lindbergh, who had split time the previous two seasons with Bob Froese, and told the 25-year-old Swede he'd be the Flyers' No. 1 goalie.

Defenseman Mark Howe had already emerged as the Flyers' top defenseman and wanted Keenan to know exactly where he stood. The two met for lunch at Kaminski's Ale House in Cherry Hill, New Jersey.

Mark Howe accepted Keenan's challenge to become the team's most heavily played defenseman.

"I said, 'Look, I would just like to have the opportunity to get a little bit more ice time than I have my last few years,'" Howe told Keenan.

"I felt if I played a little more I could help the team more. The only thing he said to me was, 'Be ready.'"

In the first period of the Flyers' first exhibition game, Keenan sent Howe onto the ice for more than 16 of the 20 minutes.

"It might have been the best period of hockey I played in my life," Howe said. "I had a feeling he'd challenge me and I had to be ready."

Howe said his performance in that game got him in Keenan's good book.

Poulin earned his stripes just a few days before.

Keenan had scheduled a 10 a.m. practice and when the clock struck 10 and Keenan was nowhere to be found, Poulin took matters into his own hands and started practice.

"Mike skates onto the ice five minutes later, comes right up to me and yells, 'If I'm not here, you're NOT running this team.'

"I said, 'Yes, I am,' and Mike skated away.

About a week later, Keenan again showed up late, this time 30 minutes after practice began. Poulin had already put his teammates through a brisk workout and at 10:30 Keenan calmly stepped on the ice and took over the remainder of the practice.

"He didn't say a word to me," Poulin said. "But I knew he was late for a reason. He wanted to see how I reacted."

Poulin remembers a game early in his tenure as captain in which the Flyers were leading 4-0 after the first period and on the way up the tunnel to the locker room, Keenan grabbed his captain and screamed, for all to hear, 'I'm not going in there, but if we lose, it's your fault.'

HARDLINE NEGOTIATOR

Bob Clarke jumped into his new role as general manager with both feet. He negotiated his first big contract with Tim Kerr, signing the sturdy right wing to a five-year contract worth $1.25 million.

"Big then," Kerr joked, "but not in today's world."

Clarke's first big trade came about a week later and tested his ability to separate team business from his personal feelings.

A few weeks before training camp Clarke promised Darryl Sittler he'd be named the Flyers' next captain. But on the day the announcement was to be made, Clarke received an offer for Sittler and traded him to the Detroit Red Wings for prospects Murray Craven and Joe Paterson.

The Flyers got off to a fast start under Keenan, losing just four of their first 26 games, but the strain of running the Flyers with no professional experience was beginning to take its toll on the 35-year-old Clarke.

"It was really difficult," Clarke said. "In hindsight, I should have never been the GM. You can't go from playing to running a business with no experience.

"All of a sudden I was trying to negotiate contracts. I remember going home from the office. I'd sit on the couch and fall asleep. I'd be just exhausted and I hadn't done nothing all day but sit in the office. Oh, I hated it. And we were winning!"

Kerr said Clarke had two things going for him as a general manager: credibility as a former player, and a single-mindedness to do what was right for the team.

"Whether he was a player or GM, the Flyers were Bob Clarke's franchise," Kerr said. "Bob never really worried about what people wrote about him or thought about him. Everything he did was to make the team better."

YOUTH WILL BE SERVED

From the start of the 1984 training camp it was clear Keenan was just as head-strong as Clarke and equally obsessed with winning.

"We didn't know a lot about him but we learned right away he demanded a lot," said Kerr, who along with Brian Propp was one of the few veterans on the team. "He wasn't just happy to coach in the NHL, he wanted to win."

Along with naming Pelle Lindbergh his starting goalie Keenan accelerated the Flyers' youth movement by giving energetic rookies Rick Tocchet, Peter Zezel, Murray Craven and Derrick Smith roster spots.

With veterans Clarke (retired), Sittler (traded), Barber (rehabbing) and Holmgren (first-year assistant coach) no longer in Flyers uniforms Keenan entered the 1984-85 season with the youngest team in the NHL.

After 26 games the Flyers had just four losses, but a four-game losing streak brought out the worst in Keenan.

During a nationally televised game against the Islanders Ron Sutter lost a key defensive faceoff that resulted in an Islanders goal from the point.

"It was an innocent play," recalls Howe. "But when Ronny came to the bench, Mike walked down to the end of the bench and shut the gate. He wouldn't let him on the bench. He made Ronny go right to the locker room.

"Ronny was a real heart-and-soul guy on our team and it was kind of degrading."

Keenan once told Ron Sutter that if he didn't play better, he'd send his twin brother, Rich, to the minors.

LOSING THEIR (CHRISTMAS) COOKIES

The Flyers entered the 2004 Christmas break with a 19-9-5 record but had lost five of their last seven games. With a short two-day reprieve for the holiday and many players already booked on noon flights home for Christmas Eve, Poulin asked Keenan if he could move practice up from 10 a.m. to 8 a.m. so players could catch their flights.

Keenan agreed and supplied some holiday cheer by pulling out a boom box and playing holiday music for his players. Poulin ordered pizzas and beer to be delivered after practice.

"It was a great practice," Poulin recalled.

After all of his practices, Keenan pushed his players through 12 minutes of lap skating — six minutes around the rink one way, followed by six minutes the other way.

"The young guys – Derrick Smith, Tocchet, Zezel – were flying around the ice," Poulin recalled. "They were excited about getting home to see their families."

Keenan had other plans. After the 12-minute skate, he lined his players up at the goal line and put them though 45 minutes of suicide skates – sprint to the near blue line and back; to the red line and back; to the far blue line and back; to the far goal line and back.

"Mike never said a word," Poulin said. "It was like the scene out of the movie 'Miracle' with Herb Brooks. All Mike did was keep blowing his whistle."

By the end of the suicide skate, several players were hunched over, throwing up on the ice. With their legs burning and their lungs gasping for air, Keenan said to them, "Gentlemen, expect the unexpected. Merry Christmas."

And with that, he left the ice.

"All we wanted to do was get away for a couple days and for those two days all we did was talk about Mike," Poulin said. "It's probably exactly what he wanted."

When the Flyers returned from their two-day hiatus, they suffered their most lopsided loss of the season, a 6-0 setback in Washington that proved to be their only shutout loss of the season.

ON THE LIGHTER SIDE

Not all of Keenan's practices were executed with whips, chains and spiked medicine balls.

To lighten things up at practice Keenan sometimes allowed his players to switch positions. Tim Kerr, who skated backwards like a penguin helplessly sliding down a ski slope, almost always volunteered to play defense.

"I was an accident waiting to happen," Kerr said. "But my dream was to play one game on defense, even if it was an exhibition game."

Keenan never relented, but in a game about a week after one of those light-hearted practices, a Flyers defenseman pinched in too deep in the offensive zone, leaving Kerr as the last recourse on a one-on-one breakaway.

"He was looking at us on the bench and we were all laughing," Howe recalled. "He took one hand off his stick and put it in the air trying to keep his balance. The guy went around him and scored. Mike Keenan was ready to blow a cork on that one."

But wait. That's not how Kerr remembers it.

"Oh, no, they didn't score," Kerr said. "I don't know who it was, but I stopped him."

ZEZEL THE SUPER MODEL

The 1984-85 Flyers weren't just a collection of good hockey players, many of them were teenage heartthrobs.

Nineteen-year-old rookie Peter Zezel had cover boy looks to go along with his lightning speed and women young and old did everything in their power to get his attention.

"Girls would send me videos of themselves; naked pictures; fan letters with stuff you wouldn't believe. It was crazy," Zezel said in one of his last interviews before passing away to a rare blood disorder on May 26, 2009. "Guys would grab the pictures and pass them around the locker room.

"It was the same with Tock. We just wanted to play hockey, but some of that stuff was out of control."

Zezel's good looks and pleasant, unassuming personality made him an easy target for veterans wanting to pull pranks on him. A native of Toronto, Zezel was excited to see his friends and family in his first visit to Maple Leaf Gardens as a Flyer.

Rookies Peter Zezel and Rick Tocchet attracted a whole new Flyers fan base – teenage girls.

"Peter always loved his looks and his hair," Brian Propp said. "We waited until just before that Toronto trip to cut his hair. Let's just say we made him look not as cute as he normally would."

Of course, that wasn't the only prank pulled on the Flyers' four rookies.

"They told us to meet them at a bar for the rookie party," recalls Zezel. "The four of us walked in and realized it was a gay bar. We turned around and got out of there pretty fast."

Zezel said any of the brow-beating tactics used by Keenan were balanced by some of the hi-jinx that brewed inside the locker room.

One veteran defenseman, whose father will be forever known as Mr. Hockey, arrived at the Flyers' practice rink early every day and would occasionally squeeze the custard out of the donuts and replace it with shaving cream.

"Ed Hospodar chugged one down in one big bite," Zezel recalled, "and guys were just rolling."

Zezel roomed with Ilkka Sinisalo on road trips during his rookie season and remembers Sinisalo hiding the television remote under his sheet.

"Because I was the rookie, I had to get up and change it myself," Zezel said. "But every time I changed it, he'd change it to another channel with the remote. This went on for a half hour. I thought, 'What the heck is going on?' I finally went down to the front desk to tell them there was something wrong with the reception in our room."

The pranks on Zezel didn't stop there. One day, Zezel pulled into the Coliseum parking lot with a brand new car. But while he was showering, teammates snuck into the parking lot and loosened the bolts on one of his tires.

"I pull out of the parking lot and my tire rolls right into a ditch," Zezel said.

The only member of that team that was un-prankable was, of course, Keenan.

"We were too scared of what Mike might do to us if we got him," Zezel said.

LEGEND OF IRON MIKE

One part drill sergeant, another part hockey genius, Keenan would try just about anything to motivate his players.

"If he saw a weakness, he went after it," Poulin said. "And if he saw toughness, he wanted to make you tougher."

Propp, the Flyers' second all-time leading goal scorer behind Bill Barber, said he took as much heat from Keenan as anyone.

"He'd give me heck and I'd smirk at him and it would drive him crazy," Propp said. "He'd yell, 'Wipe that bloody smirk off your face!'

"But if he yelled at you, the next day he'd call you into his office let you have your say. Sometimes he'd even apologize."

Like the time in Buffalo, when Swedish defenseman Thomas Eriksson blocked a shot and came to the bench writhing in pain.

"Mike's all over him because he's European," Propp recalled. "He yells, 'Get back out there! You're nothing but a wuss!'"

Eriksson went back out and finished the game. The next day an X-ray showed he had fractured his knee cap.

Ron Sutter was another one of Keenan's verbal targets. Before one game, he told Ron that if he didn't start playing better he'd send his twin brother, Rich, to the minors.

E.J. McGuire, an assistant coach under Keenan in Philadelphia, said Keenan didn't always mean what he said.

"I think what Mike wanted to say was, 'Quit worrying about your brother Rich,'" McGuire said. "If somebody came up high with a stick on Rich, Ron would lean over the boards and say, 'We're going to get you.' I think Mike just wanted Ron to worry about himself."

That said, McGuire admits he needed to be the good cop to Keenan's bad cop image.

"The joke was made to me that my job was to clear the blood off the walls after Mike's pre-game talks," McGuire said.

PRIMA TOCCHET?

Rick Tocchet recalls a game in Calgary in which the Flyers fell behind 2-0 after the first period.

As players retreated to the visiting locker room, Keenan called Tocchet a prima donna.

"It was loud enough for everybody to hear," Tocchet recalled. "I turned around and went right after him. McCrimmon had to stand between us to keep me from hitting him." Tocchet impressed Keenan by getting into a couple of fights and leading the Flyers back into the game, which they eventually lost 4-3, and afterward handed Tocchet some cash and said, "Go take the guys out for some beers tonight."

Tocchet shoved the money back in Keenan's hand and said, "I'll take them out with my own money."

As tough as Keenan was on that 1984-85 team, he drilled into them that their love of winning should be exceeded only by their hatred of losing.

Pat Croce, a strength and conditioning coach under Keenan, remembers Keenan

When Keenan called Rick Tocchet a prima donna, the two had to be separated by Brad McCrimmon.

taking Zezel into the boiler room in the bowels of the Spectrum and screaming at him until Zezel came out in tears.

"It was OK because my father was hard on me, too," Zezel said. "But Mike would get me so mad I wanted to prove to him I could play better."

Tim Kerr was no stranger to Keenan's wicked tongue but enjoyed his greatest success under Keenan's guidance, recording three straight 50-goal seasons.

"I knew the things he said weren't personal, but other guys didn't see it that way," Kerr said. "I don't like the way he treated some of the guys, but if we were at a restaurant and someone said something about one of his players, he'd stand up for that player.

"He had a great hockey mind. I knew when I was driving over that Walt Whitman Bridge that if I played well that night, I'd get a lot of ice time."

And if he didn't play well?

"He'd lose it on me."

THE BEAST IS SLAIN

The Flyers won 16 of their final 17 regular season games in Keenan's first season and rolled over the Rangers and four-time Stanley Cup champion Islanders to reach the 1985 Wales Conference Finals.

But in Game 1 against the Quebec Nordiques winger Wilf Paiement cross-checked Brad McCrimmon into the boards, breaking his clavicle and knocking him out of the playoffs.

"My collar bone was four inches above where it should have been," McCrimmon said. "I had a broken hand the same year and didn't tell anybody. By the time we got to the Finals we were held together by glue and Band-Aids."

Legend has it McCrimmon earned the nickname "Beast" because of the way he played hockey. Others say it's because he was hairier than most humans. Zezel thinks it's

Affectionately known as "Beast," Brad McCrimmon slept with his windows open in the dead of winter.

because McCrimmon, who hails from Dodsland, Saskatchewan, had thicker blood than most mammals.

"He wanted to be cold all the time," Zezel said. "I slept at his apartment one night and he kept his windows wide open in his bed room. When I woke up the next morning there was a snow drift next to his bed."

In truth, McCrimmon said he actually arrived in Philadelphia with the nickname of Beast. Former Bruins forward Peter McNabb gave him the name because …

"He had two daughters and they thought I looked like the Beast on Sesame Street."

BRING ON GRETZKY

McCrimmon was not the only casualty from the semifinal series with Quebec. Poulin had suffered broken ribs and was playing with a flak jacket, Kerr was playing on a badly sprained knee and Ilkka Sinisalo had a separated shoulder.

"Davey would sit in the shower before a game and get injections of pain killers into his rib cage," recalls Croce. "Tim Kerr was the same way. These guys were like Hell's Angels on skates."

The banged-up Flyers found a way to eliminate the Nordiques in six games and earn a date with Wayne Gretzky and the Edmonton Oilers.

With 429 goals, 1,122 points and one Stanley Cup ring on his resume through just six NHL seasons, Gretzky was the class of the NHL. That meant nothing to Rick Tocchet, a hard-nosed 21-year-old from Scarborough, Ontario, who hit The Great One every chance he got.

"He ran me the first game in Philly," Gretzky said. "I said something to him and he turned to me and said, 'Get used to it, it's going to happen every night for the next seven games.' I said to him, 'I must be in the wrong series, because we only plan on going four.'"

The Flyers won that opening game in the Spectrum, but the Oilers smoked them in four straight for their second of four Stanley Cups.

"If we have McCrimmon and Kerr that's a different series," said Propp.

TRIGGER FINGER MIKE

Along with having a silver tongue, Keenan's impatience with goaltenders is legendary. In Game 3 of the 1985 Finals, with the Flyers trailing by two goals and down two men, he yanked Pelle Lindbergh and replaced him with ice cold backup Bob Froese.

The strong play of Pelle Lindbergh forced the Flyers to consider trading young goaltending prospect Ron Hextall.

"Mike looked down at the end of the bench and yelled, 'Frozey, you're in!'" recalled Poulin. "Frozey yelled back, 'What?'"

As Froese climbed over the bench and began stretching, Miro "Cookie" Dvorak leaned over and in a thick Czech accent, said to Froese, "Good luck, my friend."

"It took everything all of us had not to break out laughing," said Poulin.

"We tried not to laugh," Tocchet said, 'but it was a classic line."

Froese stopped every shot on that power play and when it was over Keenan sent Lindbergh back between the pipes in an eventual 4-3 loss.

Two years later, in Game 4 of the Stanley Cup Finals against the Oilers, Keenan alternated between Ron Hextall and Chico Resch a total of five times.

"Why? Control," Poulin said. "It was like, 'I don't care who you are, I'm in charge.'"

The Flyers went on to lose that series against Edmonton in five games, but with the NHL's youngest team, a work ethic second to none and a Vezina-winning goaltender, many believed the Flyers would be the team to end the Oilers' reign as Stanley Cup champions.

THE TRADE THAT NEVER HAPPENED

A week after the Flyers' incredible run to the 1985 Finals, Detroit Red Wings general manager Jim Devellano saw the Flyers had themselves a goaltending dilemma.

While Lindbergh was setting the standard for excellence between the pipes, a brash young goaltender named Ron Hextall was developing into one of the NHL's brightest prospects as a member of the AHL Hershey Bears.

"Not only did we have Pelle, but we had Hextall coming," recalls Clarke. "One of them would have had to be traded. Whoever we traded would have brought us some pretty good players."

Clarke could not imagine trading Lindbergh, so he listened to offers on Hextall.

"Detroit offered us the first pick in the (1986) draft for Hextall and I turned it down," Clarke said.

Devellano decided to hold onto that pick and the Red Wings drafted Joe Murphy No. 1 overall. The Flyers selected defenseman Kerry Huffman with the 20th pick overall.

Murphy went on to play parts of 15 seasons with Detroit, Edmonton, Chicago, St. Louis, San Jose, Boston and Washington and finished his career with 233 goals and 528 points in 779 games.

Dave Poulin began the 1986–87 season with his twin daughters' health weighing heavily on his mind.

TWIN BLESSINGS

At the start of the 1985-86 season, Flyers captain Dave Poulin had more on his mind than hockey.

Pregnant with twin girls, his wife, Kim, went into labor 26 weeks into her pregnancy because of a placental abruption, which occurs when the placenta separates from the uterine wall.

"At one point, I was losing all three of them," Poulin recalls. "We had to prompt the birth."

Lindsay and Taylor Poulin were less than 2 pounds and 12 inches when they were born on Oct. 2, 1986. Taylor had a collapsed lung and bleeding on the brain. Both were in critical condition and stood only a slim chance of survival.

Eighty-three days later, on Dec. 24, 1986, the Poulins were told they could bring Lindsay home from Pennsylvania Hospital, but Taylor would need to remain on a high frequency ventilator.

"We said we're taking both," Poulin said.

Kim Poulin needed to sign a waiver because the high frequency ventilator Taylor required was not approved by the Food and Drug Administration.

Nearly 22 years later, Lindsay and Taylor Poulin accepted their diplomas from their father's college alma mater, the University of Notre Dame.

"When they walked in with their caps and gowns, it was an emotional moment for us," Poulin said. "They are young and vibrant and filled with so much promise."

LONG NIGHT ENDS IN TRAGEDY

Buoyed by the belief that a healthier team might have gone all the way against the Oilers, the Flyers opened the 1985-86 season by winning 12 of their first 14 games, including 10 straight from Oct. 19 through Nov. 9.

Following a 5-3 victory over the Bruins at the Spectrum, the Flyers had a four-day break in the schedule and several players made their way to Bennigan's Grill & Tavern in Mount Laurel, New Jersey to celebrate their 12-2 start to the season.

Lindbergh drove to Bennigan's in his sedan, leaving his prized candy apple-red Porsche 930 at his lakefront town home in the Kings Grant section of Marlton, New Jersey, where his mother, Anna-Lise, and his fiance, Kerstin Pietzsh, were visiting.

Before leaving Bennigan's, players planned an informal get-together at the nightclub adjacent to their practice facility, the Coliseum, in Voorhees, New Jersey. Lindbergh drove back to Marlton, climbed into his $125,000, Porsche and drove to the Coliseum, where he and many of his teammates partied well into the night.

"Pelle didn't drink much at all," recalls Brian Propp. "He would have one or two beers and then drink Coca Colas the rest of the night."

This night was different. Lindbergh left the nightclub around 5:15 a.m. and offered to take home Ed Parvin, a close friend whom Lindbergh had taken to Sweden the previous summer, along with Kathy McNeal, a friend of Parvin's.

Parvin climbed into the passenger side of Lindbergh's two-seat, 565-horse-power Porsche – "I barely remember leaving the Coliseum," Parvin says now — and McNeal squeezed herself onto the console between the two seats.

Lindbergh, who later was found to have a blood-alcohol content of .24 — twice the legal limit — pulled out of the Coliseum parking lot and made a right onto Preston Avenue.

"People at that time drove drunk," Dave Brown said, "and if nothing happened, it didn't matter."

"Life was different back then," agreed Kerr. "If we stopped for a couple beers and got pulled over, a couple of hockey tickets made the cops your best friends. It was totally different than it is now."

Lindbergh's affinity for speed was well known by everyone who knew him. He often did doughnuts in the Coliseum parking lot and told teammates he once reached 160 mph while driving on the autobahn in Germany.

"Pelle was a speed freak," said Kerr, who owned a burgundy Porsche at the time. "If I was going 75, he'd come by me at 110."

After turning right on Somerdale Road, Lindbergh stopped at a red light at the intersection of Somerdale Road and the White Horse Pike, waited for the light to turn green, and sped off into the darkness. Exactly what happened in the next 30 seconds remains a mystery.

Voorhees Police Department deputy chief Jack Prettyman, one of the officers to arrive at the scene of the accident, said he thinks Lindbergh hit the gas pedal with all his might when that light turned green.

"I think he floored it and took off like a jet," Prettyman said. "In my opinion, he didn't know that turn was coming. In my mind, he was showing off."

The distance between the traffic light and the hard right turn that claimed Lindbergh's life is slightly more than three-tenths of a mile. The speed limit is 35 mph with a sign that reads "Reduce Speed." Lindbergh's speed was considered undetermined at the time of the accident, but Prettyman thinks his car could have gotten up to 100 mph before crashing into the concrete steps leading up to New Life Christian Fellowship Church.

"He let me drive that car," Prettyman said. "I know how powerful it was."

Some, including Brown, believe something strange happened just before Lindbergh's car drove straight into those steps. He thinks McNeal might have been frightened by the car's speed and pulled the keys out of the ignition, locking up the steering column. Prettyman said there were only slight skid marks, about 15 feet long, and that the car's tires never shifted from left to right.

"I can't say," says Parvin. "I was sleeping in the passenger seat. I was out; I had no idea where we were going or how fast we were going. I've heard so many rumors."

Prettyman said he remembers taking photographs of the inside of the car and remembers keys being in the ignition.

"If the car's in gear, you can't take the key out," he said.

The collision was so violent the entire hood of the Porsche was forced into the driver's seat. Lindbergh suffered a broken leg, a broken hip, a broken jaw and irreversible damage to his brain stem, which controls the flow of oxygen in the body. Lindbergh and McNeal, who suffered injuries to her spleen and liver, were rushed to Kennedy Hospital in Stratford, New Jersey.

Parvin, who suffered a fractured skull and fractures to his nose, shoulder and ribs, was taken to Cooper Medical Center in Camden.

By late Sunday morning, word had spread that Lindbergh was breathing with the help of a respirator, but that there was no hope of recovery. Poulin and Kerr, who were with Lindbergh that tragic night, still believe it was speed, not alcohol, that took their 26-year-old friend's life.

"He could have been stone cold sober and he still drove like an idiot," Poulin said.

"The alcohol played a part," Kerr said, "but it was the speed that took his life."

Pelle Lindbergh's infatuation with speed was no secret to his teammates, who often saw him exceed 100 mph.

Hours after the crash Kerr was woken up by a ringing phone. His mother was on the other end, desperately hoping to hear her son's voice.

"She saw the news come across her TV that a Flyer had been involved in an auto accident involving a red Porsche," Kerr said. "She thought it was me."

Led by Poulin and Keenan, the Flyers held a vigil at Kennedy Hospital for the next two days. "Some guys went in to see him," Brown recalled. "I didn't. I didn't want to see him like that."

"We all just hung around," Propp said. "We couldn't do anything."

Lindbergh remained on a respirator until his father, Sigge, arrived from Stockholm two days after the crash and took him off life support. Lindbergh's heart, liver, kidneys and corneas were sent to patients awaiting transplants.

News of Lindbergh's fatal crash sent shockwaves throughout the hockey world.

"When I saw in the newspaper he had died I had to read the article over a couple times," said Pete Peeters, who had roomed with Lindbergh in Lindbergh's rookie season. "I was devastated."

A young Swede named Peter Forsberg, who was 12 years old at the time, said he remembers an entire nation mourning over Lindbergh's tragic passing.

"It was a national tragedy," Forsberg said. "I never met him or knew him, but I thought it was very sad. I remember thinking, 'Is he brain dead? Is he going to die?' Everything about it was so sad."

Parvin, who underwent an eight-hour surgery to repair his skull, did not learn of Lindbergh's death for weeks. He spent the next month and a half at Cooper Medical Center and could not speak for three months. His father said it took three years of speech therapy before his son could communicate freely.

"He lost a couple years of his life," said Ed Parvin, Sr.

Parvin later filed lawsuits against Bennigan's and the Coliseum for over-serving Lindbergh the night of the accident and received an undisclosed settlement.

"The money wasn't really important to me," Parvin said. "I lost a friend." McNeal recovered completely from her injuries and now lives in California.

Kerstin Pietzsh, whom Parvin described as the most beautiful woman he had ever met, is now living in Sweden, where she is married with three children.

MOVING FORWARD

The Flyers commemorated the life of Lindbergh in an on-ice ceremony before their next game against the Edmonton Oilers on Nov. 14, 1985. His locker stall was left empty that night, adorned only with a small Swedish flag.

The Flyers, wearing black patches with Lindbergh's No. 31 in white, somehow summoned the courage to beat the defending champions 5-3 that evening behind rookie goaltender Darren Jensen, who was called up from the Hershey Bears two days earlier.

The winning didn't stop there. The Flyers plowed through their grief, sinking all of their emotion into each day's practices and each night's games.

"A lot of people don't deal with death real well and for many of us it was the first time anyone close to us died," Propp said. "It affected all of us, but we knew we had a job to do."

Sensing his team's needs, Keenan organized private team get-togethers throughout the next several days and weeks, some included players' wives and families; others involved only players.

"That's when Mike Keenan was at his absolute best as a leader," Poulin said.

"He kept all of us together and he kept us talking. Sometimes the silence would be awkward, but we all got through it together."

"There was no more of an understanding person during that period than Mike," said E.J. McGuire. "He was very sensitive to the players needs."

Poulin said the events that surrounded Lindbergh'sdeath helped change the attitudes players had about the dangers of drinking and driving.

"Guys still went out," Poulin said, "but we were a lot more conscious about drinking and driving.

Later, as head coach of the Notre Dame ice hockey team, Poulin recounted the story of Lindbergh to each of his 10 teams, emphasizing the importance of players recognizing their own mortality.

Since Lindbergh's passing no Flyers player has worn his No. 31. Many wonder what kind of legacy Lindbergh would have left if he had been able to negotiate that hard turn on Somerdale Road. At the time of his death he had a career record of 87-49-15 and a 3.30 goals-against average.

"If that would not have happened I think he would have had an amazing career," said Propp, whose office wall is decorated with a photo of Lindbergh.

PELLE LINDBERGH

Adorned with Swedish flags, Lindbergh's locker stall was a haunting reminder of the beloved goaltender.

The Flyers asked fans, many of them awash in tears, for a moment of silence before their game against the Edmonton Oilers on Nov. 14, 1985.

"To this day, I think he would have been a Hall of Famer," Peeters said. "He was that good. The guy was the real deal in my books. He was such a loveable guy. He worked hard on the ice and loved life off the ice."

"It's a shame," Brown said, "but a lot of lives changed that day."

ON A MISSION

Despite the tragic loss of their friend, the Flyers kept winning, stretching their 10-game win streak to 13 and carrying a 28-10-0 record into the New Year.

Propp (40 goals, 97 points), Kerr (58 goals and an NHL record 33 power play tallies) and Howe (plus-85) enjoyed one of the finest seasons of their careers and the Flyers rolled into the 1986 playoffs with 110 points after having won 11 of their final 13 games.

"I actually thought that team was better than the ones that went to the Finals in '85 and '87," Holmgren said. "We just didn't get the goaltending in the playoffs."

Bob Froese, who led the NHL with 31 wins that season, allowed 15 goals in five playoff games and the Flyers bowed out quietly to the Rangers in six games.

NEW SEASON, NEW BULL'S EYE

Keenan's third season as coach of the Flyers (1986-87) was marked by the emergence of a pair of rookies who would go on to have long and productive NHL careers. One (Ron Hextall) Keenan loved, the other (Scott Mellanby) he loathed.

Keenan viewed Hextall as a rabid, snarling rookie hungry for a chance to prove himself as the Flyers' next great goalie. He viewed Mellanby as the college-educated, silver-spooned son of Ralph Mellanby, the executive producer of Hockey Night in Canada.

"If there was one guy Mike missed on it was Scott Mellanby," Poulin said. "Clarkie really wanted him to succeed, but Mike was determined to break him."

At a practice during Mellanby's rookie season, Keenan chased Mellanby into the corner and began cross-checking him in the back.

Scott Mellanby survived a tumultuous rookie season with the Flyers to go on to play in 1,431 NHL games.

"Mike was saying, 'What are you gonna do if a guy crosschecks you like this?'" Tocchet said.

And then Keenan would crosscheck Mellanby in the back again and again and again.

"A lot of us just wanted to go after Mike right there on the ice," Tocchet said. "But we didn't."

Mellanby survived that first season under Keenan and went on to play in more than 1,400 games in 20 NHL seasons.

GUFFAW MAKES ITS DEBUT

Brian Propp began the 1986-87 season with 266 goals, but was lacking a signature celebration. That changed in the summer of 1986 after he and a friend went to see Canadian comedian and future game show host Howie Mandel in Atlantic City.

"Howie asked the crowd if they would like to mess up the next comedian that came on stage," Propp said. "Of course, everyone said yes."

Mandel explained that instead of clapping for the next comedian, the crowd should twist their right hands into the air like mini-fireworks and called the move the "Guffaw."

When the next comedian stepped on stage the crowd broke into the "Guffaw" and broke up with laughter. Propp began using the gesture every time he greeted friends and told his friend he'd use it whenever he scored a goal the following season.

"I'll never forget my first goal at the start of the 1986-87 season," Propp said. "I had the usual crowd of players congratulating me after the goal, then as I broke away from the pack and headed to center ice, I put my right glove under my left arm and did the Guffaw as I skated toward center ice. I always said the word "Guffaw" as I was doing it."

Brian Propp began doing the "Guffaw" after seeing a Howie Mandel comedy act in Atlantic City.

Propp's signature celebration eventually made its way back to Mandel, who phoned the Flyers and asked equipment manager Turk Evers if he could speak with Propp before a 1987 playoff game against the Rangers.

"I thought Turk was playing a joke, but sure enough, it was Howie Mandel on the line," Propp said. "He thought it was great that I was using the Guffaw and he didn't mind if I used it. That was a thrill for me to get his approval."

An avid golfer, Propp still celebrates with the Guffaw whenever he shoots a birdie or an eagle on the golf couse.

"I'm not sure what I'll do when I get my first hole in one," he said, "but I'm sure the Guffaw will have something to do with it."

KING OF PAIN

While Mike Keenan's dictatorship began fraying his players' nerves, Pat Croce was busy revolutionizing the world of pro fitness at his torture chamber in Broomall, Pa.

"When I first started working with the Flyers (in the early 1980s) they drank beer like camels drink water," Croce recalled. "They carried a case of sticks under one arm and a case of beer under the other."

To keep them honest in the summers Croce often invited players to his home in Ocean City, New Jersey, where he'd put them through daily circuit training at 7 a.m.

"I think some of them came right from the bars," he said, "because they'd be throwing up between each circuit."

When players were rehabbing injuries Croce demanded they show up at his rehab center by 7 a.m. For every minute a player arrived late Croce, a black belt in karate, tacked on a wall seat, which called for a player sitting on the floor with his back against the wall and his legs in front of him at a 90-degree angle.

Strength and conditioning coach Pat Croce, shown here with Jay and Ed Snider, was known as the "King of Pain."

"I remember (76ers power forward) Charles Barkley strolling in 10 minutes late and his legs were burning from those wall seats," McCrimmon said. "Pat made it clear it was his time and not ours."

Since the Flyers and Philadelphia 76ers both trained with Croce, rehabbing athletes would often race to his office to get first dibs on the radio.

"The Flyers wanted rock and the Sixers wanted rhythm and blues or soul," Croce said. "(Flyers enforcer) Ed Hospodar would come in and take his teeth out and put them in front of the radio. The basketball guys wouldn't go near them."

Tocchet recalls rookie Greg Smyth coming into training camp slightly overweight and Croce following him down a hallway until he stopped at a vending machine and grabbed a bag of potato chips.

"Croce snuck up behind him, grabbed the bag and smashed it in front of his face and screamed, 'If you ever … eat this again, I'll … kill you!'"

APRIL FOOL'S JOKE?

In the mid-1980s no player was feared more than Detroit Red Wings pugilist Bob Probert. Someone forgot to tell that to Ron Hextall.

The Flyers' only visit to Detroit in 1986-87 came on April 1 and Hextall was foolish enough to challenge Probert to a fight.

"I'm skating up the ice and I hear the crowd roaring," recalled Kerry Huffman, one of the Flyers' more passive defensemen. "I look behind me and Hexy and Probert both have their gloves dropped and they're ready to go at it.

"I look over and Rick Tocchet, Dave Brown and Craig Berube are all on the bench and I'm out there with Ilkka

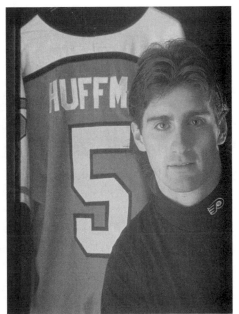

Kerry Huffman's bravest act as a Flyer was saving Ron Hextall from Red Wings enforcer Bob Probert.

Sinisalo, Pelle Eklund, Murray Craven and Mark Howe."

Fearing his goalie, still wearing his mask, would be decapitated by Probert, Mike Keenan screamed to no one in particular, 'Get in there!"

Huffman raced down the ice flew into the air and tackled Hextall into the Flyers net.

"I'm on top of him and he's throwing punches at me," Huffman said. "Probert looked at the two of us and must have thought we were crazy."

MOSQUITO BITES FOR ROYALTIES

Bill Clement's brief career in acting will best be remembered for his 1987 portrayal of an outdoorsman in a television commercial for Deep Woods Off, which ran for six years on national television.

As Clement recalls, more than 150 actors auditioned for the part before the pool was narrowed down to seven. As one of the seven, Clement was asked to fly to Orlando, Fla. on a Wednesday night to tape the commercial in the Florida Everglades.

Clement's audition happened to come in the midst of the 1987 Stanley Cup playoffs between the Flyers and New York Rangers. He had broadcast a game in Philadelphia on Tuesday and was scheduled to be in New York on Thursday for the next game.

After working Tuesday night's game at the Spectrum, Clement arrived in Orlando at 2 p.m., took a nap, then hiked to the Everglades at 9 p.m. for the moonlit shoot.

Because of truth in advertising laws, the insect repellent company took 15,000 mosquitoes and flies from the entomology department at the University of Florida, transported them into the thick of the Everglades, and released them into a mesh tent.

Clement stepped into the tent wearing only a pair of shorts and a pair of hiking boots.

``It was an eerie experience,'' he recalled, mimicking the sound of 15,000 mosquitoes.

Clement's lines went something like this:

``We filled this tent with 10,000 hungry mosquitoes and biting flies. But they're not biting me. I'm wearing Deep Woods Off. It repels even the toughest mosquitoes and biting flies. Deep Woods Off. Aerosol or pump spray. Deep Woods Off. Repels extra tough mosquitoes and biting flies.''

Clement and the crew shot the commercial 37 times before finally settling on one they liked — at 3 a.m.

Apparently, their judgment was good. The commercial ran for six years, earning Clement $90,000 in royalties — all for six hours of work — and two mosquito bites.

FIGHTING IN FLIP FLOPS

Ed "Boxcar" Hospodar and Glenn "Chico" Resch were not exactly leading men in the Flyers' 1987 playoff drive, but they both played supporting roles in one of the biggest and most memorable brawls in NHL history.

With the Flyers leading the Montreal Canadiens three games to two and a date with the Oilers in the Cup Finals hanging in the balance, Hospodar and Resch had grown perturbed at Claude Lemieux's habit of firing a puck into the Flyers' net at the end of warmups.

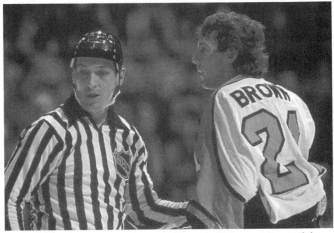

Dave Brown came out of the locker room half dressed to partici-pate in the 1987 brawl that resulted in 36 players being fined.

Several players no-ticed that whenever Lemieux scored into the unguarded net the Canadiens won that night. Hospodar and Resch were determined not to let it happen again, so before heading to their own locker room after warmups, they waited until Lemieux and teammate Shayne Corson left the Montreal Forum ice.

But wait!

Lemieux and Corson schemed up a plan before the game. Once Hospodar and Resch retreated to the visiting locker room, the two Canadiens pranksters sprung back on the ice. Lemieux took a pass from Corson and fired the puck into the empty net, much to the delight of the early birds who saw the shenanigans.

Hospodar and Resch didn't see the humor and like a bull out of a cattle chute Hospodar bounded onto the ice and began throwing overhand rights to the head of Lemieux.

Flyers assistant equipment manager Turk Evers played the role of Paul Revere, sprinting from the ice to the Flyers' dressing room to inform the troops there was a battle breaking out on the ice.

Before you could say Kung Fu Fighting, players from both locker rooms were climbing over each other to get on the ice and find a dance partner. Flyers defense-man Doug Crossman was trying to keep his balance while fighting in flip flops.

A half-dressed Dave Brown found Chris Nilan and began throwing left hooks. Don Nachbaur squared off with Larry Robinson and Darryl Stanley traded blows with John Kordic.

Keenan defiantly watched it all unfold, but when Hextall bounded up the run-way looking for some Canadiens flesh to pound, the Flyers coach held him back and ordered him back to the dressing room.

Keenan seemed more than willing to let the festivities continue unabated when Ed Snider appeared in the tunnel and ordered him to take his players off the ice.

"Ed Snider said to me, 'Go out there and stop it,'" Croce recalled. "Mike tells me, 'No, let them go.' I knew who the boss was, so I listened to Ed. But once I got out there, I didn't know what to do. I grabbed Tock from behind, but I knew as a street fighter you never hold your own guy back if it means somebody gets a free a shot at him. It was wild out there."

When all was said and done, 36 players from both teams were fined a total of $24,500 and the little-used Hospodar was suspended for the remainder of the play-offs.

To this day Tocchet believes Keenan's belligerence that night led to his firing a year later.

"A lot of people think that's when Mike's fate was sealed in Philly," Tocchet said.

HEXTALL'S CORONATION

Legend has it that when Ron Hextall climbed onto the team bus as a rookie in 1986-87, veteran Bob Froese informed him that the seat he was about to sit in was reserved for the starting goalie.

"Well then, I guess it's mine," Hextall said, confidently making himself comfortable.

In need of someone to fill the huge vacuum left by Lindbergh's passing, Keenan entrusted the keys to the Flyers' goaltending future to a wild-eyed 22-year-old from Brandon, Manitoba.

"Hexy was the exact opposite of Pelle," Tocchet said. "You could joke with Pelle before a game, but we were scared to go near Hexy."

So was any opponent who dared enter Hextall's goal crease. Hextall guarded his crease as a holy grail, clearing intruders with an ax disguised as a goalie stick.

"I couldn't believe how volatile he was on the ice and how much of a vocal leader he was in the dressing room," Flyers assistant coach E.J. McGuire said. "That was unusual for a rookie and highly unusual for a goalie."

Keenan didn't simply ease Hextall into his first NHL experience; he played him in a league-high 66 games and wrung 37 wins out of him. Hextall thrived on the workload and his brash and bravado quickly made him one of the NHL's most hated goaltenders.

"The fans in New York might have been the worst," Hextall said of his rookie experiences in Madison Square Garden. "One guy painted an ice bucket to make it look like an urn and waved it at me chanting, 'Buy a Porsche.'"

Ron Hextall's ornery style made him a popular target in opposing arenas, especially Madison Square Garden.

Hextall seemed to thrive on the emotion of the game, raising his level of play as the stakes grew higher.

"Hexy had to play at a certain level of intensity," recalled Dave Poulin. "He couldn't be above it or below it. It was up to somebody else to recognize the levels of that range. And you had to do it without taking the edge down."

Hextall's regular season brilliance extended deep into the playoffs, where he led the Flyers to a six-game victory over the Rangers, a seven-game victory over the Islanders and a six-game victory over the Canadiens to reach the Stanley Cup Finals.

Matched against one of the best teams in league history without Tim Kerr and with Poulin again hampered by broken ribs, Hextall was the Flyers' only hope of survival.

Many believe his performance in Game 6, when the Flyers rallied to win 3-2 on a late goal by defenseman J.J. Daigneault, was the best single performance they've ever witnessed.

"He was as good as Bernie that season, maybe even better because he could handle the puck," remembers Clarke.

"I've seen a lot of great goalies play and for one year he was as good as anybody I've ever seen play," said Mark Howe.

Hextall's performance in Game 6 also provoked what many believe was the loudest crowd in Spectrum history.

When the Flyers went to the Stanley Cup Finals in 1985 and 1987, Mike Keenan was the toast of the town.

"It was so loud in pre-game warmups, it went quiet," McCrimmon said. "It's like your skin stood up."

"I remember when J.J. scored the goal," Hextall said. "You're so into the game, you hear the crowd, but you don't comprehend that's the loudest that's it been in that building, possibly ever."

Hextall's most vivid memory of that Game 6 was needing a police escort out of the Spectrum and into his car.

"It was pretty funny," he said. "It was kind of like being a rock star, everyone was going nuts. It took a while to be escorted to my car because of the crowd. Back then I did have a rock star haircut. I couldn't get 'er cut because we kept winning.'"

Hextall said that after that emotional victory in Philadelphia he fully expected the Flyers to pull off the unexpected and shock the Oilers in Game 7 three nights later. The Flyers lost 3-1 in that game, but Hextall became just the fourth player from a losing team to win the Conn Smythe Trophy as the Most Valuable Player of the playoffs.

Yet more than 20 years later Hextall still refuses to watch replays of the game.

"I can't because it's too painful," he said. "I'll leave the room. I'd like to play that game again."

Years after the Oilers' seven-game victory over the Flyers, Wayne Gretzky told Rick Tocchet he never played against a team that worked as hard as the 1987 Flyers.

"They had six Hall of Famers, we had none," Poulin said, referring to Glenn Anderson, Paul Coffey, Grant Fuhr, Jari Kurri, Mark Messier and Gretzky. "We weren't healthy and they were and we still took them to a seventh game."

"That was a special team," Hextall recalled. "I was never on a team like that in all my years. The commitment of that team was almost insane. I knew it was a gritty team and a driven team, but in 15 years (of professional hockey) I never came close to the character of that bunch.

"That whole year everybody gave everything every night. Talk about squeezing a lemon and getting everything out of it, that's what Mike Keenan did with us. I look back and that's a bond that will never break and I am proud to be a part of it."

PAY THE TOLL, KID

The start of the 1987-88 season issued in a new crop of Flyers rookies, led by Craig Berube, Kerry Huffman and Greg Smyth.

One day after practice Smyth's teammates told him that when the Flyers play a game at the Spectrum the toll gate at the Walt Whitman Bridge opens for players, but only if they yell, "Flyers!" when they approach the change basket.

So, as he crossed the bridge and approached the toll basket, Smyth did as he was told, yelling "Flyers!"

The toll gate didn't budge.

So Smyth yelled again even louder, "FLYERS!"

The gate stayed still.

By now, a line of angry drivers had formed behind Smyth and many of them began honking their horns in disgust.

Finally, a police officer from the Delaware River Port Authority asks Smyth what the problems is.

"I'm with the Flyers and I've got a game to go to," Smyth barks at the officer.

"I don't give a (crap) who you are," the officer replied. "Put your money in like everybody else."

Smyth became so irate he asked for the officer's badge number and informed his teammates of how rudely he was treated.

"He honestly thought that if you said, 'Flyers!' the gate would go up," Tocchet said. "It was priceless."

GO AHEAD, HIT ME!

On the wall of Mike Keenan's office in the Coliseum hung a sign that read: "Some athletes compete against others. Champions compete against themselves."

In his first three seasons with the Flyers, Keenan became the youngest coach in NHL history to record 150 wins and the first to win 40 or more games in his first three years behind an NHL bench.

But with Hextall serving an eight-game suspension for slashing Oilers forward Kent Nilsson in the Stanley Cup Finals and tension building between Keenan and his players, the Flyers opened the 1987-88 season by winning just six of their first 22 games.

"The pressure was very extensive," Keenan said at the time. "'I, myself, didn't feel any true despair or major amount of discomfort. But there was so much psychoanalysis about what was wrong, and we had more than a few genuinely young guys. They were turning street corners in their neighborhoods worried about who would confront them next."

With a three-game break in the schedule in late November, Keenan took his players to Lake Placid, home of the 1980 Miracle On Ice, and showed up for practice in full equipment: helmet, shoulder pads, everything.

"He stood in front of us and said, 'Here's your chance. If you want to take a shot at me, do it now.'"

Tocchet recalls Lindsay Carson giving Keenan a stiff body check, but although many contemplated the satisfaction of dropping the gloves with the 38-year-old coach, no one dared.

"You never knew how he'd make you pay," Propp said.

When they returned from Lake Placid, the Flyers went on a 28-9-4 tear and it appeared Keenan had survived his biggest crisis in Philadelphia.

HELLO? SIR CHARLES? CLICK!

As a player, Rick Tocchet enjoyed fraternizing with athletes from all circles. After games, he could often be seen chatting with other professional athletes from Philadelphia.

During one game at the Spectrum, Tocchet was scratched from the lineup with an injury and was sitting in the press box with travel secretary Joe Kadlec when he spotted 76ers star Charles Barkley seated in the first row behind the penalty box.

During the game, Tocchet asked Kadlec for the phone number in the public address announcer's box and dialed down to Lou Nolan.

"My phone rings and it's Tocchet," Nolan said. "He says, 'Let me talk to Charles.' I hand the phone to Charles and say, 'It's for you.'"

"For me?" Charles asked incredulously.

"Yeah, but if a goal is scored, give it back right away because I've got to call upstairs to get the assists on the goal," Nolan informed Barkley.

"So Charles and Tock are laughing away and a goal is scored," Nolan said. "I grab the phone from Charles, hang up on Tocchet and make the call.

"After the game I see Tocchet and he says to Barkley, 'You son of a (gun,) you hung up on me."

Charles said, 'Oh, no. Not me!. It was that man right there!"

HEXY SHOOTS, HE SCORES!

By his second year in the NHL, Hextall was feeling more comfortable handling the puck around his net and often used those skills to create odd-man rushes on penalty kills.

"Dave Poulin and I would force teams to dump it in and Hexy would fire an outlet pass up to us for a 2-on-1," Propp said.

After practices, Hextall would shoot pucks the length of the ice almost as hard as his teammates.

"I wanted him to shoot more than he did," Propp said. "I always told him that if the other team pulled their goalie to go for it."

The opportunity presented itself on Dec. 8, 1987 when Hextall settled a dump-in, cradled the puck and whipped it down the middle of the ice for a goal, becoming the first goalie to ever shoot the puck into an opponent's net.

"I think it was the perfect opportunity," Hextall recalled. "The puck came right to my left side. It was a very good opportunity to take a shot at it. When I got the shot, I looked up ice and everything was clear so I knew I could clear the zone. Fortunately. it went over everybody's head and into the net."

Derrick Smith fetched the puck from the Bruins net while Hextall's teammates poured from the bench for a group hug.

"The special part to me was the whole team came over the boards and it was almost like we won a playoff round or something. Guys were real excited. I don't want to say it became a rallying point; it became a bit of a team accomplishment. Everybody was pumped after the game."

The Flyers mounted the game sheet onto a plaque and presented every player with one. The following season, Hextall scored again, this time in the second round of the Stanley Cup playoffs, to become the first netminder to score in the playoffs.

"I think if he looked more often, he would have had a lot more goals," Propp said.

KEENAN'S UNDOING

The good vibrations that surrounded Hextall's goal continued through late February, but when the Flyers began slipping again in early March, losing five of six games, Keenan again cracked the whip.

"I remember losing in overtime in Chicago (March 13, 1988)," recalled Tocchet. "It was a great game. There were three or four fights, Denis Savard was doing spinaramas and I remember saying to myself, 'That was one of the best games I've ever been a part of."

As the players undressed, Keenan stormed into the room and let his players have it.

"I think we all looked at each other and said, 'Are you kidding me?'" Tocchet said. "I'm a Mike Keenan fan, but if you ask me, that's when he lost the team."

The Flyers went on to lose six of their final 10 games, completing a 4-11-2 slide to end the season. But if the sky was falling, Keenan didn't see it.

"I didn't sense it," McGuire said, "and I don't think Mike did, either."

When the Flyers blew a three-games-to-one lead on the Washington Capitals in the first round of the playoffs, losing Game 7 in overtime on a breakaway goal by Dale Hunter, it was clear to everyone Keenan had coached his final game in Philadelphia.

Rick Tocchet and Murray Craven celebrate after winning Game 4 in overtime. It was Keenan's last victory as Flyers coach.

IRON MIKE OUT, HOMER IN

The news came on June 1 when Keenan, despite a 190-102-28 record and two trips to the Stanley Cup Finals in four years, was replaced by Paul Holmgren.

Shortly after Keenan' firing untold stories of his treatment of players surfaced.

"It was a war between Mike and the players," Clarke said. "He was so mad at Zezel he made him dress with the Zamboni. He did some cruel things to people.

"Brad Marsh hit his head in a game against the Bruins and got a concussion. He came back right away and he was struggling.

"Just by pure luck I walked down to the locker room on a game day and all of Marsh's equipment was gone. I said to Sudsy (trainer Dave Settlemyre), 'Where's Marshy's stuff?'

"He said. 'Keenan told us to get it out of here and throw it all away, he's not playing anymore.' I said, 'You get that stuff and put it back and we'll get it straightened out in a hurry.'

"You can't be cruel to people like that. It's not necessary. This is sports."

Keenan went on to have successful coaching stints in Chicago, New York,

St. Louis, Vancouver, Boston, Florida and Calgary and is revered by Rangers fans for leading them to their first Stanley Cup in 54 years.

But even today Clarke stands by his decision to fire Keenan.

"I think what happened to Mike is that it came too fast for him," Clarke said. "Right from the start he took a team that was just OK and made it a top team. But when the team didn't play good, it became the players' fault.

"Mike did a really good job, but after four or five years here he ended up blaming the players and that's when he lost them all."

Mark Howe agreed.

"Mike did a lot for me and for the organization, but because of the things he did over the course of four years, he had to go," Howe said. "I know the organization caught some hell for getting rid of him, but the time had come."

Tim Kerr and Brad McCrimmon acknowledged they had their share of disagreements with Keenan, but neither believed his intentions went beyond wanting to win.

"Mike got a bad rap for being insensitive, but as a whole he was always there for the guys," Kerr said. "I don't think Mike masked his feelings. He had a soft side to him; he just didn't show it very often.

"Mike enjoyed guys pushing back," McCrimmon said. "He had no problem with you walking into his office, closing the door and letting him have it. He liked to see that response."

Holmgren, who had the uncomfortable job of replacing Keenan after coaching under him, believes everyone who played for him became a better player.

"I always thought he was hard on players, but I think some players understood he cared for them," Holmgren said. "Some didn't believe that. But a lot of the players who wanted Mike fired benefited from him."

In fact, several years later, while golfing before Rick Tocchet's wedding, Poulin, Mellanby, Craig Berube and Murray Craven posed this question: Who was the best coach they ever played for in their careers?

"Begrudgingly," Poulin said, "we all admitted Mike was."

CHAPTER 6

THE BLUNDER YEARS
(1988–1992)

The firing of legendary captain and general manager
Bob Clarke marks the beginning of the
darkest days in team history.

HOMER'S ODYSSEY

THE FLYERS DID NOT NEED TO LOOK FAR TO FIND MIKE
Keenan's replacement for the start of the 1988-89 season. Paul Holmgren had
become a confidante for several players near the end of Keenan's tenure and his
calm demeanor made him the perfect antithesis to Iron Mike.

The Flyers won their first four games under Holmgren, but won just six of their
next 24, making everyone in the organization wonder if Keenan had squeezed so
much from his players there was nothing left.

Peter Zezel was the first sacrificial lamb when he was dealt to St. Louis for Mike
Bullard, a former 50-goal scorer who had a reputation for taking hockey a little less
seriously than his coaches liked.

"I really hated being traded," Zezel said. "And for Mike Bullard? C'mon.

"I really felt like I grew up in Philadelphia and I was hoping I'd someday get
back there."

Dave Brown, a former teammate and good friend of Holmgren's, was the next
to go, getting sent to Edmonton for Keith Acton.

The Flyers recovered from their slow start, but even with Tim Kerr and Rick
Tocchet combining for 93 goals, there were legitimate questions surrounding a
Flyers blue line consisting of Terry Carkner, an ailing Mark Howe, Kjell Samuels-
son, Jay Wells, Gord Murphy and Jeff Chychrun.

The Flyers finished the regular season a pedestrian 36-36-8 and there was no reason to believe they'd beat the Washington Capitals in the opening round of the playoffs.

They did, rallying back from a two-games-to-one deficit to beat Pete Peeters in six games. The Flyers tied that series with an 8-5 win in Washington that is best remembered for Ron Hextall becoming the first goaltender to score a goal in the playoffs.

Moments after Peeters left the ice for an extra attacker with just over a minute to play, Washington defenseman Scott Stevens rimmed the puck around the Flyers net.

Hextall quickly intercepted it, looked up the ice and flung the puck the length of the ice.

"I was thinking goal," Hextall said after a wise-cracking

Peter Zezel was angry about being traded to St. Louis, especially when he learned it was for Mike Bullard.

reporter asked if it was the longest he had gone in his career between goals. "I knew we were short-handed and that it wouldn't be icing.

"Somebody told me the other day that it had been over 100 games since I scored. I guess it was time."

WREGGET TO THE RESCUE

A wild series against the Penguins followed, with Pittsburgh grabbing a 3-2 lead in the series with an amazing 10-7 victory in Game 5.

Mario Lemieux enjoyed one of the most dominating performances in playoff history, tying NHL records for goals (five), points (eight) and goals in one period (four).

Already incensed by the night's proceedings Ron Hextall went ballistic when Rob Brown celebrated the Penguins' ninth goal with a center-ice windmill.

A humiliated Hextall sprinted out of his crease and chased after Brown before teammates intervened.

Ken Wregget celebrated a spectacular performance in Game 7 by smoking a cigarette in under the stands of the Igloo.

"It was 9-2," Hextall said afterward. "Enough is enough."

Joked Brown, "It was probably the quickest I've ever skated."

Hextall re-gained his composure in Game 6 and the Flyers rebounded to knot the series with a 6-2 win at home, sending it back to the Igloo for a seventh and deciding game.

Hextall suffered a sprained knee in Game 6 and tried to convince doctors to clear him for Game 7, but when he could barely walk to the Igloo the morning of the game, Holmgren told backup Ken Wregget he'd be making his third start in three months.

Wregget, who was recovering from mononucleosis when the Flyers acquired him from Toronto at the trade deadline, was sensational that night, stopping Lemieux on several point-blank shots and being named first star of the game.

"He was phenomenal that game," Tocchet recalled. "It was vindication for Clarke, too, because he had taken heat for giving up two first-rounders for him."

For good measure, Scott Mellanby celebrated the game's final goal by mocking the Penguins bench with a Rob Brown-inspired windmill to seal the 4-1 victory.

As reporters poured into the visiting locker room looking for Wregget, the 25-year-old goalie nowhere to be found.

A mad search found the cool-handed netminder smoking a cigarette under the stands.

"You guys looking for me?" Wregget asked with grin.

'I AM NOT A MADMAN'

The Flyers could not savor their Game 7 win over the Penguins very long. They chartered a flight directly to Montreal, where they would face the Canadiens in the conference finals for the second time in three years.

With Hextall still sidelined with his knee sprain, Wregget and the Flyers outplayed Patrick Roy and the Habs in the series opener, winning 3-1 at the Forum.

The game was marred by a vicious elbow Montreal defenseman Chris Chelios landed to the head of Brian Propp.

Propp had released the puck along the defensive left wing boards when Chelios took two steps and drove his left elbow into the head of Propp, whose head slammed the ice, creating a small pool of blood under him.

"It was a cheap shot," said Propp, who was carted off the ice on a stretcher after telling paramedics he thought he was in Pittsburgh.

Propp and Hextall missed the next two games, both losses, but returned to the lineup for Game 4, a 3-0 loss at the Spectrum. Holmgren told his players they were playing too tight, so Mike Bullard decided to have some fun in Montreal the night before Game 5.

When Holmgren caught wind that Bullard had blown curfew the night before, he put a scare in him and everyone else on the team at an optional skate the next morning.

"To this day, anytime Homer is mad, he'll grab a stick," said Craig Berube. "So when I saw him grab a stick I knew something was up."

Bullard didn't. He was slumped in his locker stall when Holmgren wheeled around, stuck his stick under Bullard's chin, and lifted him off the bench like a fisherman reeling in a marlin.

"You want to go out the night before a playoff game?" Holmgren screamed at a terrified Bullard. "Where's your commitment to this team?"

"I'm sitting there thinking, 'Holy − −! He's going to kill him!' Berube said. "Bully's feet were literally dangling off the floor. Ands he says, "I promise ... I promise I'll play good tonight."

The Flyers staved off elimination with an overtime win in Game 5, setting up a Game 6 showdown in Philadelphia.

When it became clear the Flyers were not going to erase a 3-1 deficit late in the game, Hextall charged out of his net to seek retribution on Chelios, slamming him to the ice with a body check.

Linesman Gerard Gauthier quickly intervened and after finally separating the two from the pileup, Hextall, his jersey completely off, hurled his blocker at Chelios, who was drenched with beer and sodas as he left the ice.

Still steaming after the game, Hextall was grilled by the media but did not back down.

"Did you see what he did to Brian Propp?" Hextall shot back. "C'mon. I think we owed him something. God Almighty, he just about took (Propp's) head off. I think that's good enough reason."

When a radio host suggested Hextall went after Chelios like a madman, a wild-eyed Hextall retorted, "I am not a madman!"

Ron Hextall never backed down from his attack on Chris Chelios, saying, "I think we owed him something."

Once his nerves calmed, Hextall explained his behavior to a small group of reporters.

"'I didn't intend to hurt Chelios; I intended to fight him," Hextall said. "I know I was wrong, but I also know what Chris Chelios did to Brian Propp was far more vicious than what I did to Chelios."

Propp agrees.

"Hextall went right after Chelios and as a teammate I respect that," Propp said.

NHL vice-president Brian O'Neill slapped Hextall with a 12-game suspension, fourthlongest in league history, calling his actions a "blatant and premeditated attack on an opponent."

"It was so unfair that Hextall got 12 games and Chelios got nothing for what today would have been a 20-game suspension," Propp said.

TAKE MY JET, TIM

For his incredible perseverance, Tim Kerr became the first Flyer since Bobby Clarke to win the Bill Masterton Award, but because the awards ceremony in Toronto fell on the same day as his parents, Earl and Eileen, were celebrating their 50th wedding anniversary, he informed the Flyers he would be unable to pick up his award.

"I had to decline because I wanted to be with my family that day," Kerr said.

When Ed Snider learned of Kerr's dilemma, he sent his private jet to pick up Kerr, whisk him to Tecumseh, Ontario for his parents' anniversary party, then to Toronto for that evening's NHL awards ceremony.

"The thing about Mr. Snider is that he never looked for anything in return," Kerr said. "He is truly a generous man and he's the reason the Flyers are a first-class organization."

HEX IS ON

Few honestly believed the Flyers were as good as that three-round romp through the playoffs in 1989 and the following season proved it.

It began inauspiciously when Hextall, already about to serve a 12-game sentence for his attack on Chelios, held a teary-eyed press conference to announce he would not play for the Flyers until they renegotiated his contract.

Three years earlier Hextall had agreed to an eight-year contract worth about $500,000 a season. But with more than half of that money deferred and with the NHL's salary landscape quickly changing, Hextall and his new agent Rich Winter, believed the 25-year-old goalie was worth more.

Backed into a corner by the popular goalie, Clarke came out swinging, first saying he would not renegotiate the contract, then saying he would do so only if Hextall fired Winter and hired a new agent.

Clarke, who had earlier battled with Brad McCrimmon and Doug Crossman, said he let his emotions get in the way of his negotiating in his early years as a GM.

"I wasn't good," he said. "I was too combative. In those years, I was right and you were wrong. It takes you a while to learn to compromise and be more diplomatic. It was also a time when agents were really combative, too. It was a war out there and everybody hated each other."

Hextall retained Winter as his agent and reportedly agreed to contract that began at $500,000 and escalated to $660,000 the following season.

Cynics would suggest Hextall stole the Flyers' money that season. A series of groin and hamstring pulls limited the goalie to just eight games that season and he never again showed the razor-sharp form abundantly evident in the springs of 1987 and 1989.

``In retrospect, yeah, that took a lot out of me," Hextall said of his wipeout season of 1989-90. ``I missed a whole year and I'll tell you what, it's a long road back.'

HALLOWEEN HYSTERICS

Even when wins were hard to come by, the Flyers provided plenty of laughs around Halloween.

At one party, Frank Bathe, dressed as a hobo, sat in a corner all night without saying a word.

"No one knew until the next day at practice it was him," Brad McCrimmon said.

Rich and Ron Sutter showed up at one costume party as twin soldiers and no one could tell them apart.

In the late 80s, Mark Howe remembers Dave Brown dressing up as Peewee Herman and doing the best impersonation he ever saw. And then there was Terry Carkner, a 6-foot-3, 210-pound … woman?

"He had the blonde wig, high heels, nylon stockings, shaved legs and a short skirt," Howe said with a laugh. "He stopped in a WaWa (convenience store) before the party and everyone stopped what they were doing."

P.A. announcer Lou Nolan decided to play along before a game by wearing a fake nose, glasses ands mustache.

"At one point during the game (Craig) Berube was in the box and said, 'Hey, Lou!' I turned around and there he was with the nose and glasses on."

"I think I got on ESPN that night," Berube said.

POULIN AND PROPP HEAD TO BEANTOWN

With the Flyers struggling to stay above .500 due to injuries to Tim Kerr, Mark Howe, Brian Propp and Ron Hextall, Clarke began dismantling his team, trading veteran Dave Poulin to the Bruins for Ken Linseman, then Brian Propp to the Bruins for a second-round draft pick.

Poulin, who had not seen or heard rumors about him being shopped around, was devastated.

. "Tocchet answered the phone and told me it was Bob," Poulin recalled. "Clarkie was real matter of fact. He said, 'I just traded you to Boston. Call (Bruins general manager) Harry Sinden."

Just as matter of factly, Poulin said he didn't have to call Sinden at all.

"Kim was pregnant with our third child and she was considered a high-risk," Poulin said.

After a few days of consideration, Poulin accepted the trade and moved his family to Boston.

Bob Clarke said trading Dave Poulin for Ken Linseman in 1990 was one of the worst deals he ever made.

"Did it turn out extremely well for me? Yes," Poulin said. "But I was very disappointed to leave Philadelphia."

Linseman, who by now was married with a family, admitted he was surprised to learn he'd been traded to Philadelphia. He lasted only the remainder of that season.

"I remember is being very tense that season," Linseman said. "Everyone was kind of looking over their shoulders."

Years later, Clarke admitted trading Poulin was his most regrettable trade, saying he underestimated the number of quality seasons Poulin had left in him. Poulin went on to play five more seasons in the NHL, finishing with 530 points in 724 games and reaching the playoffs in each of his 13 NHL seasons.

Unlike Poulin, Propp, who had been benched by Holmgren for his lack of production, welcomed the trade.

"I looked at it as Clarkie giving me an opportunity to go to a better team," Propp said, "We didn't have the right mix in Philly. He did me a favor."

Propp played another four seasons before retiring with 1,004 points in 1,016 career games. He remains second on the Flyers' all-time list in goals (369) and assists (480) and his third in points (849).

While Poulin and Propp flourished in Boston, the Flyers finished with a 30-39-11 record, missing the playoffs for the first time since 1972. As the Flyers' worst season in 18 years melted away, fans in front of Clarke's executive box at the Spectrum began booing him and chanting, "Bob Must Go!"

A LEGEND IS FIRED

A week after the Flyers completed their most disappointing season in years, Jay Snider asked Clarke to devise a long-range plan that would restore the Flyers to their perch as one of the NHL's elite teams.

When Snider asked Clarke to meet him in his Center City office on April 16, 1990, Clarke was prepared. But not for the news he received.

Snider explained to Clarke the team needed to go in a new direction and said he would find a suitable role for Clarke in the organization.

"I was in shock," Clarke said. "I remember having to drive home from Jay's office and thinking, 'This can't be happening.' I was 40 years old, I had four kids. And even though the Flyers had been very good to me financially, I had to work for a living.

"For the first time in my life, I had to go out and look for a job."

In his press conference, Snider said "philosophical differences" had developed between him and Clarke and that the team needed to move in a new direction under different leadership.

Ed Snider seemed bewildered over how far apart his two "sons" had grown.

"If I had known their differences were that serious, I wouldn't have allowed it to happen," Snider said at the time. "Bob Clarke is like a son to me."

At first, Clarke was defiant over his firing, saying he was a victim of the team's mounting injuries to key players.

"I honestly believed that where we got caught was when those guys got hurt," Clarke said, referring to Howe, Kerr and Hextall. "We had built up draft picks for a few years down the road and I think we would have remained competitive until guys like (1990 draft pick) Mike Ricci developed. But the injuries forced us to fill in huge gaps and it just didn't work."

Today, Clarke acknowledges Snider may have had no choice.

"The spirit of the club was not good," he said. "Once that happens there's almost no way of changing it without replacing the coach or the manager. You have to start it over again and they decided to replace me.

Some speculated that Bill Barber, who was the Flyers' director of pro scouting at the time, had a hand in Clarke's dismissal, something Barber vehemently denies.

"That was a crock," Barber said. "Somebody sold me out and I'll never forget that. I was loyal to Bob Clarke. I've always been honest and straightforward with the people in the Flyers organization."

Today, Clarke is more introspective about his 1990 firing, saying Ed Snider's decision to move to Malibu, Calif., and allow his son to run the Flyers created an unstable work environment that trickled from the executive offices to the locker room.

"I didn't have much contact with Mr. Snider during those years," Clarke said. "Ed was the head of the ship and when he was gone we were all looking for our own place. We all had to figure out where we fit in all the mess.

"Jay's a good guy, but I think he was still in competition with his dad at the time. He wanted to have his own team and I was from his dad's era. All that, I think, played into it. In fairness, maybe I deserved it. I was as much to blame as anybody."

Tocchet believes the Flyers lost their identity when Jay Snider took over for his father and that it took years to get it back.

"In that era, there was a lot of tension," Tocchet recalled. "Jay was trying to change stuff and it was no longer a Mr. Snider/Bobby Clarke team."

CALLING MR. FARWELL

With Philadelphia sports fans still stunned by Clarke's dismissal, Jay Snider went to work on finding his replacement. After interviews with Dean Chynoweth, Bill Watters, Brian Burke and Bryan Murray, Snider settled on a bright, bespectacled man from Calgary named Russ Farwell.

But before he took the job, Farwell called the legend he was about to replace and asked if they could meet.

"I met with him and Russ said, 'Jay wants to hire me. Do you think I should take the job?'" Clarke said. "I said, 'Christ, yeah. Don't pass this up. They are a terrific family to work for. I think you'd be foolish not to take it.'"

Farwell accepted and at his introductory press conference, he said he would retain Holmgren as coach and did not feel the Flyers needed a complete overhaul.

"Whether you are going to take a run today or you are going to bring in young guys and build, you need character and strength in older players," Farwell said. "I think we have that, so I don't think sweeping a great number of guys out would be my plan right now."

Farwell's first big decision as GM came at the 1990 draft, where the Flyers owned the fourth pick overall. Owen Nolan, Petr Nedved and Keith Primeau went 1-2-3 and Jaromir Jagr was still on the board.

Flyers scout Jerry Melnyk thought Jagr had the talent to be an explosive NHL player, but Farwell had not seen him. The Flyers instead went with the safer choice, taking Mike Ricci with the fourth pick overall.

Picking fifth, the Penguins snatched up Jagr.

Farwell might not have seen the star potential in Jagr, but he saw NHL coaching potential in two young coaches, Craig Hartsburg and Ken Hitchcock, and hired them as Paul Holmgren's two new assistants for the 1990-91 season.

Farwell cleaned house by refusing to re-sign Bullard, Linseman and Ilkka Sinisalo, but retained the heart

The Flyers passed over Jaromir Jagr and took Mike Ricci fourth overall in the 1990 NHL draft.

of the team by extending Rick Tocchet's contract for four more years and Ron Hextall's for five.

Tocchet pulled his weight that season, scoring a team-high 40 goals, but Hextall repeatedly pulled his groin, forcing Holmgren to use a three-headed rotation of Peeters (26 games), Wregget (30 games) and Hextall (36 games).

None of the three managed to sport a winning record and Tocchet had very little offensive support as the Flyers finished four games under .500 and missed the playoffs for a second straight season.

Losing had begun to take its toll on Holmgren.

"One game Homer was so mad he grabbed a stick and did a two-hander over the shopping cart we used to throw our dirty laundry in," Berube said. "Terry Carrkner was sitting next to me and he reached down and put his helmet on. I started cracking up."

A TREE LOSES ITS BLOOM

Tim Kerr was in his hotel room in Pittsburgh on the morning of Oct. 16, 1990, when the phone woke him from his sleep.

His wife, Kathy, had given birth to a daughter, Kimberly, 10 days earlier and

Kathy had remained in Pennsylvania Hospital with a pelvic infection. Kerr had spoken to Kathy over the phone the day before and both were excited she would be leaving the hospital the next day.

When a doctor on the other end of the phone told him that Kathy had passed away, Kerr could not believe his ears.

"It was crazy," he said. "I needed all the support I could get."

An autopsy later determined that Kathy had died of the pelvic infection for which she was being treated.

Tim Kerr says the support of the Flyers and their fans helped comfort him in the loss of his wife, Kathy.

Tim and Kathy also had an adopted 10-month old named Kayleigh and a 7-year-old girl, Jackie, from Kathy's first marriage.

Jay Snider and Russ Farwell took a private jet to Pittsburgh, where they picked up Kerr and brought him back to Philadelphia. The Flyers won that night in Pittsburgh, then returned home to comfort their grieving teammate.

Two weeks after his wife's passing, Kerr pulled on his uniform and returned to the Flyers lineup, receiving a long ovation from the Spectrum fans the moment he stepped on the ice.

"People say I've had terrible injuries and personal tragedies and I have," said Kerr, now the proud father of five children. "But I never look back and say, 'What if?' I handled the situations I was given because I had to. Anyone else would have done the same thing. I don't think about what I don't have. I appreciate what I do have and I consider myself very fortunate."

HUNTER BECOMES THE HUNTED

Off the ice, Dale Hunter was one of the NHL's great guys. On the ice, he was one of the NHL's grate guys.

As a Flyer, Craig Berube hated no player more than Hunter and their disdain for each other touched off one of the wildest and most entertaining brawls in Flyers history.

In a 1991 visit to Landover, Craig Berube unsuccessfully carried out Paul Holmgren's orders to dispose of Dale Hunter.

In a Feb. 10 visit to the Cap Center, Flyers defenseman Gord Murphy was knocked out of the game when Hunter leaped into him and drilled his head into the glass with an elbow.

"Homer went wild on the bench," Berube recalled. "He yells down bench, 'Where's Chief, Acton and Kushner?' We all stand up and he says, "I want that Hunter dead!"

When Berube, Keith Acton and Dale Kushner jumped out for their next shift, Hunter wasn't on the ice, so when Washington goalie Don Beaupre went behind the net to play the puck, Berube checked him into the boards and was jumped by Nick Kypreos.

"Kypreos said, 'What are you doing?'" Berube said. "I said Hunter wasn't out there so I had to hit somebody."

Berube was immediately sent off the ice but the fireworks were just getting started. Holmgren grabbed a stick, stood on the bench and began smacking it on the glass that separated him from Capitals coach Terry Murray.

Kushner went-to-to-toe with Washington's Mike Lalor and when that fight ended Kypreos grabbed Kushner and pounded him with several balled fists. Murray Baron came to Kushner's defense and was greeted by Al Iafrate, who took off his sweater and elbow pads and chucked knuckles with Baron. Even Pete Peeters got into the act, racing down the ice and yanking Beaupre's mask off in a brief scuffle.

Meanwhile up in the stands, Flyers assistant coach Ken Hitchcock and an injured Rick Tocchet were jawing with fans. When Hitchcock tried going after a fan, Tocchet tried holding him back and twisted his knee.

"All that and I don't even get a chance to fight," Berube said. "Kushner walks into the dressing room bleeding and says, "Where were you. I just got my ass kicked three times?"

HOMER OUTFOXED

After a season of relative inactivity that earned him the nickname Rip Van Farwell, the second-year GM put on his reconstruction hat in the summer of 1991, unloading Ron Sutter, Craig Berube, Scott Mellanby, Mike Bullard, Murray Baron and Jeff Chychrun and replacing them with Rod Brind'Amour, Dan Quinn, Steve Duchesne and Steve Kasper.

When those moves produced only lukewarm results early in the 1991-92 season, Farwell kept the revolving door moving by exchanging Murray Craven, Gord Murphy, Brian Dobbin, Tony Horacek, Rick Tocchet, Kjell Samuelsson and Ken Wregget for Kevin Dineen, Garry Galley, Wes Walz, Ryan McGill, Mark Recchi and Brian Benning.

It was an insane season of player movement as 39 different men suited up in orange and black.

But Farwell's biggest move came just 24 games into the season when, with the Flyers limping along with an 8-14-2 record, the Flyers' general manager decided it was time for Holmgren to be replaced. He just wasn't sure who should replace him.

Bill "The Fox" Dineen, a 60-year-old scout Farwell had hired when he first took the job in Philadelphia, was scouting in Seattle when he received a call from Farwell.

"The Flyers were playing poorly and Russ asked me to come in and take a look at the team," Dineen recalls.

Dineen caught a morning flight to New York, where he saw the Flyers fall to the Rangers 4-2.

"We went to some high class restaurant after the game and he asked me my opinions," Dineen said. "We were there from about midnight til 3 in the morning and then Russ says, 'What would you think about coaching?'"

Kevin Dineen was stunned to learn that his father, Bill Dineen, had replaced Paul Holmgren as coach.

"I don't know what you're drinking there, Russ," Dineen responded, 'but you can't be serious."

Farwell said he was and Dineen told him he'd talk it over with his wife, Pat. The next day Dineen flew back to his home in Rochester, N.Y., found the skates he had tucked away in the basement and said to his wife, "What if I start wearing these again?'"

The next day he became the oldest head coach in the NHL.

"Pat was excited," Dineen said, "and so was I."

The next day's practice was delayed until 1 p.m. so that Dineen could drive down to Philadelphia and familiarize himself with a team he had seen play just twice that season.

Kevin Dineen, who had been acquired for Murray Craven just two weeks earlier, didn't know his father had been hired until he walked into the Coliseum that afternoon.

"I walked past Kjell Samuelsson and he said, 'They let Homer go," Dineen said. "I said, 'Oh, man.' Then he said, 'Billy's having a meeting.'

"Billy who?" Dineen replied.

And in his thick Swedish accent, Samuelsson said, "You're Daaaad."

Some players who were close to Holmgren were resentful of the switch and didn't mind saying it.

"There was just too much change at once," Tocchet said. "Russ came in and there was a changing of the guard. Guys were a little uneasy. They told Homer to play the young guys and I think he took the bullet for those teams."

FROM ROD THE REED TO ROD THE BOD

One of the few highlights of 1991-92 season came on Jan. 18 when the Spectrum hosted the NHL All-Star Game. Ten of the players from that game, including captains Wayne Gretzky and Mario Lemieux, have been inducted into the Hockey Hall of Fame.

The game, won by the Campbell Conference All-Stars 10-6, was the first penalty-free All-Star Game in league history.

The Flyers' lone representative was a muscular center named Rod Brind'Amour. But Rod the Bod didn't always have nulging biceps and washboard abs.

To hear his father tell the story, Rod joined and quit hockey teams twice by the time he was 7.

"I was heartbroken, said Bob Brind'Amour, a former pipefitter and senior league player from Prince Huber, British Columbia. "I was sort of a hero in my town and now my oldest son wouldn't play hockey."

It wasn't until just before his eighth Christmas that Rod had a change of heart.

When Rod Brind'Amour was 12 years old, his father brought him to the doctor thinking he was anemic.

"One day he came to me and said, 'Dad, I want to play hockey,'" the elder Brind'Amour said. "I said, 'You quit twice, what's the sense of doing it again?' And he said, 'No, I'm serious. I want to play.'"

Wary of his son's dedication to stick it out, Bob Brind'Amour made it known that if Rod was not up and out of bed in time for his 5 a.m. practices, he would not participate.

"Every day, he'd come in my room and wake me up," Bob Brind'Amour said. "I knew then he was ready to play."

But there were hurdles to overcome.

"He was a skinny kid," Bob Brind'Amour said. "I took him to the doctors and told them he was anemic. He wouldn't eat, he wouldn't put on weight. I thought he was sick."

As it turned out, the young Brind'Amour was perfectly healthy. He just hadn't matured physically.

Bob Brind'Amour managed to find a team that would take his son in midseason that year, then coached him as a 12-year-old, forcing him to play defense before allowing him to move back to his natural position as a left wing.

"`He amazed me," Bob Brind'Amour said. "He must have been studying the game all those years he wasn't playing because he knew every rule and every situation."

But he was still built like a weeping willow.

When Rod turned 12, his father summoned him to the weight room and asked him to begin 10-minute workouts each morning. They gradually worked their way up to 20 minutes, 30 minutes and more.

By the time he was 18 years old, Rod was leading his Notre Dame junior team to the Saskatchewan league championship, ending the season with 107 points in 56 games. The St. Louis Blues made him the ninth pick overall in the 1988 draft and after a year at Michigan State, Brind'Amour found himself scoring a pair of goals for the Blues in the 1989 Stanley Cup playoffs.

He was acquired by the Flyers on Sept. 22, 1991 along with Dan Quinn in a trade that sent Ron Sutter and Murray Baron to the Blues.

Brind'Amour played parts of nine seasons in Philadelphia and ranks among the top 10 in all-time goals (235), assists (366) and points (601).

TOCCHET'S LAST STAND

The Flyers were five games under .500 when Tocchet learned he had been traded, along with Samuelsson and Wregget, to the Penguins. Bittersweet might be too strong a word to describe his feelings.

Rick Tocchet says his 157 career fights were more popular with fans than his 440 career goals.

"To be honest, at the time I thought, 'Perfect. I'm going to play with Mario Lemieux.'" Tocchet said. 'Pittsburgh had just won the Cup. Get me there."

The Penguins did not visit the Flyers until the following season, but when they did, Tocchet felt like …

"A traitor," he said. "Of all the places I've played, I never had a better relationship than with the fans in Philly," he said. "I can only think of great stories. If I scored a couple goals, I'd go out for a beer after the game and everybody would say, 'Good game, Tock.'

"But if I got into a couple of fights, they'd buy me drinks all night. Philly and me were made for each other. If I started my career somewhere else, who knows? Maybe I would have never even made it to the NHL. We were the perfect fit."

Kerr said he always admired Tocchet because he showed great respect for the game and his role within the structure of a team.

"He took the mantle from me in terms of scoring and ice time, but he never disrespected me," Kerr said. "Some guys forget that, but he had a great deal of respect for the guys who had paid their dues."

Tocchet went on to win his first and only Stanley Cup that season, recording 19 points in 14 playoff games.

HEXTALL THE LEADER

The Flyers were in the midst of a four-game losing streak in January and after a listless first period in Detroit, Bill Dineen was ready to show his dark side with a locker room rant.

"I was really wound up to give it to them and when I walked in, Hextall was going from guy to guy, breaking sticks and screaming at everyone," Dineen said. "He did everything I wanted to do."

GREAT COLLAPSE

The slim chances the Flyers had of making the playoffs in 1992 evaporated in the cloud of a 2-5-0 finish and Spectrum chants of "Bob Must Go!" were replaced with chants of "Jay Must Go!"

When Snider was questioned about possibly being replaced by prodigal son Bob Clarke, he rolled up his sleeves and showed the same spunk that epitomized his father.

"I'm going to be here and I'm going to see this thing through," Snider said. "I'm not going to be run out of here by anyone. Our fans are frustrated and they're taking it out on me. I can live with that. At least they're here and at least they're emotional and they care.

"It's very popular to say that as soon as I took over the Flyers the thing has gone downhill. That's not true. I got involved in 1983 and we were going downhill then. The fan base was off, we built it back up with an exciting product, and had a heck of a run. We're going to do it again."

Ed Snider also rushed to his son's defense.

"We're down now at it's easy to kick us. We're trying hard. We're not a bunch of idiots here."

Although the Flyers finished that 1991-92 season five games under .500, the roster had been completely retooled by Farwell. Only six players remained from the team he inherited from Clarke two years earlier: Kerry Huffman, Mark Howe, Pelle Eklund, Terry Carkner, Ron Hextall and Ken Wregget.

Within a month, two of those players would be included in the most controversial trade in NHL history.

PRODIGAL SON RETURNS

Bob Clarke's exile from the NHL did not last long. Within two months of his firing in Philadelphia, the Minnesota North Stars had chased down Clarke and made him their general manager.

"Initially, there was a lot of anger toward the Flyers," Clarke said. "It was like, 'I'll show you I can do this job.' But that didn't last very long. You don't gain anything good by flaunting what you've done."

Maybe so, but Clarke spoke volumes about his general managing abilities when he directed the overachieving North Stars to the 1991 Stanley Cup Finals in his first year in Minnesota.

The elation of that surprising playoff run ended quickly, however, as the North Stars finished the following season 10 games under .500.

Clarke, who kept his home in Ocean City, returned to the Jersey shore in the summer of 1992 and in a conversation with Ed Snider was offered the job of senior vice president of the Flyers. Clarke accepted and on June 10, 1992, the lifelong Flyer was back.

"I never felt Minnesota was my home," Clarke said. "The people there were great, but it was always my intent to return to Philadelphia. That's where my friends are."

Clarke said the summer of '92 was enjoyable. He golfed, fished and reacquainted himself with old friends. But when the 1992-93 season began, he became a third wheel in the Flyers' decision-making group. He had a title and a nice paycheck, but his role with the Flyers had been reduced to handling occasional player contracts and acting as an advisor to Farwell. For a man who had built a career on hard work, it just wasn't enough.

"I guess there are a lot of people who would love to be in the position I was in," Clarke said, "but it wasn't me."

Clarke remained with the Flyers through the first three months of the 1992-93 season, but when he found little responsibility at the NHL's Board of Governors meeting in December, he decided he needed a new challenge.

"All the guys down there were involved in something and I wasn't," he said. "I could have sat in a beach chair. That's when I realized I couldn't go on the rest of my life like that."

Clarke called then-NHL president Gil Stein and asked if he would mention to Florida Panthers chairman Wayne Huizenga that he was interested in running Miami's expansion team.

Within three months, Huizenga hired Clarke as the Panthers GM and Clarke left the Flyers once again. Only this time, it was on his terms.

"I thought long and hard about it," Clarke said of his decision to relocate to Plantation, Fla. "It was something I felt I had to do."

Clarke said leaving Philadelphia the first time made it easier for him to leave again.

"You get a little more cautious with your heart," he said. "My whole adult life was with the Philadelphia Flyers and they were exceptionally good to me. It's not like they owed me anything, but it's your first taste of business.

"It wasn't that I ever felt I couldn't be replaced, but I put my whole life into it and all of a sudden I'm standing on the street corner. I didn't have a job. The Flyers were exceptionally good to me financially, but I had my whole adult life pulled away from me. You learn a lot from that and I made sure it wouldn't happen again."

CHAPTER 7

GREAT (88) EXPECTATIONS

(1992–1994)

A young star named Eric Lindros bursts onto the scene with Gretzky-like fanfare and points the Flyers in a new direction.

LITTLE E ON A BIG WHEEL

From the time her son could hop on his Big Wheel and motor around the hardwood floors of their London, Ontario home, Bonnie Lindros knew she would need to get her son Eric involved in some form of physical activity.

"Eric was so full of energy," she said. "He was nonstop."

When he was in kindergarten, after being snubbed by a group of older boys playing football at a playground in London, Ontario, Eric got into his first fight, beating up a third grader.

By the time he was 15, the hockey rink was Eric's personal playground and if there was bullying to be done, he was the one dishing it out.

Bill Dineen and Neil Smith had heard all about 6-foot-4, 229-pound man child, so the coach and general manager of the Adirondack Red Wings drove through a rainstorm before finally settling into their seats to watch Lindros play for the St. Michael's Buzzers.

"We were curious about how good this kid was," Dineen said. "He got into a fight and got thrown out in the first two minutes of the game!"

At 16, Lindros was drafted first overall by the Sault Ste. Marie Greyhounds of the Ontario League, but refused to report and was eventually traded to the Oshawa Generals, where he scored 149 points in 57 games.

"He was literally head and shoulders above everybody else," said Dineen, who estimated he saw Lindros play 30 times before he turned pro. "If his team was down a goal, he'd start knocking people down and you could just see the other teams back up. There was nothing stopping this kid from being a star."

Touted as "The Next One" and "Eric The Great," Lindros made it clear before the 1991 NHL draft that he would not play for the small-market Quebec Nordiques, who owned the No. 1 pick.

The Nordiques picked him anyway and when Lindros refused to pull on the Nordiques' jersey the day of the draft, a very personal and public feud began between Nordiques owner Marcel Aubut and the Lindros family.

"There were cartoons of Eric dressed up as a Ku Klux Klan member," Carl Lindros said. "It turned into a political and racial thing that was never intended."

"It was part of Marcel's campaign to disunite our family," Bonnie Lindros said.

Lindros played the following season for the Canadian national team and midway through that season Farwell and Jay Snider made a strong but quiet pitch for him.

The complicated proposal would include two of the following players – Rick Tocchet, Ron Hextall, Steve Duchesne and Terry Carkner — along with two more of the following players – Kimbi Daniels, Wes Walz, the first pick in the 1992 draft and the first pick in the 1994 draft. The Flyers would also send the Nordiques $15 million.

Aubut did not consider the offer, believing he could either convince Lindros to play in Quebec or peddle his rights at the 1992 June draft in Montreal.

Aubut's attempt to sell Lindros on Quebec City failed miserably.

"The argument would be made, 'Eric, come to Quebec City and you'll be a god,'" Carl Lindros said. "Eric never wanted to be a god."

"In the middle of one of our meetings," Eric Lindros said, "he said to my parents, 'If your kid grew up in Quebec, he'd be a better person.' Once, he told me he wanted me for life. All I could picture is me with (prison) stripes on my shirt."

DEAL OR NO DEAL?

In June of 1992, at the end of a pre-draft press conference, Russ Farwell was asked his opinions on Lindros, who almost certainly would be traded by the Nordiques at the upcoming draft.

"Just like Gretzky and Lemieux made kids want to pivot, Lindros might make kids want to run people over," gushed Farwell, normally the master of the understatement. "We're following it, but we don't know yet what the price will be."

The Flyers went into the Lindros Sweepstakes with only two players deemed

Once they learned he'd be making his home in Philadelphia and not New York, the Flyers trumpeted Eric Lindros' arrival.

untouchable: Mark Recchi and Rod Brind'Amour. The Flyers had high hopes for Peter Forsberg, whom they took sixth overall in 1991, but were told that Forsberg would be playing one more season in Sweden before turning pro.

"I saw Eric play in junior and I talked to Terry Crisp, who had him in World Juniors and Crispy loved him," Clarke said. "I told Russ that. I know some of the scouts weren't as crazy about him and wanted to keep Forsberg."

Farwell later said that if Forsberg had committed to coming to Philadelphia in 1992 the Flyers might not have made a pitch for Lindros at all.

Aubut was prepared when the Flyers paid him a visit upon arriving in Montreal for the draft. He wanted Brind'Amour, Ricci, Hextall, Duchesne, Kerry Huffman and first-round picks in 1992, 1993 and 1994. And he wanted either Forsberg or prospect Viacheslav Butsayev.

The Flyers said they would not surrender Brind'Amour and would offer no more than two first-rounders.

The Blackhawks, Maple Leafs and Rangers were also in the bidding, with Chicago's offer including Ed Belfour and Steve Larmer; Toronto's offer including Felix Potvin, Wendel Clark, Dave Ellett and Craig Berube; and the Rangers' package including Doug Weight, Tony Amonte, Alexei Kovalev and John Vanbiesbrouck.

When Aubut handed Jay Snider a piece of paper with the final list of players he would accept in a trade — Ricci, Hextall, Duchesne, Forsberg, Huffman, the Flyers' first pick (seventh overall) at the following day's draft, along with the Flyers' first pick in 1993 and $15 million — Snider said he'd sleep on it.

The next morning, Aubut gave the Flyers permission to speak to Lindros, who confirmed to the Flyers that he would play for them.

After a long and sleepless night, Jay Snider, Russ Farwell and the rest of the Flyers management and coaching staff finally had their man.

Less than a half hour later, with the draft about to begin, there was a knock on the door of the Flyers' hotel suite. Aubut informed Snider and Ron Ryan that he had traded Lindros to the Rangers.

The Rangers deal included Weight, Amonte, Kovalev and Vanbiesbrouck, along with first-round picks in 1993, 1994 and 1995.

Ed Snider, who was on his way to Montreal to celebrate the acquisition of Lindros, told his son to speak to NHL president John Ziegler to see if the botched trade could be mediated.

Ziegler appointed Larry Bertuzzi as the arbitrator of the case and after a full week of hearing statements from the Rangers, Nordiques and Flyers, Bertuzzi ruled Aubut had a deal with the Flyers before he had one with the Rangers and by granting the Flyers permission to contact the Lindros family he had relinquished his rights to trade Lindros a second time.

"It was a very, very complicated set of circumstances," Betuzzi said. "I wrestled with the decision. I found myself on an emotional roller coaster. ... I devoted a full 12 hours just re-reading over 400 pages of notes that I made. I was emotionally wrecked at the end of it."

The Flyers were on an emotional high.

"We're elated," Ed Snider said. "With Lindros on the team and Bob back in the organization I feel like we're whole again."

I'M TRADED? CLICK!

If Bertuzzi wanted real proof the Nordiques made a deal with the Flyers on draft day, all he needed to do was call Kerry Huffman.

On the day of the draft, Huffman, who was coming off the best offensive season of his career with 14 goals, was enjoying a couple beers with friends at his lakeside cottage in Peterborough, Ontario when Nordiques general manager Pierre Page called him on the phone.

"Kerry, this is Pierre Page of the Quebec Nordiques and we've traded for your rights," Page informed Huffman in a thick French accent.

"Hah, hah!" replied Huffman, who thought Page was a friend playing a prank on him. "Get out here and have some beers with us!"

Huffman hung up on Page and a few seconds later his phone rang again.

"I thought it was my buddy with a really bad French accent," Huffman said, "so I hung up again."

Finally, Huffman's agent, Steve Mountain, called and said it was true; he had been traded to Quebec.

"Talk about embarrassing," Huffman said. "I hung up on my new GM twice on the day I was traded."

Meanwhile, Ron Hextall was trying to come to grips with moving his family from South Jersey to Quebec while leaving a team that had felt like family.

"It was one of the hardest things I've ever been through in my life," he says now. "I put my heart and soul in that organization and now I was being sent away."

MARRIAGE MADE IN HEAVEN?

While Lindros' father, Carl, and agent, Rick Curran, hammered out Lindros' first contract with the Flyers, Bill Dineen and Eric went golfing on the west side of Toronto.

"Eric was a little wild with his golf swing," Dineen recalled. "His ball was traveling a lot of different directions."

Lindros was even more wild behind the wheel of his golf cart.

Ed Snider, Russ Farwell and Jay Snider were thrilled to sign Lindros to a six–year, $20.5 million contract.

"It must have been 10 years old and Eric was pulling U-turns all over the place," Dineen said. "He terrified me."

Lindros and the Flyers settled on a six-year deal worth $20.5 million. The contract also stipulated that Lindros' average salary would not fall below the top three in the NHL.

After the Flyers brass returned to Philadelphia with the signed contract, Snider's jet was sent back to Toronto for Dineen, Lindros and his two buddies, Jeff Hardy and Shannon Finn.

"Those kids were on Cloud Nine," Dineen said with a laugh.

After a night at the Four Seasons Hotel in Philadelphia, Lindros was introduced to the Philadelphia media at a press conference attended by his parents and Curran.

After repeatedly being asked how he felt about making more money than

Lindros was both relieved and confident at his introductory press conference, saying, "I'll earn the money."

established teammates Mark Recchi, Rod Brind'Amour and Kevin Dineen, Lindros tried to rationalize that his contract should not be the ultimate measuring stick of his value.

"Just because I make more money doesn't mean I'm better than anyone else," he said. "We're all the same. I'm not better than any one of you. I might have a different career, but we're all the same."

It was a nice attempt, but even at 19 Lindros knew the money he was promised without ever playing an NHL shift made him different than every player in the NHL who had worked his way into the league.

"I'll earn the money," Lindros said, his lips tightening. "I'll give the effort and I'll earn the money. I'm not worried about that."

Neither, apparently, was Jay Snider, who likened the six-year commitment to Lindros to a marriage, "and of course, we all feel it is one that will last forever."

DIAPERS, BONNETS AND PACIFIERS

The Flyers decided to get Lindros away from the media spotlight by arranging the first week of their 1992 training camp on Prince Edward Island. But when the Flyers arrived at their practice rink, O'Leary Recreation Center, more than 1,200 fans greeted them.

Lindros did not disappoint, throwing his body around and scoring a goal in his first scrimmage.

"I remember getting on that plane to P.E.I.," Kevin Dineen said. "Eric was a little quiet around us, but he was the talk of Canada. He was THE guy. And he made a splash. He brought back a fun factor that had been missing. There was this new-found optimism."

"He plays like Messier," Mark Recchi said after Lindros' first practice with the Flyers. "He gets this look in his eyes that says, 'I'm getting there, and whatever's in my way I'm running over.'"

Dominic Roussel had the pleasure of playing against Lindros in the camp's first scrimmage game.

"It was like having a bus in front of me," Roussel said. "No, make that a freight train.,

Dineen recalled a preseason game against the New Jersey Devils when Lindros grabbed one of their bigger players – "I can't remember which one" – and threw him around like a rag doll.

"On the bench we all looked at each other and said, 'Wow!'" Dineen recalls. "Eric was a big, beefy man and he played with the hammer down."

Bill Dineen said he liked Lindros right away, but wasn't sure how Lindros felt about him.

"He was pretty leery of me at first. I think it was a month or two before he realized I was all right. By then he would drop into my office for chats."

With Quebec fans still incensed at Lindros' refusal to play in their city and his assertion the Nordiques "lacked a winning spirit," Dineen wisely sat his 19-year-old rookie out of an exhibition game in Quebec. But when the Flyers arrived there four games into the season, Dineen and Lindros had no choice.

Lindros' first visit to Le Colisee was tantamount to a public lynching.

Hundreds of grown men dressed in diapers, bonnets and bibs, waving rattles at the villainous No. 88, whose refusal to play in Quebec fueled the tensions between the French- and English-speaking residents of Quebec.

"Those people in Quebec were really passionate and the hatred they had for Eric was incredible," Huffman recalled. "Even the days leading up to the game was a circus. Hexy, Ricci and I were talking before the game and we wondered if they might actually try to kill Eric. That's how nuts it got."

The jilted fans in Quebec arrived in Le Colisee with profane, hand-written posters that ridiculed Lindros' mother, Bonnie, and throughout the game they executed three-word chants that ended in "... You, Lindros!"

A Quebec radio station distributed thousands of baby pacifiers, referred to as "soothers" in Canada, and fans gleefully threw them on the ice throughout the contest.

It was as if Mardi Gras revelers made a wrong turn on Bourbon Street and ended up in Quebec City.

"That was wild," recalled Dineen. "It was the craziest thing I've ever seen at a hockey game."

Lindros temporarily silenced the crowd with a pair of goals, but Ricci started a three-goal rally and solid goaltending from Hextall preserved a 6-3 victory for the Nordiques.

As a rookie, Lindros was maligned in every NHL city but Philadelphia, where fans embraced his rugged style.

Lindros was remarkably cool-headed after the game.

"I guess I'll have plenty of soothers if I ever have a baby," he quipped.

Even today, Hextall is unapologetic when asked about the rabid fans in Quebec that night. At the time, he too, hated the manchild wearing No. 88.

"I probably had as much hatred (for Lindros) as anybody in that building," Hextall says. "He was the one who got us all traded and it's probably a good thing I was in goal."

As for the cascade of pacifiers, Hextall said that was mild compared to what he heard in the stands that night.

"Really, what did people expect? Here's a guy who said, 'I don't want to play for the Nordiques.' If Eric got drafted by Philly and said he didn't want to play for the Flyers I'd be furious at him. The reaction, to me, was appropriate."

Hextall was unapologetic when asked about the rabid fans in Quebec.

"If anybody understands emotion I can," Hextall said. "I think our fans have the right to express themselves."

The Flyers' loss in Quebec marked the start of a 1-8-2 slide that exposed the Flyers for what they were: a watered-down team with a superstar uncomfortable with the glare of the spotlight.

"When Eric came here it was an absolute circus," said Hitchcock, an assistant under Dineen in Lindros' rookie season. "That game in Quebec was a nightmare. But I remember going into some other cities — other than Toronto, where he was loved — and it was a nightmare there, too. It was hard on him; it was hard on the team. It was not a fair evaluation."

One thing was certain to all who watched Lindros freeze goaltenders with his snap shot, set up linemates with uncanny passes and pummel opponents along the boards. This young man was a beast on skates.

"He kind of changed the dynamics of the game because after Eric came in it became a big man's game," Hitchcock said. "You had to change your roster to have somebody compete against him. You couldn't do it with small players. You had to have bigger players that could skate to try to cover up because he could control games. He was a scary player to play against because he played reckless. He didn't care where the physical play was, he found it."

Clarke, who became one of Lindros' closest confidantes in his rookie season, believed Lindros' blend of skill, speed and brute strength put him in a class with the game's all-time greats.

"I thought he would be one of those players who dominated an era, like Gordie Howe did or like Wayne Gretzky did, or like Mario Lemieiux did," Clarke said years later. "He should have dominated. He was so big and strong and powerful and fast. He had everything."

GOING KOO KOO

It took less than two months for Lindros to suffer his first injury of the season and less than two weeks later he got another taste of negative publicity when Oshawa police issued a warrant for his arrest.

A 24-year-old woman filed a complaint that Lindros poured beer on her while on the dance floor of Koo Koo Bananas, a nightclub in Whitby, Ontario. Lindros was more defiant than apologetic when asked about the incident, saying he was only acting like a typical 19-year-old college student.

When Lindros arrived in Toronto he was told to put on handcuffs and was transported to Oshawa, where he was fingerprinted. Photos of Lindros in handcuffs made national news and Durham police later admitted they were wrong in asking Lindros to wear them.

Lindros returned to the lineup, but injured the same knee a few weeks later.

That's when Lindros began what would become a long and contentious relationship with Philadelphia sports talk radio station 610-WIP.

A caller to one of the shows said he had seen Lindros in a Voorhees nightclub breaking up a fight between a friend and another

As a captain, Kevin Dineen welcomed Lindros into his home and treated him like a brother.

patron. There were assumptions made that Lindros reinjured his knee during the fracas but he denied them, saying he was simply coming to the aid of a friend.

"Anyone would do the same thing I did," Lindros said of the incident. "It's ridiculous."

Farwell and Bill Dineen were growing concerned about their star player's taste for trouble and Lindros admitted he was not real keen on living alone.

As a group they decided Lindros would move into the home of Kevin Dineen and his wife, Anne.

"Basically, it was Eric's call," Kevin Dineen said. "He had this gorgeous condo (in Voorhees) that was decorated real nice with a full kitchen, but he realized he was there by himself a lot and he was a little bit lonely."

The Dineens were living in a small rental home in historic Haddonfield and Lindros was given their attic.

"It was unfinished with studs in the walls and a bathroom that had a tub and a sink, but no shower. Eric would go up there and sit in the tub. Here's a guy making $4 million a year and he's living in an attic for a year and a half."

Aside from the awkwardness of Lindros inviting an occasional date over for dinner, the living arrangements proved beneficial to Lindros and the Dineens.

"Eric and I would fight the odd time," Dineen said. "We'd be throwing each other around and Anne would walk in and say, 'Look at you two. You're like brothers.' But when we were having our first baby, Eric really enjoyed the process."

Lindros went on to miss 21 games in his rookie season in Philadelphia but still finished with 41 goals — most ever by a Flyers rookie — and 75 points. He finished fourth in Rookie of the Year voting behind Teemu Selanne, who set an NHL rookie record with 76 goals.

"Yeah, but did you check his birth certificate?" Lindros said, pointing out that Selanne was 2 years and 7 months older than Lindros.

Bill Dineen is still convinced that if Lindros had been healthier his rookie season the Flyers would have made the playoffs – they missed by three points – and he might have kept his job as head coach.

"I don't think we had the talent of a playoff team that year," Dineen said, "but if Eric played in seven or eight more games we would have made the playoffs. Without him we just didn't have enough."

THREE CHEERS FOR MARIO

Philadelphia fans have never been known for their hospitality toward opposing players. In fact, they recently were voted the most intimidating fans in the league in an ESPN poll of NHL players.

But on the night of March 2, 1993, they showed their hearts can be as strong as their vocal cords.

About 7:15 that evening, when Penguins center Mario Lemieux skated onto the Spectrum ice for warmups, thousands of fans embraced him in a warm ovation.

Lemieux, diagnosed with Hodgkin's disease two months earlier, had spent the previous month undergoing intense radiation treatments. Wearing a black collar to protect the abrasions left by the radiation, Lemieux stepped onto the ice for the opening faceoff.

Fans remained standing from the national anthem and continued a long, loud ovation for the player who would go on to haunt them for another 10 years.

"Every time you have an injury like that or cancer, you have to have a lot of courage or you're just not going to win the battle," Lemieux said after the game. "I didn't have any choice. I had to fight back."

Paul Coffey, a defenseman for the Penguins who later played for the Flyers, said Philadelphia was one of Lemieux's favorite places to play.

"Mario's the type of player who liked to come into hostile environments and walk out a winner," Coffey said.

BLIZZARD OF 1993

When the Flyers and their fans reminisce about 1993, they undoubtedly will talk about the events of Saturday, March 13.

With a driving snow that accumulated at a rate of more than two inches an hour, it was amazing to learn that the Flyers and Los Angeles Kings would go ahead with their scheduled 1:05 p.m. starting time. More amazing was the fact that all of the players arrived at the arena with little problems.

"Kevin made us stop and help three people on the way in here," Lindros said of his roommate, Kevin Dineen. "We would have been here a lot sooner if we didn't help push people out."

"You call this a storm?" Russ Farwell said with a laugh before the game. "I'm from Calgary; I had no problem getting in here."

The same could not be said for the fans who braved treacherous road conditions as the clock ticked closer to game time. By the middle of the first period, about 2,000 fans had arrived at the Spectrum and they let out a boisterous cheer when public address announcer Lou Nolan invited everyone from the upper levels to filter down to the $50 seats.

The game took on a collegiate atmosphere as the players' voices and the sounds

In 1992–93, Mark Recchi scored 53 goals and set a Flyers single–season record by registering 123 points.

of skates and sticks bounced off the hollow walls of the Spectrum. But then came the sound of broken glass.

With the snow and high winds increasing in intensity outside the Spectrum, a large pane of glass shattered onto the concourse just minutes before the end of the first period. One woman sustained minor cuts. If the glass had blown out minutes later, a crowd of fans would have been in the concourse with the chance of multiple injuries.

Concerned with the safety of the fans, Flyers president Jay Snider huddled with coaches Bill Dineen and Barry Melrose, along with the three officials working the game.

Weather reports indicated the storm was gaining strength and it was announced that in an effort to protect their fans, the Flyers had postponed the game.

Farwell, who had joked earlier in the day about Philadelphians' over-reaction to winter storms, needed his car pushed out of the Spectrum parking lot by the 60-year-old Dineen.

SECOND COMING OF KEENAN?

The Flyers rallied to win their final eight games of the 1992-93 regular season and Mark Recchi finished with a career-high 53 goals, but that didn't stop Farwell and Snider from quietly offering Mike Keenan a five-year contract offer to return as coach of the Flyers.

Keenan said he would consider it, but within a week he was offered a more lucrative five-year deal from the Rangers and bolted for New York.

Farwell waited until the summer to replace Dineen with Terry Simpson, then saw Jay Snider step away from the Flyers to pursue business interests in the Far East.

Meanwhile, Ed Snider's involvement in a new, 21,000-seat arena across the parking lot from the Spectrum brought him back from California and closer to the day-to-day operations of the Flyers.

A MORE MATURE LINDROS

By the start of his second season, Lindros seemed more at ease with himself and the expectations of those around him. He moved himself out of Dineen's house and into his own condo and at 20 years old, seemed more equipped to handle the pressures of being the league's next superstar.

"I'm not going to try to live like so many people expect me to live," Lindros said. "It's not going to work. We went through all that last year."

"In a lot of respects, I have (grown up)," he said. "A lot of life skills

have improved. Everything seems to be even now; nothing's out of whack. Everything seems to be together and moving along slowly. That's the way it should be."

Farwell, who had been critical of Lindros' conditioning in his rookie season, agreed.

"I think he's very focused in his approach," Farwell said. "The shape he was in when he came into camp and the way he's approached every request has been very good. I think it tells you how committed he is this year."

With Lindros one of the most marketable players in the NHL, the Flyers found themselves on ESPN six times in the first month of the season and interview requests had become a part of Lindros' daily routine.

"People like to find interest in other people's lives and that's fine to a certain extent," Lindros said. "But let's talk about why he's here. He's here because he plays hockey. He's not here because he gets speeding tickets in his car or does other things off the ice. Talk about the guy because he plays hockey. That's my perspective."

NICE SHOT, WRONG GOAL

The Flyers opened the 1993-94 season like gangbusters, winning 11 of their first 14 games. Recchi, who had recorded a club record 123 points the previous season, was on his way to another 100-point season.

Garry Galley's "own goal" against the Blackhawks in 1993 was one of the most comical plays in Flyers history.

But between Nov. 6 and Feb. 16 the Flyers won just 15 of 45 games to fall three games under. 500.

One of the most embarrassing moments in team history occurred during that stretch, in a Dec. 18 home game against the Chicago Blackhawks 1993.

Referee Kerry Fraser, who'd been officiating NHL games for 12 seasons, had never seen it happen.

Neither had Flyers coach Terry Simpson, who'd been coaching 21 years, or Flyers goalie Tommy Soderstrom, who had been playing hockey since he was 6.

Flyers defenseman Garry Galley would just as well have people remember him for something else.

With less than 6 minutes remaining in the second period of the Flyers' 2-2 tie against the Chicago Blackhawks, on a delayed penalty to the Blackhawks, Galley shot the puck 180 feet down the ice and into his own net. It was as comical as it was dramatic.

It all began when Fraser raised his arm to signal a high-sticking penalty on Chicago defenseman Steve Smith. As is routine on such calls, Soderstrom broke from his net and headed toward the Flyers' bench to give his team a sixth skater.

However, halfway to the bench, Soderstrom was shocked to see the puck heading back in his direction. Galley, who was down around the Blackhawks goal line, heard teammate Kevin Dineen shouting for the puck at the blue line.

His pass never found Dineen and sent Soderstrom on a wild goose chase toward the runaway puck. The puck won.

"The puck didn't look too fast in the beginning," Soderstrom said, "but then it just flew away from me."

Galley said he knew his errant pass would be catastrophic as soon as it left his stick.

"I saw Kevin was there and I thought maybe I could throw it back to him,"

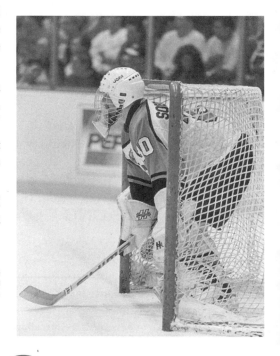

Goaltender Tommy Soderstrom once got a date with a female fan during warmups before a game in Toronto.

Galley said. "As soon as I saw Kevin miss it, I knew it was going in. I was hoping it would hit a snowman or something."

It wasn't until after the puck rested in the Flyers net that Soderstrom realized he had a second option - throwing his stick. In hindsight it would have been a better choice than chasing the puck like a runaway puppy.

"If a player on the ice threw his stick, it would have been a penalty shot," Fraser said.

"If a player off the ice threw his stick, that would be an awarded goal."

Galley's goal, which was credited to Chicago's Christian Ruutu, gave the Blackhawks a 2-1 lead, but the Flyers rallied to tie and the game ended in a 2-2 deadlock.

TOMMY THE BACHELOR

Tommy Soderstrom was a likeable Swede who always seemed distracted by good looking women.

One night before a game in Toronto, Rod Brind'Amour recalls Soderstrom leading his team onto the ice for warmups, but abruptly stopping at the end of the tunnel, bringing the procession of teammates behind him to a halt.

"When we asked Tommy what the holdup was," Brind'Amour said, "he said, 'See that girl up there in the stands? I got a date with her tonight!'"

FOPPA STRIKES GOLD

With Eric Lindros missing 19 games with injuries and the Flyers on their way to a fifth straight season out of the playoffs, Russ Farwell had to be second-guessing his blockbuster trade for Lindros when he saw Peter Forsberg celebrating his shootout goal in Sweden's gold medal-clinching victory over Canada in the 1994 Winter Olympics in Lillehammer, Norway.

"He's a great player and a great kid," Farwell said. "But from the time we made that trade, I haven't worried about who we traded. We have to make this work and go from there. I'd love to have him, but that's the way it is."

TRADING SNIDERS

On March 1, Jay Snider, saying he's had his fill of public scrutiny, officially resigned as Flyers president after 11 years in that position.

"I've been baptized," he said. "When you're in the public eye, you're going to take your shots. I took them before and I had to be confident in myself and make the best decisions I could make. I'll take pride in hiring Russ Farwell and in helping bring Eric Lindros here.

"I paid the price. I came in (as president) at age 25 and heard about the silver spoon in my mouth and all that. We went out and hired Mike Keenan and everybody loved him. Then we started going downhill and I was the reason. Now, we have Lindros and people come up to me and say, 'We love you, you're great for going out and spending the money for a guy like Lindros.'

"One night, you're a hero, the next night you're a bum."

Ironically, that's exactly the way his team was playing when Snider resigned.

But with the Flyers' record teetering just below .500 and neither Dominic Roussel nor Tommy Soderstrom able to seize the No. 1 job in goal, Ed Snider went out on a limb by predicting the Flyers would win the Stanley Cup within three years.

"I definitely predicted it and I'll stand by the prediction," Snider said at the time. "I can sit on top of my ivory tower and say things like that and get away with it.

"I'll take the heat if I'm wrong."

Lindros believed that with a few more pieces, Snider's vision could be fulfilled.

``I'm dying for a good party," Lindros said.

PRODIGAL SON RETURNS (AGAIN)

Ed Snider had every intention of keeping Farwell as his general manager, but when Bob Clarke expressed interest in a second return to Philadelphia, Snider jumped at the opportunity, hoping Clarke and Farwell could somehow co-exist.

Clarke was hoping Farwell could take over contract negotiations and the draft while he handled trades and player personnel.

"Russ has a lot of strengths that I don't have and I have some that he doesn't have," Clarke said. "I'm hoping he stays and works with us. Obviously, he has to be able to deal with his pride and we have to have a position that is good for him, and we think we do. Hopefully, I can convince him to stay. I'd really like him to."

But on the same day Clarke was introduced as the Flyers' new president, general manager and minority owner, Farwell quietly acknowledged the Flyers' front office wasn't big enough for the two of them.

"Right now, my concern is that it will be like two mothers-in-laws in the same kitchen," Farwell said. "It might be better for us to be friends from a distance than in (a working) relationship. I don't think it's healthy to stay under that arrangement," Farwell said.

Bill Dineen said he still believes Farwell got a raw deal from the Flyers, saying it was a "big mistake" to replace him.

"If they stayed with Russ they would have had success. I thought Russ had things going in the right direction."

Months after his departure Farwell felt the same way.

"There are a lot of things you would have liked to have done better," he said, "but I think we did the best we could with what we had. We started over twice when I was there. I think the team's at a point now where they have to stop looking down the road. They have to do it right now. Guys like (Rod) Brind'Amour and Lindros have had their break-in time. They've got to be steady, solid players. And I think Renberg, in another year or so, will be a real force in the NHL."

Farwell proved to be prophetic, but at the time Clarke was not convinced. He inherited a roster without a single player remaining from the one he left in 1990.

"Oh, it was horrible," Clarke recalled. "We had about six NHL players on that team: (Michael) Renberg, Lindros, Brind'Amour, Galley, Recchi. They gave up so much to get Eric and a couple draft picks didn't work out. We had some work to do."

CHAPTER 8

LEGION OF DOOM
LOWERS THE BOOM

(1994–1997)

Newcomers John LeClair and Mikael Renberg unite
with Eric Lindros to become the most intimidating
line in team history.

'PART OF SOMETHING SPECIAL'

WHEN BOB CLARKE RETURNED TO PHILADELPHIA HE WAS
determined to turn over a roster that had gone 136-150-42 during Russ Farwell's
four-year tenure.

In Clarke's opinion the Flyers had lost their identity as one of the NHL's hard-est-working teams and he thought Terry Murray, who had been fired by the
Washington Capitals the year before, would restore that personality.

"The Flyers used to be about hard
work and dedication," Clarke said shortly
after being re-hired. "Bernie Parent, Billy
Barber, Rick MacLeish, all those guys
poured their blood and sweat on that ice.
So did the players of the '80s with Rick
Tocchet, Brian Propp, Dave Poulin and Tim
Kerr.

"Now it's time for these guys to put it
together. It's not a question of preserving
history. It's establishing a work ethic and a
pride within themselves that can make
them proud to be part of something special.
And it has to begin right now."

When he returned as general manager
in 1994, Bob Clarke wanted to restore
the Flyers' hard-edged image.

Clarke thought the Flyers had gotten soft since his departure and in his first move as GM he traded Yves Racine to the Canadiens for hard-hitting defenseman Kevin Haller.

He also addressed the shaky goaltending situation by trading the happy-go-lucky Tommy Soderstrom to the New York Islanders for the fiery Ron Hextall.

Identity restored.

"I'm pretty adamant about not getting pushed around in this league," Clarke said. "I know what it's like. We got the crap beat out of us the first couple years I was here (as a player) and it wasn't fun. But when we started getting tougher, we started getting better."

BIG E BEGINS WITH C

Joining Terry Murray behind the Flyers bench were Keith Acton, a respected veteran who had retired after 14 seasons in the league, and Tom Webster, who had worked with Clarke with the Florida Panthers.

Clarke and Murray decided that after two seasons in the NHL, Lindros was ready to be anointed the Flyers' leader and on Sept. 6, 1994, at the age of 21, Lindros succeeded Kevin Dineen as the youngest captain in team history.

Mark Recchi, 26, and Rod Brind'Amour, 24, replaced Dave Brown and Garry Galley as assistant captains.

"I believe there's a lot of leadership inside of that guy that will start to come out now over the

With Terry Murray as his new coach, Eric Lindros became the youngest captain in Flyers history at the age of 21.

next 10-15 years that he's going to be a Flyer," Terry Murray said of Lindros. "He's certainly regarded as one of the premier players in the league and with the change in management and the coaching staff we felt a change was needed in the dressing room, as well."

Lindros seemed ready for the challenge. His relationship with Clarke was strong – "He's one of the best general managers in the league, if not the best," he said at the time – and although he was younger than all of his teammates, the shadow he cast was large.

Clarke said he hoped Lindros would grow into his role while still leaning on Dineen, Brown and Recchi.

"You can't expect a 21-year-old to know everything and I don't think Eric will be shy about asking questions," Clarke said. "He's bright. Just let him be himself."

Lindros seemed just as guarded about following in the footsteps of Clarke, Poulin, Sutter and Dineen.

"I'm not going to act like there's a loaded gun in my back and if I falter it's going off," he said.

Brind'Amour said he'd ride shotgun with Lindros and if a teammate's play dipped, he'd be quick to pull the trigger.

"A lot of things that went on last year won't go on this year," Brind'Amour promised. "I'm not going to let things slide."

ANOTHER PREDICTION

While NHL players were planning a work stoppage that would erase the first half of the 1994-95 season, Flyers owner Ed Snider was digging up dirt at the site where JFK Stadium once stood.

The same location where more than 100,000 Flyers fans gathered for the celebration of their last Stanley Cup victory would become the footprint of their new home. The two-year project, at the time named Spectrum II, would be home to the Flyers and Sixers and would open its doors in time for the 1996-97 season.

"I'm going to get in trouble," Snider said at the groundbreaking, "but I can see a Stanley Cup final in this building the very first season."

Players noticed Snider's renewed involvement with the Flyers and believed that with him overseeing the operation better days were just around the corner.

"Mr. Snider getting back into the organization was a huge commitment of wanting to win this," Mark Recchi said. "They want to get back on a level where we're challenging for the top. That's something that's really appreciated."

SNIDER THE DEFENDER

Ed Snider has always been passionately protective of his players and Rod Brind'Amour discovered just how much one night.

After Brind'Amour was tossed out of a game with a 10-minute misconduct for arguing a call, Snider left his box at the Spectrum and stormed into the Flyers dressing room just as the final horn sounded.

"He asked me what happened and I just told him the ref made a bad call," Brind'Amour said. "I didn't have to say another word. Mr. Snider ran right to the refs' locker room and started screaming at the guy. It just showed me how much he cared about winning and how he would back his players."

It wasn't the first time Snider berated an official, and it wouldn't be the last.

A REX FOR A RICO AND A JOHNNY

The Flyers started the lockout-shortened 1995 season as if they were still on a sabbatical. They lost seven of their first 11 games under Murray and Lindros was sputtering along with just four goals.

Clarke questioned his captain's conditioning during the long offseason but recognized his team needed a change in personnel. With defenseman Garry Galley overworked and Lindros in need of some help along the corners, Clarke called Montreal Canadiens general manager Serge Savard and asked if he was interested in Recchi.

Savard desperately wanted an infusion of offense and asked what it would take to get Recchi. Clarke asked for defenseman Mathieu Schneider and a big winger and when Savard countered with Eric Desjardins and center John LeClair, Clarke agreed.

"Bob told me what he had working," Ed Snider said, "but it was his call all the way."

Montreal winger Gilbert Dionne was thrown into the deal and on Feb. 9, 1995, one of the biggest trades in club history was completed.

"That was straight luck," Clarke says now. "We were after Desjardins and we needed a big forward so we took LeClair. At worst, in our minds he could be a good checking player. We wanted John, but we didn't think he'd score 50 goals."

Eric Desjardins was nervous about leaving Montreal in the trade that also netted John LeClair and Gilbert Dionne.

Desjardins and LeClair were shaken when they heard the news. They had won a Stanley Cup with the Canadiens less than two years earlier and had never been traded in their careers.

"We were all worried," Desjardins said, recalling the two-hour plane ride from Montreal to Philadelphia. "We were nervous and John finally said, 'You know what, guys? We'll be all right.'"

DON'T MESS WITH HEXY

It took Hextall four weeks to earn his first victory as a return Flyer and he celebrated by punching Rob Pearson's lights out.

The Flyers had a 5-1 lead on the Washington Capitals when Pearson was given a game misconduct for high sticking Flyers defenseman Ron Zettler.

On his way off the ice, Pearson yanked on the jersey of Hextall, who was who had taken off his mask for a breather.

"He got closer and closer, and when he got real close, I knew something was going to happen," Hextall said. "What am I going to do? Let him beat me up?"

Hextall unloaded a flurry of punches on Pearson, dropping him with an overhand right before a pileup ensued behind the Flyers net.

Hextall remained in the game and missed scoring his third career goal by about 10 feet when his rink-long shot rolled wide of the open net.

Washington forward Keith Jones didn't appreciate Hextall's bravado and backed his way into the goalie's crease with about 3 seconds remaining in the contest.

Hextall cross-checked Jones in the back and both were slapped with match penalties.

LEGION OF BELIEVERS

At the advice of Clarke, Terry Murray put the 6-foot-3, 226-pound LeClair on a line with the 6-foot-4, 229-pound Lindros and 6-foot 2, 218-pound Mikael Renberg and ...

"Nobody could stop them," Kevin Dineen said. "Once they got the puck in the corners, no one was big enough or strong enough to get it away from them. It was scary."

Two nights after the trade LeClair scored his first goal as a Flyer in a 3-1 win in New Jersey and two games after that he netted his first career hat trick in a 5-2 win in Tampa Bay.

Ed Snider called the Legion of Doom line of John LeClair, Eric Lindros and Mikael Renberg the best he'd ever seen.

"When I got my first hat trick, that's when I really thought, 'I can score,'" LeClair said. "Once I did it, I expected it of myself."

Two weeks after the trade LeClair scored his second hat trick as a Flyer, this time in front of his friends and family in Montreal in a 7-0 Flyers rout.

"You wouldn't believe the amount of hats that came down from the Forum that night," recalled LeClair's father, Butch. "And they were all for John."

During the early dominance of the Lindros-LeClair-Renberg line, teammate Jim Montgomery was asked to describe the play of the three muscular forwards.

"They're the Legion of Doom," he replied.

By the middle of March, the entire league was abuzz over the Doommates and after the line combined for five goals in an 8-4 win over the Canadiens to run the Flyers' win streak to eight, people were running out of superlatives.

Montreal coach Jacques Demers called it the best line he'd seen in 10 years. Ed Snider went one step farther.

"It's the best line I've ever seen," Snider said, passing over the famous triumvirate of Reggie Leach, Bobby Clarke and Bill Barber. "I don't see how anybody can stop them. It gives me goose bumps."

GOING MY WAY?

The Flyers have always prided themselves in the close relationships they've formed with their fans.

That relationship was taken to a whole new level late one night after the Flyers' team bus broke down on Interstate-95 on the way home from a game in Landover, Maryland, against the Washington Capitals.

"There was a fire in the back of the bus and guys were all scrambling to get out," Kevin Dineen recalled. "Fans who were following our bus pulled over and they all started offering us rides."

Dave Brown and three teammates wedged themselves into one fan's Ford Focus and started down the highway.

"The guy's defroster didn't work and we had to keep jumping out of the car and wiping down his windshield for him," Brown said.

Dineen, Shjon Podein and Lindros climbed into another car with a fan whose excitement was surpassed only by his fear of bridges.

"He must have lived in Pennsylvania and he had never been across the Walt Whitman Bridge," Dineen said of the players' trek back to their homes in New Jersey. "He was absolutely terrified. He went about 20 miles an hour in the center lane of the bridge and he never took his eyes off the road.

"I don't know how he ever made it back home."

BABE RUTH OF HOCKEY?

Eric Lindros and John LeClair enjoyed their first of five straight All-Star Game appearances in 1995-96.

For Lindros, sitting beside Eastern Conference teammate Mark Messier was like a fledgling guitarist strumming a few chords with Eric Clapton.

"When I was a kid, my birthday present always used to be to go to Maple Leaf Gardens when Mark Messier was in town," Lindros admitted. "The bus to and from the Gardens ran about three blocks from my house. And when I was in high school I kept Messier's hockey card on my desk."

LeClair's All-Star debut was highlighted when he cranked out a 98 mph slapshot during the NHL skills competition.

"He's the Babe Ruth of hockey," Lindros marveled. "He can bring the heavy artillery, and he's pinpoint accurate."

The following year, LeClair felt like a Johnny on the spot when he lined up again for the hardest shot competition.

Eric Lindros celebrated his All–Star Game debut with teammates Craig MacTavish, John LeClair and Eric Desjardins.

LeClair skated across the blue line, cocked his stick, and fired ... wide of the open net. The speedometer reading: 00.0.

LEGION OF PEACE?

As tough as the Legion of Doom was to play against in the mid-1990s, two-thirds of that line – Renberg and LeClair — rarely dropped the gloves.

Renberg, the only son of a gas station owner, grew up playing soccer in Pitea, Sweden and was staunchly against fighting.

"Hockey is not about fighting," he said. "It's about skating fast and shooting the puck. And it's about playing hard and playing tough. Fighting is not going to go away, but the game has more of a European style now. It's a better game."

BRINDY TO THE RESCUE

Rod Brind'Amour will go down in history as one the ultimate Flyers and on the night of April 16, 1995 he showed why.

The Flyers were in danger of having their five-game win streak snapped at home against the Penguins when Brind'Amour was slammed into the boards on a vicious cross-check by Troy Murray.

Blood trickling down his left temple, Brind'Amour looked like a moose that had just been struck by a hunter's bullet. He stalked his attacker in front of the penalty box, but with 48.3 seconds remaining in the third period, Brind'Amour reluctantly skated away from Murray, allowing the Flyers to go on a game-breaking 5-minute power play.

"I almost lost my cool," Brind'Amour said. "But I realized the situation. Hopefully, (Murray) will be around next year."

With 19.9 seconds remaining in regulation, Brind'Amour set up Mikael Renberg's game-tying goal and minutes later he tipped Eric Desjardins' overtime

Known as the ultimate warrior, Rod Brind'Amour recorded a career–high 110 penalty minutes in 1995–96.

slapshot past Penguins goaltender Ken Wregget for a thrilling 4-3 win.

"He wasn't coming off the ice," Flyers right winger Kevin Dineen said. "We were trying to get him off just to wipe the blood off his face. But he had that fire in his eyes where you knew something good was going to happen."

JAGR WINS BY AN EYELASH

Five players in Flyers history have recorded 100 or more points in a season. Bobby Clarke did it three times, Mark Recchi did it twice, and Rick MacLeish, Bill Barber and Eric Lindros did it once each.

But never in the club's history has a Flyer won an NHL scoring title.

It almost happened in the lockout-shortened 1995 season.

With two games remaining in the regular season, Lindros held a three-point lead on Pittsburgh's Jaromir Jagr when his own slapshot boomeranged off the hip of Rangers defenseman Jeff Beukeboom and struck Lindros in the left eye.

Lindros was forced to miss the final game of the regular season while Jagr picked up three points in his last two games. Both players finished with 70 points, but since Jagr had 32 goals to Lindros' 29, he was awarded the scoring title.

A JOYFUL SIGHT

Just before the start of the 1995 playoffs, the Flyers received a scare when Nathan MacTavish, the 3-year-old son of Flyers center Craig MacTavish, pushed through a screen and fell from the second-floor window of his home in Voorhees, suffering small fractures in his hip.

Nine days after the accident, Nathan wheeled himself into the Flyers dressing room, lighting up the room with his smile.

``He'll (recover) at his own pace,'' MacTavish said. ``The only thing keeping him off his feet is the pain. Once that goes away, he'll be bouncing around like he was before.''

The Flyers took turns pushing Nathan around the dressing room and giving him high-fives.

``It's great to see him OK,'' Rob DiMaio said. ``It's a good pick-me-up for us and I'm sure it is for him. It's hard not to like that little guy.''

GET THAT KID A HOCKEY STICK

At an exaggerated 5-foot-10, 190 pounds (he was closer to 5-7, 170 pounds) Rob DiMaio fought his way into the hearts of South Philly fans who saw themselves in him.

Born and raised in Calgary, DiMaio was the son of Italian immigrants and his father didn't know the first thing about hockey when he arrived in Calgary.

"What's funny is that a neighbor saw me push a kid into a seesaw once and told my dad I should play hockey," DiMaio laughed. "He didn't have a clue what hockey was. But my mom was the one who would dress me and drive me to the rink in the freezing cold. Now, she's always worried about me getting hurt. I guess that's all part of being a mother."

WE WANT HEXTALL

When the Flyers hosted the Buffalo Sabres in Game 1 of the Eastern Conference quarterfinals on May 7, 1995 a six-year playoff wait spanning 2,233 days and more than 70 players finally ended.

The Flyers began the series without their captain and when Lindros returned from his eye injury before Game 4, Flyers goaltender Ron Hextall issued this proclamation: "Eric is one of the best captains in the league and he has a chance to become one of the greatest captains of all time."

Despite missing Lindros for the first three games of the Buffalo series, Hextall outplayed a rattled Dominik Hasek in a five-game rout.

Mark Messier and the Rangers were next up and the crowd at Madison Square Garden made it clear at the end their first-round victory whom they hoped to meet in Round 2 with chants of "We Want Hextall!"

The year before, as a member of the Islanders, Hextall was blitzed for 16 goals in a series sweep by the Rangers and fans in Manhattan figuref he'd be road kill on their road to a second straight Stanley Cup.

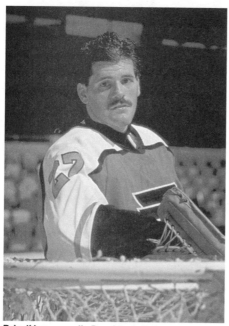

Brind'Amour calls Ron Hextall the greatest goalie he's ever played with. "He hated losing and that's what made him great."

Hextall enjoyed every second of the Flyers' four-game sweep of the Rangers, wagging his head at the Garden fans as the Flyers put the finishing touches on a 4-1 victory in New York to complete the sweep.

"We all felt great for Hexy," Brind' Amour recalled. "I still tell people he was the greatest goalie I've ever played with. It wasn't that he was incredibly flexible, or had really quick feet or a great glove. He was just a battler and so competitive. He hated losing and that's what made him great."

Former Rangers coach Colin Campbell hated losing to the Flyers for other reasons. After Eric Desjardins scored an overtime game-winner in Game 2 at the Spectrum a fan behind the visitors' dropped a beer on the coach.

Campbell reacted by grabbing the stick of one of his players and swinging it in the direction of the fan. The stick hit the plexiglass separating the Rangers bench and the first row of seats and no one was injured. Campbell left the ice without further retaliation as fans littered the ice with cups of soda and beer.

Campbell was fined $200 by the NHL and said he'd bill the Rangers an extra $2,000 to have his suit cleaned.

NOT THIS TIME, PEPE

Claude "Pepe" Lemieux had so much fun in the 1987 pre-game brawl between the Flyers and Canadiens he thought he'd try his warmup antics again before Game 1 of the Eastern Conference Finals between his Devils and the Flyers.

This time, the Devil didn't get his due.

Lemieux stayed on the Spectrum ice long after pre-game warmups, waiting for a chance to shoot a puck into the Flyers' net before leaving the ice.

One by one, the Flyers headed for the dressing room and the drama unfolded. Lemieux stood lurking at the edge of the Devils tunnel. The Zamboni sat waiting. And so did Flyers left winger Gilbert Dionne.

Dionne stayed on the ice until Lemieux retreated down the Devils' tunnel without incident — a full three minutes after the horn sounded for the players to leave the ice.

STEVENS VS. LINDROS, PART I

During the Legion of Doom's reign as the best line in hockey there may have been no better theatre than the one-on-one battles between Eric Lindros and Devils defenseman Scott Stevens.

They fought each other like two pit bulls locked in a closet and in the 1995 playoffs their first snarls could be heard.

Late in Game 2 of their series, with the Devils on their way to a commanding 2-0 series lead in Philadelphia, Lindros snapped Stevens' head back with a vicious elbow to the temple.

As Lindros turned back at Stevens with a menacing scowl, the Devils captain broke out in a broad smile, blood streaming down the side of his face.

Lindros headed for the penalty box. Stevens and the Devils headed for their second straight win.

"I love it," Stevens said of getting the best of Lindros, who stood two inches taller and weighed 19 pounds more than Stevens. "It's a lot of hard work, but it's very satisfying afterward. I guess, when we win, I know we're doing a good job on him."

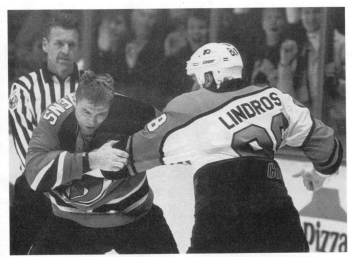

Every time they hit the ice together, Eric Lindros and Scott Stevens provided hockey's most primitive theatre.

One look at the first two score sheets could tell you that. Lindros had three shots and one goal.

Lindros and the Flyers battled back to win Games 3 and 4 at the Meadowlands to restore their home-ice advantage. The Flyers had stolen momentum from the Devils and were returning home for a pivotal Game 5.

The teams tugged back and forth — Martin Brodeur and Hextall matching one another save for save — until, with 44.2 seconds remaining in a 2-2 game, Lemieux broke down the right wing boards and blasted a shot from just inside the blue line past Hextall for a 3-2 series lead.

"I take full responsibility for the goal," Hextall said. "I should have stopped it."

Two nights later Hextall was forced to stop three breakaways in a lopsided 4-2 loss, ending the Flyers' remarkable playoff run.

"I think we gave everything we had," Hextall said. "Every single one of us."

GOTTA HAVE HART

On July 6, 1995 Lindros joined Bobby Clarke as the only Flyers ever to be named the NHL's Most Valuable Player. Still just 22 years old, many believed it would be the first of many Hart Trophies for the talented young center.

"The sky's the limit for him," said Craig MacTavish, who played alongside nine-time Hart winner Wayne Gretzky and two-time Hart winner Mark Messier. "He's the MVP of our league this year and that's just touching the outskirts of what he can accomplish."

"He can be the greatest player ever," gushed Clarke, who normally threw around superlatives like manhole covers. "I mean, the kid's only 22."

Lindros held back tears as he accepted his award at the Metro Toronto Convention Center, just a few miles from the backyard rink on which he learned to play.

After accepting the Hart Trophy from rock legend Neil Young, Lindros breezed through his acceptance speech cleanly until it came time to thank the fans of Philadelphia. Ignoring background music to signal his exit, Lindros remained on the stage long enough to work up an emotional promise.

"In closing, I'd just like to say thank you to the fans of Philadelphia," Lindros said, his voice beginning to waver, "who supported us even when we weren't so good. (an exaggerated pause) We're getting better and we're gonna do it."

Afterward, Lindros said the rare show of emotion was the product of four trying years, beginning with his refusal to play for the Quebec Nordiques.

"I think it's the whole thing," Lindros said. "The trouble coming into the league, the trouble that we had in the first couple years in Philly, and (the fans) always staying with us.

"It gets better than this," he said. "You gotta win a Cup. That's as good as it gets."

DELLY'S YELLOW SHOES

The Flyers have had their share of pranksters over the years and Chris Therien, a rookie on that 1994-95 team, was among the best.

Therien spent most of his 11-year career rooming with John LeClair, which meant every road trip was an adventure.

Chris Therien ranks as one of the Flyers' all–time pranksters. Most came at the expense of road roommate John LeClair.

"I moved Johnny's entire bed into the stairway once," Therien said. "I'd get up and turn the shower on and then leave the room. Johnny would wake up and think I'm in the shower and think, 'Geez, he's in there a long time!'

"I've hid in closets and waited for Johnny to come in and just before he opens the closet to put in his clothes I'd jump out at him."

Of course, being a practical joker comes with its share of risk.

After squirting yellow mustard on the shoes of teammate Andy Delmore during a team dinner, Therien fell victim to his own prank.

"I was standing at an ice-cream bar at a team meal in Chicago and Delly hid under the table," Therien recalled. "I'm standing there and all of a sudden I see his hand pouring caramel sauce all over my shoes. I lifted up the curtain and there's Delly under there."

Therien got Delmore back by cutting the sleeves off his overcoat, while leaving a few threads attached to the shoulders.

"When he put it on, the sleeves just fell off," Therien said.

For good measure, on a road trip to Buffalo, Therien poured mixed concrete into Delmore's new shoes.

Craig Berube grew tired of Therien's pranks and got revenge one night when he gave him a backward Mohawk.

"When he was asleep I shaved his head down the middle, from the front to the back," Berube said. "He never even woke up."

SHUFFLING THE DECK

From the time the Flyers were eliminated by the Devils in the 1995 conference finals to the time they began the 1996 playoffs against the Tampa Bay Lightning, Kevin Dineen, Brent Fedyk, Craig MacTavish, Garry Galley, Rob Zettler, Andre

Faust, Dominic Roussel and Anatoli Semenov had been replaced by Petr Svoboda, Dale Hawerchuk, Garth Snow, Pat Falloon, Trent Klatt, Dan Quinn, Bob Corkum, Tim Cheveldae, Kerry Huffman and John Druce.

Lengthy battles with abdominal strains kept Mikael Renberg out of the lineup for 31 games that season, but Lindros and LeClair were unstoppable as Big E finished with a career-high 115 points and LeClair netted a career-high 51 goals.

"I never really thought I would get 20 goals," LeClair said. "My first year in the league (Canadiens teammate) Russ Courtnall told me if I scored 20 I could play in this league a long time."

SVOBODA HITS THE DECK

They were the longest seven minutes of Petr Svoboda's life and he'll never remember them.

From 9:01 p.m. until 9:08 p.m. on Thursday, Feb. 1, 1996, Svoboda lay on the CoreStates Center ice, the victim of a vicious elbow to the jaw by Montreal Canadiens center Marc Bureau.

With the Flyers on the power play, Svoboda was cruising through the neutral zone when he released a backhand pass to Eric Desjardins. But just as the puck left Svoboda's stick he was leveled by Bureau in full stride.

The hit jarred Svoboda's helmet loose and the back of his head smacked the ice, leaving a pool of blood under the 29-year-old defenseman.

"I don't remember much after I got hit," said Svoboda, who was forced to retire from the game five years later because of post-concussion syndrome. "I woke up in the ambulance. It's a good feeling, even though you don't really know why you're there."

MR. ULANOV, MEET
MR. LINDROS

Although he finished the 1995-96 season with a career-high 163 penalty minutes Eric Lindros spent much of the season trying to master the art of restraint.

The Flyers' addition of linebacker-turned-winger Shawn Antoski allowed Lindros to skate away from most on-ice altercations but in Game 6 of the Flyers' opening-round war against the Tampa Bay Lightning, Lindros let out 11 days worth of pent-up frustration on the face of Tampa defenseman Igor Ulanov.

After the Flyers' grind line of Antoski, Corkum and Klatt scored three goals to give the Flyers a commanding 6-1 lead in front of 27,189 fans inside the Thunder-Dome, Lindros unleashed his vengeance.

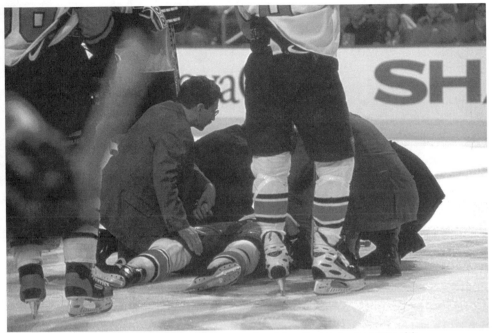

Petr Svoboda's scariest moment in hockey came when Marc Bureau leveled him with an open–ice check.

With 2 minutes, 4 seconds remaining in the contest, Lindros dropped his gloves and pummeled Ulanov mercilessly. Lindros yanked Ulanov back and forth with his left hand and hammered away with his right. ·

The bloody beating on Ulanov was so brutal Tampa Bay winger Jason Wiemer stepped in to break things up and suffered a similar fate as Lindros punched him into submission as well.

"He was just a beast," Huffman recalled. "After that, no one wanted any part of Eric."

Just as lasting in the minds of Flyers teammates was the courage John LeClair showed in coming back from a serious ankle injury to play in Games 4, 5 and 6.

"I've been playing a long time and I've seen some incredible things in the play-offs," marveled 34-year-old Joel Otto, "but what Johnny did in this series I'll be telling my grandchildren someday."

STUNG BY THE BEEZER

The Flyers grabbed a two-games-to-one lead on the Florida Panthers in Round 2 of the 1996 playoffs, but with John Vanbiesbrouck stopping everything in sight, the Panthers rallied to win Game 4 in Miami and Game 5 in Philadelphia, both in overtime.

Figuring the Flyers had just absorbed Florida's best punch, Lindros tore a page out of Mark Messier's book of guarantees and made this bold statement following Game 5: "We're coming back home," the Flyers captain said, "and we're going to win."

Vanbiesbrouck saw Lindros' comments in the next day's newspaper and was the best player on the ice as the Panthers eliminated the Flyers under a shower of plastic rats in a 4-1 victory in Miami.

"There's not a guy in this locker room who didn't take notice of what he said," Vanbiesbrouck said of Lindros' declaration after Game 5. "You know, there are no guarantees in hockey. You've got to learn that lesson early."

PASS THE WATER BOTTLE

Eric Lindros spent an entire career inflicting pain on opponents, but in 1996-97 he put himself and his teammates on the injured list with freak mishaps.

The first came during training camp when Lindros tripped over Ron Hextall's goalie pad while participating in a skating drill, tearing his own groin and missing the first 23 games of the season.

The Flyers struggled without their captain, going 12-10-1 to start the season. When Lindros returned he led an incredible 14–0–3 run but nearly lost his eye in another freak collision involving Lindros.

The Flyers were going through the paces during a Sunday morning skate-around when Lindros headed toward the bench to grab a water bottle. Hextall was stretching with his skate propped up on the boards and as he lifted his skate to bring it back to the ice, Lindros bent over for the water bottle.

"I really didn't see him," Hextall said. "I didn't know what happened. I looked up and I saw blood and he was grabbing his eye."

With blood streaming down his face, Lindros was helped off the ice by teammate Daniel Lacroix. Lindros needed 20 stitches to close the wound and even after the rink was resurfaced the ice was still stained crimson red.

Lindros recovered in time to join his teammates and their families at the Flyers' annual Christmas party at the CoreStates Center.

"I told him to stay away from me," Hextall joked. "A long way from me."

BETTER THAN THE PENGUINS?

When Paul Coffey came to Philadelphia in a trade for Kevin Haller midway through the 1996-97 season he compared the Flyers to the Stanley Cup champion Penguins of 1991 and 1992.

Paul Coffey says the biggest hit he ever absorbed came when he and Eric Lindros collided in 1997.

"When I got to Pitt in 1988, they had Mario (Lemieux), but they didn't have the cast that they have here in Philadelphia," Coffey said. "Of course, you've got Eric (Lindros) and the list goes on and on. That (Legion of Doom) line alone is one of the best lines in the league. We have great goaltending; a great second, third and fourth line. I think we have a lot more talent here than we had in Pittsburgh."

Coffey's memory of those Pittsburgh teams – not to mention what he had for breakfast that morning — was put to the test two weeks later when, in a game in Vancouver, Lindros inadvertently steamrolled No. 77 at full speed. Coffey crumbled to the ice, where he lay unconscious for five minutes before being carted off on a stretcher.

When he awoke, Coffey said he thought he was still a member of the Detroit Red Wings, for whom he played the previous season. Later he said it was the most frightening injury of his 17-year NHL career.

"I've had my bell rung a couple times," Coffey said, "but I've never had anything like that. I hope it's the worst of my career. I don't want to get anything worse than that. Eric never hit me like that when I played against him."

TWO FLEW OVER THE CUCKOO'S NET

Ron Hextall and Garth Snow shared more than just a goal crease in 1996-97. They shared an affinity for fighting. Hextall led NHL netminders with 31 penalty minutes that season and Snow was second with 30.

"They're both really off the wall," Clarke said at the time. "We don't put them together on the road. They'd need bars on their windows."

Hextall piled up 29 of his penalty minutes in a post-game fight with Toronto goaltender Felix Potvin on Nov. 10. Hextall said he only chased down Potvin because the Leafs goaltender took a slash at teammate Daniel Lacroix just before the final siren.

Goaltender Garth Snow fought three different Sabres goalies in his first two seasons with the Flyers.

"None of that would have happened if their coach (Mike Murphy) hadn't put Tie Domi out there," Clarke said. "The guy plays five minutes the whole game and he puts him out there at the end to start something. I don't like Ron doing what he did, but that's a decision he has to make for himself. What if one of those guys breaks his hand out there? If Potvin breaks his hand, it doesn't look like a real smart move putting Domi out there, does it?"

The next day Hextall showed up at practice with a welt above his left eyebrow.

"You need to carry a can of mace," a teammate suggested.

"Not a bad idea," Hextall yelled back. "I'll stick it in my pants pocket."

Not to be outdone, Snow picked up 14 minutes for attacking Rob Ray and Dominik Hasek in a Feb. 4 war against Buffalo.

"If Hexy was in that game against Buffalo, they would have had the cops breaking it up in riot gear," Snow said. "He's a little bit of a menace on the ice, a psycho."

Snow actually fought three Sabres goalies — Hasek, Andrei Trefilov, and Steve Shields – in his first two seasons with the Flyers.

ERIC VERSUS WIP

First came rumors he injured his knee while coming to the aid of a friend in a bar. Then came reports he left Flyers tickets for Philadelphia mob boss "Skinny" Joey Merlino.

Eric Lindros had his share of controversies spill onto the airwaves of 610-WIP in his stormy career as a Flyer, but nothing compared to the firestorm near the end of the 1996-97 season when radio host Craig Carton reported that Lindros missed a Feb. 15 afternoon game in Philadelphia because he was hung over from drinking the night before. Lindros said he rented movies that night and was suffering from back spasms the next day.

"It's been going on for a long time," Lindros said of the radio rumors. "What are you going to do? I don't know what to say other than it's a joke. It's too bad, really."

Lindros said that despite the reports and the criticisms that followed he remained loyal to the fans of Philadelphia.

"It's a great city to play in," he said. "It's too bad we have this kind of (stuff) that happens all the time. It's wrong. I have a great time here. I love the area, I love the team, but this extra stuff is horrible. I don't understand it. I don't get it. Maybe somebody I'll figure it all out. Fat chance."

Flyers coach Terry Murray said he spoke with Lindros before that Feb. 15 game and asked him how his back was responding to treatments. Lindros had fallen hard to the ice on a check from Ottawa's Janne Laukkanen two nights earlier and had not participated in the team's practice the day between the Ottawa and Pittsburgh games.

"It's outrageous," Murray said of the report. "It's ridiculous. I spent time with Eric in the morning talking to him about playing the game. I know that he got treated in the medical room with our trainers and our doctors. I know he went out on the ice for the warmup. It's absolutely ludicrous, these accusations."

The Flyers' fight with WIP did not end there.

On March 5, Ed Snider announced the team had filed a lawsuit against the station and threatened to pull broadcasting rights from the station, which owned them since 1973.

"We are going to pursue this fully, completely and as long as it takes," Snider said in a news conference at the CoreStates Center. "They finally went over the ledge. We were willing to give them the benefit of the doubt last time. We're not willing to do that any longer. We're not going to sit back and take it. We understand that they have the power of the airwaves, but we have the power of our integrity and our pride and we're not going to sit back and take this garbage."

Ironically, it is Snider who created the all-sports format now used at WIP. Snider and his company, Spectacor, formed the talk show in 1987. Subsequently the station was purchased by Infinity.

"When the station was created, I had thought, I guess in my own ignorance, that it would be a great station," Snider said, "informing the sports public what was going on in sports throughout the area. If it was critical, it was critical. If it's warranted, it's warranted. If it's positive, it's positive. Never in my wildest imagination did I think that it would become some vehicle for ratings and entertainment; a vehicle which reporters do very, very little background checks and instead are looking more for entertaining their customers."

Clarke said it was the responsibility of the Flyers to stand up for their player and said the same action would have been taken if similar comments were made about any other Flyer.

"I think it's absolutely the right thing to do," Clarke said. "If management and ownership don't support the players, you don't really have a team."

The suit resulted in an out-of-court settlement in which the station issued apologies for the report and fired Carton, who stood by his story. Lindros said he wouldn't let the incident distract him from his work or affect his relationship with the media.

"They can blow wind at the candle," he said. "But I don't see my candle going out."

HEXY VS. POTVIN

One of the best goalie fights in NHL history took place on Nov. 10, 1996 when Ron Hextall went toe-to-two with Felix Potvin of the Toronto Maple Leafs.

As time ran out on the Flyers' 3-1 win over the Leafs at the CoreStates Center, Flyers winger Daniel Lacroix cross-checked Toronto defenseman Larry Murphy. Potvin took a wooden whack at Lacroix's ankles and before Wendel Clark could jumped on top of Lacroix, Hextall was in full sprint mode down the ice.

He and Potvin yanked off each other's mask and began throwing roundhouse rights and lefts. Hextall threw 24 punches, mostly rights, and landed one of them cleanly on Potvin's jaw. Potvin threw 17 punches and caught Hextall with an uppercut.

"Yeah, Potvin bled all over me," Hextall says now with a laugh. "You didn't think that was my blood, did you? I thought I got him really good, just ask me."

CLARKE DELIVERS MESSAGE

On March 9, 1997, after watching back-to-back losses to the Devils and Penguins, Clarke walked out of his second-floor office at the Coliseum, marched into the Flyers' dressing room and slammed the door behind him.

"The one message I remember was, "Get your head out of your rears and start playing," Brind'Amour said of Clarke's tirade. "He said, 'Listen, we're not making any more moves. We're in this together and this is how we're going to stay. Now start playing better.'"

The Flyers answered by winning six of their next nine games and ended the regular season with a 45-24-13 mark.

SNOW IN THE FORECAST?

When it came time for choosing a goalie to start the 1997 playoffs, Murray had a difficult decision to make. Should he start the postseason with 27-year-old Garth

Snow, who went 14-8-8 with a 2.52 GAA in the regular season? Or 33-year-old Ron Hextall, who went 31-16-5 with a 2.56 GAA but had struggled down the stretch?

"I've always been a coach who would stick with the one guy who has the hot hand," Murray said. "That's no different now. At this time of year, if you have a hot goaltender, go with him."

Murray went with Snow and the confident young goalie made the move pay off when he stopped Mario Lemieux and the Pittsburgh Penguins in a five-game opening-round victory.

LEMIEUX BIDS ADIEU

The final game of that 1997 series against the Penguins was an emotional one for Lemieux. Weeks earlier the 31-year-old center had decided to call it a career, even though he was on his way to a second straight scoring crown with 122 points.

On April 26, 1997, with time running out in Game 5 and the Flyers ahead 4-1, fans in the CoreStates Center stood as one and gave Lemieux a heartfelt ovation similar to the one he received four years earlier at the Spectrum.

"It was great," Lemieux said. "These are the fans I came back to from my first cancer treatment to play my first game. They did the same thing four years ago. I have nothing but great memories from Flyers fans. They're great fans who appreciate you for what you're trying to do out there."

Coffey, who spent parts of five seasons with Lemieux in Pittsburgh, said he didn't know what to say when the two met in the post-series handshake line.

Mario Lemieux wished Lindros well when they shook hands at the end of the 1997 Conference Quarterfinals.

"The only thing I asked him was, 'Are you happy?'" Coffey said. "He said, 'Yeah.' I said, 'That's great because you deserve to be happy.'"

When Lemieux and Lindros met at the end of the handshake line, chants of "Mario!" cascading from the rafters, the Penguins superstar put his arm around Lindros and whispered in his ear.

"It's your time," Lemieux said to the 24-year-old captain.

"Does it put pressure one me? No, it's a little boost," Lindros said the following day. "Actually, it's a big boost. It's something I'm going to remember the rest of my life."

MATTHEW THE MOUTH

When the Flyers met the Buffalo Sabers in the second round of the 1997 play-offs, they faced off against a team at war with itself. Coach Ted Nolan was feuding with general manager John Muckler and goaltender Dominik Hasek was suspended three games for grabbing the neck of Buffalo News columnist Jim Kelley, who suggested in a column that Hasek was faking a knee injury.

Despite the antics of Sabres antagonist Matthew Barnaby, who earlier in the season had played possum before attacking Garth Snow, the Flyers breezed past the Sabres in five games.

"I never liked that guy," Rod Brind'Amour said of Barnaby. "I mean, who draws attention to himself for being an idiot? The guy put a tattoo on his tooth. My 8-year-old wouldn't even do that."

The series was filled with verbal battles between the two sides, with Nolan accusing Snow of doctoring his shoulder pads.

"We weren't sure if they called up the goalie from the Philadelphia lacrosse team," Nolan said. "We had a couple of shots we thought were going in before they hit those pieces of wood in his shoulder pads."

Asked if he was using anything to prop up his shoulder pads, Snow smiled and said, "Two by fours."

"Actually, that's muscle," he continued. "Tell him I've been working out. We've got a better strength program than them."

LIGHTS OUT

After having the heat turned up in his team's visiting dressing room and being forced off the ice in Buffalo by a Zamboni driver, Flyers general manager Bob Clarke gave the Sabres a taste of their own medicine when the series shifted to Philadelphia.

When the Sabres tried to take the ice at the Center, Clarke made sure two Zambonis blocked their entrance to the rink and had both nets hung on a wall. Clarke said he was simply returning the favor.

"I don't have a problem with Muckler," Clarke said. "He's a good guy. Nolan's a ... idiot."

The next day Clarke gave the Sabres one hour of ice time beginning at 10 a.m. And with the Sabres still practicing, the lights were turned off at precisely 11 a.m., leaving players skating in the dark."I thought I was done that when I was 10 years old," Sabres center Donald Audette huffed. "It's terrible."

Nolan went on to be named coach of the year and Muckler was named executive of the year. But both were fired by the Sabres two weeks later.

"Our team is a debacle," declared Barnaby. "A complete and utter schmozzle."

Trent Klatt had some explaining to do after literally knocking his brother–in–law out of the NHL.

KLATT FAMILY FEUD

Flyers right wing Trent Klatt, one of the most polite players to wear a Flyers jersey, owed his wife and sister-in-law an explanation after giving his brother-in-law, Rangers forward Ken Gernander, a concussion and separated shoulder in Game 3 of the Flyers' second-round playoff series with the Rangers.

Klatt's wife, Kelly, and Gernander's wife, Kirby, are twin sisters.

"I knew it was him," Klatt said of his big check on Gernander, "and when I realized he didn't get up, I thought, 'Oh, no."

Klatt and Gernander were linemates for two years at the University of Minnesota. Klatt began dating Kelly in high school and Gernander began dating Kirby in college.

The two couples were married a year apart and spent their summers in adjacent cottages in northern Minnesota. Kelly and Kirby were sitting together at Madison Square Garden when Gernander was helped off the ice.

"It was a very uncomfortable situation," Klatt said.

Gernander did not return in the series and never played another game in the NHL.

'GO GET IT'

Having won four of the five games against Buffalo, Flyers coach Terry Murray opened the conference semifinals against the Rangers with Garth Snow in goal and the move paid off with a series-opening 3-1 victory.

But when Snow was riddled for five goals in a 5-4 setback in Game 2, Murray whistled in Hextall. The Flyers took control of the series by winning back-to-back games in New York.

When the Flyers returned home to clinch their first berth in the Stanley Cup Finals in 10 years the 20,051 delirious fans at the CoreStates Center began chanting, "We Want The Cup!"

As Janet Jones, the supermodel wife of Wayne Gretzky, comforted her sobbing son, Ty, in the stands, Rangers captain Mark Messier reached out a congratulatory hand to Lindros and said, "Go get it!"

MURRAY-GO-ROUND

With five days off before they hosted the Detroit Red Wings in the Stanley Cup Finals, there was plenty of time to speculate whether Terry Murray would return for a fourth season as Flyers coach.

Asked if winning the Eastern Conference for the first time in 10 years was worthy of a contract extension for his coach Clarke replied, "If he wants to be, yeah. Why would he want to go anywhere else? We don't want him to go anywhere else."

Murray said he and Clarke had talked before the playoffs and that Clarke told him not to worry about his contract, saying, "We'll get things taken care of."

Opinions in the Flyers locker room seemed splintered on the future of their coach.

"That's not my decision," Hextall offered. "That needs to go on when the season is over and not a second before."

"He's done a great job behind the bench," Lindros said. "The way he's working the goaltending situation, my hat's off to him. He's done a tremendous job for us, that's for sure."

While Murray contemplated his next move in goal, Red Wings coach Scotty Bowman was devising a strategy that would bring Detroit its first Stanley Cup in 42 years.

Instead of using shut down defenseman Vladimir Konsantinov against the line of Lindros, LeClair and Renberg, Bowman surprised the Flyers by going with the puck-moving pair of Larry Murphy and Nicklas Lidstrom.

Bowman figured his two best puck-moving defensemen would allow the Red Wings to get out of their zone before the Legion of Doom unleashed its will on the forecheck.

The second half of Bowman's strategy mirrored the one Fred Shero had used against Bruins defenseman Bobby Orr in 1974. He instructed his players to hit Flyers defenseman and former Red Wing Paul Coffey as much as humanly possible.

"He's not one of my favorites," Bowman had said of Coffey a few months earlier. "A guy that can skate like he can and has all that talent, why can't be play defense?"

Bowman also stung Coffey with this zinger:

"He didn't win the Cup in Pittsburgh," Bowman said of the future Hall of Famer. "Mario won the Cup in Pittsburgh – Mario and (former coach) Bob Johnson."

The Red Wings followed their coach's orders and in the first two games of the series Coffey was on the ice for six of Detroit's eight goals and in the penalty box for a seventh. When Darren McCarty dropped Coffey to the ice with a concussion late in Game 2 in Philadelphia, the tone of the series was set.

With Coffey sidelined the remainder of the series Murray was forced to dress little-used defenseman Michel Petit when the series shifted to Detroit. Meanwhile, his decision to go with Hextall in Game 1 and Snow in Game 2 had backfired and the Flyers flew into Detroit with identical 4-2 losses.

"I don't like to play musical chairs," Murray said, "I was going on a hunch in the second game at it didn't work out, obviously."

"Terry made the right calls to get us there," Clarke recalls. "But we probably didn't have the confidence we should have had in either (goalie). For a team that went to the Finals, we still hadn't settled on a goalie and that's our fault. One or the other should have been the No. 1 guy."

Some wonder if it would have mattered against the Red Wings.

"Switching goalies wasn't really a big deal to us," Brind'Amour said. "I'm sure for the goalie who got pulled it sucked. But we had to go out and play the games."

The Flyers could have had a stone wall in front of the net for Game 3 and the Red Wings would have found a way to score. They pumped six goals past Hextall, including a 60-footer by Lidstrom between his pads, en route to a 6-1 rout.

Through three games, only Brind'Amour (three goals) and LeClair (two goals) had scored for the Flyers. Lindros and the rest of his teammates seemed to be playing in a fog.

'CHOKING SITUATION'

About 14 hours after the lopsided defeat in Game 3 and with his team on the brink of elimination, Murray was asked at a press conference about his team's sudden loss of confidence.

"'I wish I could find it," Murray said. "I wish I could find the answer for that. I don't know where it's gone. But many teams have been through this before. It's basically a choking situation, as I call it, for our team right now."

Every jaw in the room hit the floor. Murray's press conference lasted another 15 minutes, but the remainder was spent on what he meant by the word "choking" and with each response he dug himself deeper.

Terry Murray never imagined uttering two words would ultimately cost him his job as Flyers coach.

"Competition brings out the best in you," he said, "but sometimes it brings out the worst in you. If you keep competing, inevitably, you'll get to the best. If you stop competing, you are never going to break through and you are going to be in one of those teams that were also-rans your whole life. You're going to choke. You're going to get into competitive situations and you're not going to know how to get the job done. , you're not going to know how to break through, you're not going to know how to get the job done."

Murray said he was unconcerned about how his players would react to his harsh words.

"If we are going to be that fragile and collapse because of the things I am saying right now, we don't have a chance."

It turned out to be a gross miscalculation. Murray could not have imagined just how painful his words would be to the ears of his players.

When reporters filed into the visiting locker room seeking a response from Lindros, the captain had already exited the building and was on his way back to the team hotel.

"Aye, yie-yie," Desjardins said in disbelief. "I don't know why he said that. I don't know what he thinks it will do for us. But it's certainly hard to take as a player coming from your coach."

Brind'Amour and LeClair agreed.

"If he's trying to light a fire, I don't think we need it now," Brind'Amour said.

"It's kind of tough to use those words," LeClair said.

Today, Brind'Amour thinks Murray's "choking" comments were blown way out of proportion.

"I don't think he meant it literally, but we weren't playing the way we had been," Brind'Amour said. "So, in a sense, he was just telling it like it was."

The morning after Murray's comments Lindros explained he had an obligation to his teammates, not an inquiring media.

"We had a team meeting in our (locker) room and talked about a number of things," Lindros said. "Terry was having a press conference and you guys were all over there. I didn't skate, a lot of guys didn't skate. After that I went back to the hotel."

As for Murray's choking comments, Lindros said they hurt.

"They're a little tough to swallow when they're coming from your coach," he said. "But I guess that's the way things are, and we'll just have to stick together as a team and go out and win as a team."

Clarke now believes Lindros' quick exit was a harbinger of things to come from his captain.

"In hindsight, Lindros didn't want the responsibility of being a captain and being a leader and standing up with his team," Clarke said. "He would have rather run away and let the other guys take the heat. We kind of ignored it and hoped it went away. It was poor management on our part."

END OF THE ROAD

The Flyers played their best game of the Finals in Game 4, but by the time Lindros scored his first goal of the series with 14.8 seconds remaining fans at The Joe were already celebrating a 2-1 victory and the Red Wings' first Stanley Cup since 1955.

After the game, Murray called his players "champions," but they certainly didn't feel that way.

In a sullen Flyers locker room Lindros stared blindly through the glare of dozens of television cameras and assessed his play in the series, in which he recorded one goal and two assists.

"It went by so quick," Lindros said in a whisper. "We expected more from ourselves. I'm shocked about what happened. It was just a blur. We couldn't stop the bleeding."

Lindros acknowledged the obvious when he said, "I'll be the first to admit that I didn't have a great series. But I'm not going to go jump off the Walt Whitman Bridge. Just get back on the saddle and ride 'er again."

Today, Clarke admits the Flyers were an inferior team to the Red Wings and that Lindros would have needed to provide a herculean effort to lead the Flyers to a championship.

"If we were going to beat Detroit, I felt the only way we could do it is if Lindros, LeClair and Renberg dominated with their size," he said. "Renberg had a bad groin and the other two guys weren't very good.

"I don't think we competed very hard. They were beating us with Bowman playing Larry Murphy against Lindros and that's not a good sign. If Lindros had wanted to compete he would have run over Larry Murphy and that would have been the end.

"Eric had been through these things his whole life almost. He played in the Canada Cup, in World Juniors. He had been on center stage his whole life. I'm not sure he liked being there. If you don't like it, it's hard to perform well and we weren't going to win unless he played well."

MURRAY GETS THE AX

In the days that followed the Flyers' collapse against the Red Wings, the hottest topic was the future of Terry Murray as head coach.

"If going to the Stanley Cup Finals is a problem, then it's going to be a huge surprise to me," Murray said. "...The growth of the team in the last three years has been outstanding."

Indeed, Murray's teams went 118-64-30 and had the fourth-best winning percentage in Flyers history, behind only Fred Shero, Mike Keenan and Pat Quinn. But there were concerns about Murray's strained relationship with his captain.

"I think my relationship with Eric has been very good," Murray said, "and I don't see any change whatsoever."

But on June 14, one week after the Flyers were swept by the Red Wings, Clarke announced the team had fired Murray. It marked the first time in NHL history a coach had been fired after leading his team to the Stanley Cup Finals.

"The problems didn't just surface," Clarke said at the time of the firing. "They've been basically over the last couple of years. We solved some and we haven't been able to solve others."

While some players defended Murray, Rod Brind'Amour said it was clear at the time Lindros was "running the show."

Clarke said the firing was the worst thing he ever had to do as a manager, adding "he has the right to hate me for what I've done."

Years later, Murray said the demands he placed on Lindros ultimately grated the star center and led to his dismissal.

But Clarke said too many players were hurt by Murray's "choking" comment to bring him back and Ed Snider agreed.

"I think it was inevitable," Snider said. "…The bottom line is no team can be successful when the players are rebelling against a coach."

Today, Clarke says a simple apology from Murray might have kept him from getting his walking papers.

"When Murph said we were choking, the players were really offended by it," Clarke said. "Those comments were irreparable. Obviously, I'm good friends with Murph and it was really a hard decision.

"I asked him to just explain to the players why he said it and apologize and it will all go away. He's stubborn and didn't want to. It was tough for him to do. He's an honest man and I don't think he knew Lindros was against him. I probably was wrong, but you have no way of finding out once you do it."

Today, Brind'Amour says he was not surprised to see Murray let go after the emotional roller coaster of the 1997 playoffs.

"Terry showed no emotion," Brind'Amour said. "He wasn't a coach that inspired you, and at the time Eric was running the show."

CHAPTER 9

END OF AN ERA

(1997–2000)

Follow the tragic fall of Eric Lindros, from a near-death experience in Nashville to his public feuding with Bob Clarke and the crushing hit that defined his career.

CASHMAN, KEENAN OR BARBER?

THE SUMMER OF 1997 WILL BE REMEMBERED AS MUCH FOR who the Flyers didn't hire as Terry Murray's replacement as for who they did.

In the three weeks between the time Bob Clarke fired Murray and hired Wayne Cashman, two very interesting candidates emerged. Mike Keenan made it known that after four trips to the Staley Cup Finals in 10 years he was the right choice to lead Lindros and the Flyers to the Promised Land.

"I am very interested in the coaching job," Keenan said at the time. "I feel I've developed strong coaching skills that I can impart on a team like the Flyers, which I consider a favorite to win the Stanley Cup."

Bill Barber, who had led the AHL Philadelphia Phantoms to a 49-18-3-10 record the previous season, did not apply for the job but quietly hoped Clarke would offer it to him.

"Am I capable? Yeah," Barber said. "Do I have a desire to coach in the NHL? Yes, I do. Could I handle it? Could I work with the Flyers? Yes, but they haven't come to me. If I'm not a candidate they have their reasons."

The prevailing assumption was that Keenan and Barber would be just as demanding on Lindros as Murray – perhaps even more demanding – and that Clarke was looking for a more player-friendly coach.

On July 7, Clarke gave Cashman, a longtime assistant coach for the Rangers, Lightning and Sharks, his first head coaching position in the NHL. Barber was not among the candidates interviewed for the post and he was clearly hurt.

``Am I upset? No," he said. "Am I shocked? No. Would I have liked the opportunity? Sure, I would. But I don't know if my record with the players is what they want. I'm honest and fair with my players and I'm not sure that's what they're looking for."

Barber believed he had what it took to lead Lindros and the Flyers over the final hump.

"In the 14 years since I played, I haven't been playing tiddly winks or watching TV," he said. "I've been involved on almost every level. I can dance with the best."

Asked if there were doubts about his ability to handle Lindros, Barber responded, "I've dropped the hammer on the (the Phantoms) and they've become warriors for me. If I had to deal with him tomorrow, I''d be very, very straightforward."

Still, Barber wondered if his chance to coach the Flyers had just flown out the window, never to arrive again.

"I know I'll get my chance to coach in the NHL," he said. "I just don't think it will be with the Flyers."

GRATTON'S SMUDGED ARRIVAL

Eric Lindros was not the only Flyer who needed an arbitrator to determine his fate in Philadelphia. In August of 1997, after the New York Rangers signed Colorado's Joe Sakic to a $21 million offer sheet — $15 million of it up front — Clarke decided to jump in the free-agent fray, signing Tampa Bay's Chris Gratton to a $16.5 million offer sheet, with $15 million up front.

But after Clarke faxed his offer sheet to the office of Gratton's agent, Pat Morris, Lightning general manager Phil Esposito orchestrated a trade with the Blackhawks that would send Gratton to Chicago for either Ethan Moreau or Eric Daze, and Keith Carney, and Steve Dubinsky, along with several million in cash.

Esposito claimed he called the NHL's central registry to report his trade with the Blackhawks before he received the Flyers' offer sheet and that the Flyers' offer should be voided because in the transmission from Philadelphia to Tampa Bay the figures on the contract were smudged.

Two arbitration hearings later it was ruled the Flyers had indeed signed Gratton before Esposito made the trade with Chicago. As compensation, Esposito received four first-round draft picks, which he traded back to the Flyers in exchange for Mikael Renberg and Karl Dykhuis.

The Legion of Doom was history, making way for a short-lived and grossly over-hyped Chris Gratton era.

BIG WIN, YOU'RE FIRED

The Flyers were rolling along with a 27-11-9 record through mid-January, but a failed trade – Pat Falloon, Vinny Prospal and a second-rounder for Alexandre Daigle – kicked off a 3-8 stretch and it became clear to Clarke that his players were not responding to Cashman.

Clarke had secretly phoned Roger Neilson, an assistant coach in St. Louis, and offered him the job before the Flyers' March 8 overtime victory against the Penguins. Word spread throughout the CoreStates Center press box that Neilson would be arriving at Philadelphia International Airport during the game.

The Flyers rallied to win the game on an overtime goal by Daigle and just minutes after Cashman hugged his coaches and players for their efforts, he was asked at a press conference if he realized he was about to be fired.

Cashman looked dumbfounded and the next day Neilson was announced as the Flyers' next coach. Cashman, who had two more years remaining on a $2.45 million contract, accepted a role as assistant coach.

"To be honest, I thought Cash was relieved," Ron Hextall said. "He was much more suited to be an assistant coach than a head coach."

Wayne Cashman's replacement was already in Philadelphia when he coached his final game.

MR. MAGOO ARRIVES

At 64 years old, Roger Neilson arrived in Philadelphia as the second-oldest coach in the NHL, behind only Detroit's Scotty Bowman, who was a year older. He had coached more teams – seven — than any coach in NHL history.

But that didn't necessarily mean he could tell a stick room from a coach's office.

After his first practice as head coach of the Flyers, Neilson left the ice, wandered through the stick room, the locker room, the changing room, down a hallway and was standing in the foyer when he spotted Ron Hextall.

"Hexy, can you help an old guy find his office?"

Hextall broke out in laughter.

"He was standing right in front of it," Hextall said. "I thought, 'Oh boy! This really is Mr. Magoo!'"

Neilson's self-deprecating humor brought a much-needed breath of fresh air to the Flyers.

He rode to work every morning on an outdated English racing bike, arriving around 8 or 9 in the morning and staying long into the night.

"I think he slept there some nights and didn't tell anybody," Rod Brind'Amour said.

If he did, it wasn't the first time Neilson took residence in a hockey rink.

As a teenager, Neilson said it was not uncommon for him to attend an amateur hockey game at Maple Leaf Garden in the afternoon then hide in the men's room waiting for the Leafs to play that night.

"I would stand on the toilet so the guy who came in to mop the floors wouldn't see my feet," Neilson said proudly.

As an adult it was no different. Neilson admitted that when he coached the Leafs in the late 1970s, he often slept in a cot in his office in the bowels of Maple Leaf Gardens.

"I felt something run across my feet one night," he said, "and when I told one of the workers he said, 'They're just our rats. Don't bother them and they won't bother you.'"

It didn't take long for Neilson to make himself right at home at the Flyers' practice rink. He often walked around the Coliseum in bare feet, shorts, T-shirt and a ratty old Roots baseball cap and when he was forced to get dressed up for games, he always opted for an obnoxiously colored tie.

"I don't like wearing ties," he said. "So, it was kind of my way of protesting."

Neilson bought most of his ties from hawkers on the street corners of New York when he was coaching the Rangers. None cost him more than $3.50.

Roger Neilson said wearing colorful ties was his way of protesting against getting dressed up.

Neilson's tie collection multiplied dramatically when the Rangers players presented him with 300 ties after winning his 300th NHL game in 1992. He said he never wore the same tie twice in the same season.

"At the end of the season, I leave all the ties I don't like for the players," Neilson said. "They don't take many of them."

MEET YOU IN THE PARKING LOT

Dan Lacroix was one of the more colorful players in Flyers history. An avid painter off the ice, he once illustrated Christmas cards for the Flyers to send to their season ticket holders.

On the night of April 8, 1998, Lacroix was the color of crimson and it was not the prettiest of pictures.

Late in a 6-1 in over the Lightning, while the Flyers' Dan Kordic and the Lightning's Sandy McCarthy were tugging at each other's jerseys Tampa forward Andrei Nazarov grabbed Lacroix and the Flyers forward responded with an an open glove to Nazarov's face.

"About 30 seconds later, he suckered me," Lacroix said. "It was out of the blue."

Lacroix dropped to his knees just as Kordic, McCarthy and Joel Otto were being escorted to the penalty boxes, leaving four Lightning players on the ice and three Flyers. Lacroix went after Nazarov and engaged in a fight, then found himself in a second fight with Darcy Tucker, who pummeled him with a series of right hands to the left eye. By the time the fight was over, Lacroix was a bloody mess, needing 48 stitches to close the cut above his eye.

"You would think when a guy sucker punches someone, he would be the guy taken away," Lacroix said.

The Flyers were so incensed by Nazarov's actions six of them, including Lindros, waited for him in the parking lot of the Ice Palace.

"I thought they might try to jump me," Nazarov said. "They could have. It would have been six to one. I told them to save it for the ice. If you want me, come and get me on the ice."

Lindros would not get into specifics about what happened in that parking lot.

"If I say something, I could get fined," he said. "Let's just say what happened the other night won't be forgotten."

Clarke said the players only exchanged a few words in that parking lot and applauded his captain for his actions.

"I think Lindros was right in what he did," Clarke said. "They came at us just to fight. They didn't care about winning the hockey game."

Two days later, his eye swollen shut, Lacroix was informed of his teammates' actions two nights earlier.

"They really did that?" he said. "I like to see that. I like to see that a lot."

As for Nazarov, Lacroix said he would keep him in his thoughts.

"I won't forget his face," he said. "And he won't forget mine."

FROM POTATO PEELS TO 50 GOALS

When John LeClair became the first American-born player to score 50 or more goals in three straight seasons in a nationally televised 2-1 win over the Buffalo Sabres, his parents, Butch and Beverly, were beaming in the living room of their modest St. Albans, Vermont, home.

The fourth of five children, LeClair grew up in a small, four-bedroom house with one bathroom.

"It was tiny," he said. "But when you're a kid, you don't know any better. It was a little crazy waiting in line for the bathroom, but it was fun."

LeClair's first experience on an ice rink came before he could even walk. While his older sisters were in elementary school, John's mother would take him to public ice skating sessions for women.

"I'd sit him on the ice, fill his pockets with chocolate bars, and he'd sit there for an hour or so," Beverly LeClair recalled. "He seemed to like it."

LeClair could throw and hit a baseball at two years old and could ride a two-wheeler by the time he was three.

"It was scary to see him on a bike, riding into my flower garden," Beverly said. "Falling was the only way for him to stop."

Since the ponds in St. Albans would remain frozen from late December through the beginning of March, LeClair spent countless days and nights playing on a home-made rink in the backyard of his neighbor, Jeremy Benoit. The rink had plywood boards and floodlights and nearby was a warming shack with a hot stove.

"John would come back frozen, stiff as a board," Butch LeClair said.

When LeClair wasn't playing hockey he worked at his parents' diner, Pud's Lunch Bar, a popular restaurant that served breakfast every morning and sodas and milk shakes in the afternoon.

"It was a place where Fonzie from Happy Days would have hung out," Beverly LeClair said.

LeClair mostly peeled potatoes in the diner's kitchen and sorted returnable soda bottles in the stock room.

Long before Eric Lindros called him the Babe Ruth of hockey, John LeClair made a living peeling potatoes.

"He didn't do a very good job," Butch LeClair said with a laugh, "but it kept him active."

LeClair went on to attend the University of Vermont and was drafted by the Montreal Canadiens in 1987. He now ranks fifth on the Flyers' all-time goals list with 333, behind only Bill Barber (420), Brian Propp (369), Tim Kerr (363) and Bobby Clarke (358).

"In all my years and all the guys I played with, he's probably the hungriest to score," Flyers goaltender Ron Hextall said after LeClair's milestone goal. "He wants to score and he wants to score bad. Whether it's diving for a puck or holding somebody off in front of the net. This guy is possessed to score."

NOW OR NEVER?

When the 1998 playoffs began the Flyers were the overwhelming favorite to represent the Eastern Conference in the Stanley Cup Finals. Many, however, believed their window of opportunity was beginning to close.

Eric Desjardins and John LeClair were about to turn 29. Rod Brind'Amour was creeping up on 28. The time to win was now.

"It's human nature," said Flyers defenseman Petr Svoboda, who was 32 at the time. "If somebody is chasing you with a gun, you run a lot faster than if he's chasing you with a baseball bat."

THE MOUTH AND THE RAYZOR

The Flyers have had their share of playoff rivalries but few were as entertaining as their bouts with the Sabres in the late 1990s.

In 1998, a pair of thugs from upstate New York named Matthew Barnaby and Rob Ray took center stage.

"I'll get at least a half dozen death threats," Barnaby said before the series began. "And I'm sure they'll have some snipers up there in the top row (of the CoreStates Center)."

Maybe the Flyers should have had extra security in the tunnel that leads from the visitors' bench to the visiting locker room because they had their $210 million pleasure palace vandalized on the night of April 24, 1998.

It all started during a very chippy 2-1 Flyers victory in Game 2 – their only win in the series - when Sabres forward Geoff Sanderson was pushed into the Flyers bench and punched in the head by a couple of men in orange and black.

The Sabres were quick to reply when someone conveniently opened the door to their bench just as Lindros was approaching. When the Flyers captain tried to make his way off the Sabres' laps, he did so with a helicopter swing that left players and fans ducking.

When Flyers defenseman Eric Desjardins was checked into the Sabres bench and butt-ended by Buffalo forward Michal Grosek, who earlier in the game sticked Flyers defenseman Dan McGillis in the face, all hell broke loose.

Barnaby and Ray got ejected by referee Stephen Walkom and decided to take out their frustrations on any object they could find, moveable or otherwise. Barnaby was the first to get tossed after jawing with the fans he called the best in the NHL.

Ray then tore a page from Barnaby's book of temper tantrums when he did a hatchet job on the canopy leading from the ice to the visiting dressing room, tearing it down with one fell swoop of his stick.

Ray then turned into Jack Nicholson's Jack Torrance character from "The Shining."

He splintered his stick with several whacks against the door leading to the dressing room and dropped its remains on the tunnel floor. Barnaby, who earlier in the game busted a telephone in the penalty box, decided there were still a couple good whacks left in Ray's splintered stick and battered it against a cinder block wall.

Ray then drop-kicked two electric fans, sending them flying with his right skate. The poor PowerAde container was next, getting thrown into the shower. Ray even grabbed the wooden spoon they used to mix the PowerAde and tried to break it. But by then, his energy level was spent.

"You want me to tell you the truth?" Ray said when asked what really went on in the dressing room. "Sometimes you come off the ice after something like that and you sit in the dressing room 10 or 15 minutes later saying, 'What just happened?' You don't even know."

Ray was asked if he might expect to see a repair bill in his mailbox.

"Our playoff bonuses will probably be signed over and sent back to Philly," Ray said with a chuckle. "Ah, well, it was worth it."

Had he worn orange and black the Rayzor probably would have been a fan favorite. He was certainly a welcome visitor in the penalty box, a place he frequented on a regular basis.

"He sat down once and said, 'Hey, boys, how you doing?'" recalled PA announcer Lou Nolan. "I said, 'Good, Rob, how are you?'

"Well, my wife just left me. My truck blew up, my ice time's down and Barnaby always calls me collect. So I'm not doing too good."

LINDROS FEUD GETS PERSONAL

Bob Clarke began the summer of 1998 saying that if Eric Lindros wanted to be paid as the best player in the game – he was making $8.5 million a year — he needed to start playing like one.

Lindros, 25, was coming off an injury-plagued 30-goal season and had managed just one goal in the five-game playoff upset by the Sabres.

At the suggestion of Ed Snider, the Flyers were prepared to offer Lindros a deal comparable to the one the one Jaromir Jagr signed with the Penguins the previous summer — four years at $38 million. Jagr's deal averaged $9.5 million and topped out at $10.4 million.

But Clarke said he wanted someone other than Carl Lindros, Eric's father and agent, to handle the negotiating.

"I think it is more difficult because everybody views their own children as special," Clarke said. "You want to criticize another man's son in negotiations, so there is more difficulty. But Carl and I and the Flyers have always seemed to get over that."

Carl Lindros did not relent and when the Flyers drew up a detailed 100-page, five-year proposal worth about $43 million in base salary, the Lindroses came back with an unusual demand: Eric wanted a written guarantee that he would not be traded during the life of the contract.

"The bottom line is I want the opportunity to remain here," Lindros said. "And with talk this summer about me being offered around the league, I want to do what I can to stay here in Philly. There's going to have to be re-assurances that's going to be the case."

The Flyers pointed out that the NHL Collective Bargaining Agreement explicitly stated a player could not request a no-trade clause until he turned 31 years of age.

"Unfortunately, the league rules absolutely prohibit us from entering into any assurances regarding the no-trade position," Snider said. "There can't be any side deals. That would just be going against league rules and we'd be subjected to a major fine."

Clarke recently admitted he quietly sought to trade Lindros that summer.

"Oh yeah, we talked to teams every once in a while," he said. "There were a couple times it got going a little bit. We had one real good offer. But I won't say what it was."

Lindros, meanwhile, was trying to recover from the summer criticisms of his general manager.

"I wasn't too enthused with what he said," Lindros said. "But I'm not going to go and buy advertising in every paper across North America and air my frustration out on him."

Instead, Lindros tried turning to Snider, only to find an equally cold shoulder.

"What's irritating," Lindros said, "is that Ed Snider has been in any negotiation I've ever been a part of. The first one (in 1992), we agreed to a (salary) number on the phone and we stuck to that number. He was there on the second deal. And I need his reassurance on this deal that I'm not going to be shipped."

Snider said he was "very involved" in developing the Flyers' five-year offer and would step in when the negotiations neared a conclusion.

"Our motive is really simple," Snider said. "We want Eric here a long time. We just don't want to be negotiating every year because it's a big distraction. We just want it to end and know we have him for a while. We wouldn't put this many dollars at risk if we didn't believe Eric could be and would be a major part of our future success."

Lindros said he thought his no-trade request showed his own commitment to the Flyers.

"This whole thing came up because I was being shopped around before I was even offered a contract," Lindros said. "How would you feel? You sit out an entire season (1991-92) to come to a team that wants to win. You want to stick with it. We had a setback last year and everybody's disappointed about it. It was a bump in the road, but the road doesn't end there."

Actually, it did. The Flyers took their offer off the table and Lindros agreed to play out the final year of his contract.

COAT ON A RACK?

It didn't take a Ph.D. to recognize the Flyers were in desperate need of a goalie in the summer of 1998. Clarke's trading deadline gamble of trading Garth Snow for Sean Burke backfired in the playoffs.

But when Clarke signed 34-year-old John Vanbiesbrouck to a two-year deal worth $7.25 million, fans and media railed against the general manager, saying Mike Richter or Curtis Joseph would have been far better, albeit more expensive, choices.

The backlash was so strong that even the Beezer was forced to defend himself at his own introductory press conference.

Asked if he considers himself a bargain, Vanbiesbrouck widened his eyes and said, "I don't consider myself a coat on a rack."

John Vanbiesbrouck's introductory press conference was more like an inquisition by a skeptical media.

Vanbiesbrouck had fewer wins (18) and a higher goals-against average (2.87) than Joseph (29 wins, 2.63 GAA) and Richter (21 wins, 2.66 GAA), but said too many people tried to make him the ugly duckling in a free-agent beauty pageant.

"Whether or not I'm the right fit, I'll let people speculate on that," he said. "But I'm very proud of the fact they want me here."

Clarke was agitated by all the second-guessing, but not nearly as much as Ed Snider.

"There are 50 general managers in this town who think they know more than he does," Snider said. "I think he's done a damn good job. I don't know how long Bob can take this crap.

"I've been around 30 years and I haven't seen anything like it. He's a big boy and he can handle it, but it's gotten beyond ridiculous."

Today, Clarke acknowledges his biggest mistake of the Lindros era was never landing a goaltender good enough to win a Stanley Cup.

"More than anything we were a goaltender away," he said. "The year we signed John Vanbiesbrouck we could have gotten Curtis Joseph and we should have. I like John a lot and Roger (Neilson) wanted Vanbiesbrouck. Beezer was a lot cheaper, but I think if we had taken Joseph he would have given us a much better chance. He was a better goalie."

ALPHABET SOUP

In case you were wondering (and even if you weren't), John Vanbiesbrouck owns the longest name in Flyers history. His 13-letter surname is two letters longer than the former record holder — Dennis Ververgaert.

THE STORY BEHIND NO. 88

Speaking of trivial trivia, ever wonder how Lindros came to wear the No. 88?

"As a kid, I always wore the number 8," he said. "When I was traded in juniors, our captain Iain Fraser, wore number 8. The only numbers I considered were 24 or 88, so I chose 88."

Lindros said he wore the number in memory of "a great friend and person," the late John McCauley, who died in 1988 after many years as the NHL's director of officiating. McCauley was a close friend of the Lindros family.

BUT CAN THEY SPEAK FRENCH?

When the Flyers gathered for their first training camp under Roger Neilson he looked down his roster and said, "I hear these two French goalies are going to be good."

He was referring to Brian Boucher, who is from Woonsocket, Rhode Island, and Jean-Marc Pelletier, who is from Atlanta, Georgia.

APE? WHO SAID APE?

You can't believe everything you think you see.

That was the message Flyers left wing Chris Gratton gave the media after he was exonerated by the NHL following reports he allegedly called Florida Panthers enforcer Peter Worrell an ``ape" during a first-period scuffle in a game on Nov. 12, 1998.

The allegations angered Gratton, who was struggling through the worst start of his six-year career with no goals in 15 games.

"I would never, ever say that and disrespect Peter like that," Gratton said. "I respect him as a player and a person and I respect the players in the league too much. ... It's a serious, serious accusation to make. This is about people's

At $10 million, Chris Gratton may go down as the biggest single-season bust in Flyers history.

lives. I don't know who started this but it's unbelievable. I just feel really sick right now. I'd apologize, but I never said anything."

Gratton was so upset about the allegations he phoned Worrell, 21, and the two tried to put the incident behind them.

"I can't help it if people say things to me," Worrell said. "But it's like the teacher on Charlie Brown. I'm not really listening to the words. I'm not hearing them talk, they're not saying anything to me."

HOLY MOSES!

The Flyers were in the midst of a seven-game winless streak when Clarke traded the popular Shjon Podein to the Avalanche for the equally popular Keith Jones.

When Roger Neilson put Jones on a line with Lindros and LeClair the Flyers went on a tear, losing just three of their next 26 games.

During the incredible run, teammates set up a lounge chair under Jones' locker stall at their practice rink and placed cigars and sports drinks on a table beside it.

"They started calling me Moses because we couldn't lose after they got me," Jones said. "Truth is, my knee was so bad I didn't even practice. I just played in the games and sat in the lounge chair on practice days."

DID I SAY 'CHOKING?'

It wasn't until he faced the Flyers as the new coach of the Florida Panthers that Terry Murray addressed the "choking" comments he made 17 months earlier in the 1997 Stanley Cup Finals.

Speaking to a group of Miami reporters, Murray said he did not regret saying what he said, "but the word 'choke' should not have been said. ... I wasn't accusing any players of choking. That wasn't the context. But I shouldn't have said it. It's the wrong word because it's never interpreted right. If it comes from writers or journalists, then that's one thing. But to be said in-house, that was wrong. It should have been kept in the locker room, not in a public forum."

ROGER THE VISIONARY

Many thought he was crazy at the time but Roger Neilson was among the first NHL coaches to think outside the box when it came to deciding games that were tied after regulation.

"I think there should be a shootout," he said. "No overtime, just a quick shootout. It's strictly for the fans. But I think it's exciting and you're playing for a point."

According to Neilson's plan, teams would be guaranteed a point if they played to a tie in regulation. Instead of a five-minute overtime, however, each team would have five shooters take turns on breakaways against opposing goalies. The team that wins the shootout, according to Neilson, would get an extra point in the standings under a category next to ties that would read SP for shootout points.

"What I don't like about the 4-on-4 overtimes is that six forwards sit back and say, 'Oh, we'll just be cheerleaders.' That's what they've got to be thinking.

"I'd rather have the shootout. Can you imagine Eric Lindros and John LeClair against Eddie Belfour; and Mike Modano and Joe Nieuwendyk against Beezer? The fans would be taking bets on which five guys we'd use. Would we use a defenseman? It would be so much more fun."

Seven years later the NHL adopted Neilson's plan.

'A SPOILED LITTLE GIRL'

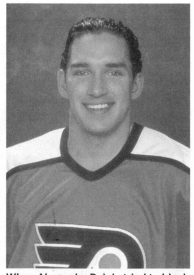

Bob Clarke has called a lot of players a lot of things over the years, but when Alexandre Daigle blocked a trade to Edmonton by saying he would not report to the Oilers, Clarke called the 23-year-old right wing "a spoiled little girl" and kicked him off the team.

Daigle, who drew comparisons to Mario Lemieux when he entered the NHL, had three goals and two assists when he asked to be traded in mid January.

Eventually, Edmonton general manager Glen Sather orchestrated a three-way trade in which the Lightning got Daigle, the Oilers got winger Alexander Selivanov and the Flyers got Andrei Kovalenko, who had reportedly missed an Oilers team flight because he overslept after a late night on the town.

When Alexandre Daigle tried to block a trade to Edmonton, Bob Clarke called him "a spoiled little girl."

"We can't find him guilty of anything until we get him here and talk to him," Clarke said. "There have been lots of guys that drank a lot of beer in their life and still scored a lot of goals and played good hockey."

Five weeks later Clarke traded Kovalenko for Adam Burt.

ERIC THE ANTIQUER?

Eric Lindros rarely let people see the softer side of him, but when he did he revealed some interesting interests. Like that he collected antiques.

When he wasn't playing hockey or at home wrestling with his 185-pound spotted great dane, Bacchus, Lindros enjoyed rummaging for unusual items to decorate his log cabin off Lake Muskoka, about an hour north of Toronto.

Over his years with the Flyers Lindros collected a pool table built in 1876 for one of the Smith brothers, the same Smith brothers made famous for their cough drops.

"Somebody found it in a woman's attic in Philadelphia," Lindros said. "It came with a letter of authenticity and it was in terrific condition. I had it delivered up to the cottage."

Lindros also came across a roll top desk and antique cabinets for his lakeside summer home, but his most prized possession is a hand-carved 30-foot war canoe that he erected in a corner of his cabin.

"This guy carved it out himself," Lindros said. "It has shelving built in and I use it for picture frames and things like that."

An avid fisherman, Lindros wondered what it might be like to own a horse. So, during the NHL lockout of 1994, he visited a ranch north of Toronto with the intention of purchasing his first horse.

"I found one and went up to ride it," he recalled. "His name was Gentle Ben. I got up on the sucker for about 10 seconds and it bucked me off and chased me around the inside of the arena. I think they named him that as a joke. Guys were all sitting back laughing as the horse tried to bite me."

RODDY THE IRON MAN

On Jan. 30, 1999 at precisely 6:54 p.m., Rod Brind'Amour busted out of the tunnel that leads from the Flyers dressing room to the ice surface of the First Union Center. No one in the crowd thought twice about it. But his teammates and trainers did.

Brind'Amour was playing in his 449th straight game – a streak lasting almost six years –

Two nights earlier, in the closing minutes of a 4-2 win over the Coyotes, Brind'Amour had been driven into his own players' bench, chest-first. He crumbled to the ice in pain and had to be hoisted over the boards and onto the bench by Eric Lindros.

He sat there, hunched over in pain, the rest of the game.

"He was in all kinds of agony," Roger Neilson said. "The trainers told us that the rib can sometimes pop out and then go in again. They figured he'd be out at least two weeks."

A few minutes after the game, Brind'Amour made his way to the shower and seemed to be feeling better.

No Flyer has played in more consecutive games than the 484 churned out by Rod Brind'Amour.

"Then all of a sudden he kind of collapsed on the way out (of the Center)," Neilson said. "They brought him back into the trainer's room then took him to the hospital for an X-ray. He was in a lot of pain going to the hospital."

X-rays showed no fracture and a CT scan showed bruised cartilage around the ribs.

"We need to treat it as a fracture," Flyers athletic trainer John Worley said.

Neilson was convinced Brind'-Amour's Iron Man streak was in "big-time" jeopardy and asked if he could have Peter White recalled from the Phantoms to take Brind'Amour's place.

Clarke knew better and told Neilson he had little doubt Brind'-Amour would be in the lineup, flak jacket and all.

"When you play as hard as Brind'Amour does every game and you go that long without missing a game, it tells you a lot about the man," Clarke said. "He's played with injuries a number of times, probably because he's stubborn. Stubborn and tough. That's what you want in a hockey player."

PARTING SHOTS AT ZUBIE

Less than three years after Dainius Zubrus became the youngest player ever to wear a Flyers uniform – 18 years, three months and 20 days – he was traded to the Montreal Canadiens along with a pair of draft picks, for Mark Recchi.

On his way out, Clarke gave Zubie a verbal kick out the door.

"To me, he's a young kid who got a pile of money and hockey became second in his life, to cars, to girls," Clarke said. "The first year he came in here, he looked like he was going to be a star in this league. But he's got to get his priorities straight.

"I like Zubie, but I went down and looked at the weight chart and he's 227 pounds. That's more than 10 pounds heavier than he was last year. He said it was his mom's cooking. I said, 'Push yourself away from the table.' He just kind of got lazy, I think.

But I also think that if he goes up (to Montreal), he'll get lots of ice time and he'll do good because he's got the ability."

So what did Zubrus do on his first shift on a line with Saku Koivu and Brian Savage? He scored his first goal in 23 games. He's now in his 13th NHL season.

A VERY LONG NIGHT IN NASHVILLE

The Flyers have had their share of gruesome injuries over the years.

Barry Ashbee was struck in the eye with a deflected puck and was forced to retire.

Ron Sutter spent weeks slurping strained vegetables through a wired-shut jaw, just so he could have the stamina to continue to play.

A stray skate blade dug a crooked path from Mikael Renberg's chin to the bridge of his nose.

Luke Richardson once had his orbital punched out of its socket, then had it sewn back in so he could finish the season.

"They didn't put it in real straight," he joked, "but you can hardly notice, can you?"

Jeremy Roenick's jaw was shattered so badly when he was struck by a puck that the bones needed to be threaded back together.

On April 1, 1999 Eric Lindros suffered an injury that could have been fatal, yet no one, not even Lindros, is certain how it happened.

During the third period of a 2-1 win in Nashville, Lindros was the recipient of a seemingly harmless check to the midsection by Predators defenseman Bob Boughner.

A few shifts later Lindros came back to the Flyers bench and told athletic trainer John Worley that his right ribcage "hurt really bad." Lindros played the remainder of the game and had the ribs iced for 20 minutes after the game.

After talking to reporters, Lindros met a few teammates at a restaurant around the corner from Nashville Arena.

"I didn't think much of the hit," he recalled. "It wasn't a big deal. I've bruised my ribs periodically, and that's what I thought it was. After the game I iced it down and got some stimulation. I felt pretty good. I went out and had a cheeseburger and beer with the rest of the guys. I wasn't feeling too good at the restaurant and I told the guys I was heading back to my room.

"That's when things started to turn. I couldn't fall asleep, I had trouble getting comfortable. I thought maybe it was a little shortness of breath from the ribs. So I got up and I laid in a bathtub."

At around 12:30 a.m., Lindros' roommate, Keith Jones, arrived back at the room and found Lindros in the bathtub filled with water, trying to relieve the pain in his chest.

"It wasn't that unusual because Eric got so banged up in the games he would sometimes take baths when we got back to the hotel," Jones recalled.

When Lindros tossed and turned all night without sleeping Jones said he realized something was not right.

"I knew something was strange because Eric is such a tough guy," Jones said. "He likes to suck it up and not say anything, that's his personality. He's the type where he doesn't want to bother people if it's just a rib."

By 7 a.m., Jones was concerned enough to phone Worley in his hotel room. Worley had spent most of the night in Baptist Hospital with Mark Recchi, who was admitted after vomiting and experiencing post-concussion symptoms.

When Worley arrived, Lindros was holding his right side and was unable to take deep breaths.

"It was clear things had gotten worse than we expected," Jones said. "He was starting to look pale and he was definitely in a lot of pain."

Worley immediately called Baptist Hospital and asked paramedics to come to the hotel. He then phoned Bob Clarke, who was in Philadelphia, to inform him of Lindros' condition.

"They called me and said Lindros had this problem and they were going to take him to the hospital," Clarke recalled. "I didn't know how serious it was. I said, 'Do the doctors want to fly him back to Philly so our own doctors could look at him?'"

Worley said it would be better for Lindros to be seen immediately and within minutes of his conversation with Clarke a team of paramedics were carting Lindros out of the hotel on a stretcher in a semi-reclining position.

Even Eric Lindros would admit the biggest assist of Keith Jones' career came in a Nashville hotel room on April 1, 1999.

"Thank God for Jonesy," Lindros said. "He got on the horn and called our training staff. I probably wouldn't have made it to the hospital in the time that I did if not for him."

Lindros, who stood 6-foot-4, 236 pounds at the time, was carted to an X-ray room, where it was discovered that a micro tear in his right lung had caused the lung to collapse. As a result Lindros' chest cavity filled with about three quarts of blood during the night.

An average chest cavity is capable of holding 3 to 5 quarts of blood, so instead of taking him to an operating room, Predators team internist Richard Garman cracked open Lindros' chest and inserted a vacuum tube to siphon out the three quarts of bloody fluid.

"When they stuck that tube in me, we hit a geyser," Lindros said. "The doctor tried to hold it in with his thumb. It was flying everywhere. We overflowed the reservoir."

It was then that Lindros realized what had caused him all that pain.

"I was thinking, 'This is not bruised ribs.'"

By that evening, Lindros was in stable condition in the intensive care unit, his diet limited to Popsicles and Mountain Dew.

The tube drained Lindros' chest cavity of about four additional pints of blood. Under normal circumstances, it takes a patient a month to replenish one pint of blood. Lindros was given medication to increase his blood count at a faster rate and was close to normal within three days.

The chest tube also was used to re-inflate his right lung and it was recommended by Garman that Lindros not play hockey again until the following season. Before being released from the hospital seven days after being admitted Lindros held out hope he'd return to the lineup sometime during the playoffs.

"I am not going to sit here and rule anything out right now," he said. "Worst case scenario is that I don't come back until September. But I think because of the jump-start we had here, and the good care that I've had, I might be on my way to something a lot sooner than that."

Lindros was overwhelmed by the support he received from Flyers fans all across North America, but mostly by the people of Nashville.

"You should see my room, it's wall to wall flowers," he said.

"I think when something like this happens, you stop. Things just slow down. You don't worry about the next game. You don't worry about the first round (of the playoffs). You worry about what's going to happen in the next hour."

Upon returning home, Lindros was admitted into the Hospital of the University of Pennsylvania Hospital, where he was released on April 10.

NO E AND NO O

Before suffering his collapsed lung Lindros had put together an injury-free 40-goal, 93-point season. But without him the Flyers scored only 13 goals in their final seven regular-season games.

It was a harbinger of things to come.

With Lindros increasing the length and intensity of his daily skating, the Flyers split the first four games of their first-round series against the Toronto Maple Leafs despite managing just seven goals.

Following their Game 4 victory to knot the series, Lindros predicted he'd be strong enough to play in the second round.

"No disrespect to the Maple Leafs, but I have to admit I'm looking ahead to the second round," said Lindros, who declined an invitation by Neilson to stand behind the bench in the first round.

"I might be the only guy in the room who is, but what do you expect? We better win this round. I haven't done all this work for nothing. I didn't set a date at first because I didn't want to disappoint myself. But now I know I can play in the second round. I know I'll be ready then."

WHERE'S HE FROM, ANYWAY?

While the Flyers' offense sputtered against Maple Leafs goaltender Curtis Joseph, it was a bad angle goal allowed by John Vanbiesbrouck in Game 5 that gave the Leafs a 2-1 win in overtime and sent the series back to Philadelphia for the deciding Game 6.

A tense scoreless tie was placed in jeopardy when John LeClair was whistled for elbowing Mikael Andersson with just under three minutes remaining in regulation. Replays showed LeClair got his elbow up, but it was a debatable violation considering referee Terry Gregson had allowed Rod Brind'Amour to get tripped by Kris King without raising his arm.

When Sergei Berezin scored on the ensuing power play with 59 seconds remaining to give the Leafs the win and the series, the normally placid Neilson was rattled and Ed Snider was livid.

"Mr. Snider came right into the locker room and said to me, 'Say whatever you want,'" recalled Keith Jones. "So I really laid into Gregson. I don't remember what I said, but for the next two years I had no friends among the officials."

Jones was fined $10,000 for his comments, but he was kind compared to Snider.

"When the official decides a game, it's a disgrace," Snider screamed outside the Flyers locker room. "Everybody in the stands knows what that guy did.

"I understand I'm going to get fined, and I don't care how much I get fined. The truth is there. Everybody in the city knows it. It's a disgrace to the game. If Gregson can sleep tonight, God bless him.

"Where's he from, anyway?"

A frantic search for Gregson's birthplace found he was from Erin, Ontario, about 50 miles outside Toronto.

A HANDSHAKE AND A THREAT

Keith Jones spent most of the 1999 playoff series trying to frustrate Mats Sundin and Steve Thomas. He must have done a good job because when the players lined up to shake hands, Thomas said to him, "I swear on my kids' heads I will kill you the next time we play next season."

Jones underwent offseason knee surgery that summer and his first game back happened to be against the Leafs.

"Craig Berube called me all day telling me I was going to get killed," Jones recalled.

On the first shift of the game, Jones speared Thomas in the gut. The two dropped their gloves and Jones recorded one of his few victories as an NHL fighter.

"I looked at the Toronto bench and yelled, 'Who's next?'" Jones said. "Tie Domi's head almost popped off."

HEXY FORCED INTO RETIREMENT

Ron Hextall played in just 23 games in the 1998-99 season but was hoping to play another season or two as Brian Boucher's mentor before retiring as a Flyer.

Only July 1, 1999, while Hextall was on a fishing trip in British Columbia, he received a phone call from his agent, Steve Mountain, informing him the Flyers had placed him on waivers.

"I didn't want to retire," Hetxall says today. "I wanted to play the rest of my life. I know my skills were slipping

Ron Hextall considered a two-year offer from Calgary before deciding to retire as a Flyer in 1999.

and my body had just about had it but I didn't want to make that decision."

Hextall pondered a two-year contract offer from the Calgary Flames for three weeks, but when he dragged his feet the Flames signed veteran Grant Fuhr and Hextall's decision was made for him.

"Even now I wonder why I waited so long when it was so obvious," Hextall said.

There were no tears and very few regrets from Hextall, who at 35 retired as the winningest goalie in Flyers history.

"It's been a fun ride, it's been a long ride," Hextall said at the time. "When I set out on my pro career, I set out to play 15 years and that's exactly what I did. Though it's not very thrilling to announce it, to announce it as a Flyer is the best way I could do it."

GENE HART PASSES

When Gene Hart passed away on July 14, 1999 at the age of 68, less than two years after being inducted in the Hockey Hall of Fame, he left behind stories that would be retold for generations.

And not all of them involved hockey.

Long before Hart was hired as the Flyers' public address announcer in 1967, he was entrenched in the entertainment business. His mother, Fritzie, was a Viennese opera singer and his father, Charles, was a Hungarian acrobat.

In the summer, Hart's father ran the water show on the Steel Pier in Atlantic City and his mother was billed as "Miss Fritzie," the lady who climbed atop the famous high-diving horse at the conclusion of the show. Later, Hart's wife, Sarah, was billed as "Miss Sarah" and also rode stop the diving horse.

Hart's pre-hockey resume included stints as a gun boy for a lion tamer; a Hawaiian high diver; a member of the Russian linguistic unit of the U.S. Army Intelligence; bill collector and re-possessor of motor vehicles; foreign sports car salesman; operator of an FM music radio station; teen talk show host; teaching principal in a three-room school; president and chief negotiator for a teacher's union; teacher at a state prison; and teacher for high school students with learning disabilities.

But if you ask Bobby Taylor, Hart might have been most proud of his exploits as a baseball player.

"He told me he hit the longest home run ever hit out of Pleasantville Park," Taylor said of the New Jersey town in which Hart grew up. "He took me there once and showed me where it landed."

Taylor said Hart often joked that he had to hit the ball out of the park because he was never nimble enough to get around the bases.

Hart's weight — he was over 250 pounds while the Flyers were in their heyday in the 1970s — was often the subject of good-natured humor.

In 1969 the Flyers were forced to spend a night on their team bus because of a blizzard. By noon the following day, players were so giddy they began a pillow fight.

Feathers were flying and Bernie Parent decided to open a window to let the feathers out. Instead, the cold air made the feathers sticky and most of them landed on Hart, who was in a deep sleep. He awoke with a sneezing fit, hundreds of feathers stuck to him and an entire bus shaking with laughter.

"He used to wear those loud Hawaiian shirts and I always told him it was to hide all his mustard stains," Taylor said. "He'd say, "Chief, you drink so much that when you die, your ashes are going to burn for three months."

Hart said he considered himself fortunate to tell the tales of a team that was so fun to be around.

"It was like describing a three-ring circus with all the hoopla that surrounded those teams," he said after learning of his induction into the Hall of Fame. "My temperament fit the team. I'm a little wacky and the team was a little wacky."

TERTYSHNY DIES TRAGICALLY

Just nine days after the passing of Hart, Flyers 22-year-old defenseman Dmitri Tertyshny went from enjoying an early evening boat ride with his teammates to dying in one of their arms.

Defenseman Dmitri Tertyshny was just 22 when a leisurely boat ride with teammates turned tragic.

A promising rookie who played in 62 games for the Flyers he previous season, Tertyshny had just completed a two-week power skating clinic in Kelowna, British Columbia when he and two players from the AHL Phantoms — Francis Belanger and Mihail Chernov — decided to rent a 17-foot runabout with a 90 horsepower outboard motor.

The three players, along with a female passenger they had met on the beach, were not wearing life preservers when their boat hit a wave on Okanagan Lake. Tertyshny, who was kneeling near the front of the boat, fell overboard and the boat ran over him. The propeller severed his neck and arm several times.

Tertyshny managed to swim toward the boat and was helped onboard by Chernov. He died of massive blood loss within minutes and was pronounced dead in Chernov's arms at 7:35 p.m., just five minutes after the accident occurred.

"He was a nice, quiet kid who worked hard all the time and always had a grin on his face," Bob Clarke said. "He had lots of potential because he had a lot of skill and brains."

Eric Lindros, who was playing in John LeClair's golf tournament in St. Albans, Vermont, said he was "just shocked" by the news.

"He was a real gamer," Lindros said. "He was kind of quiet, with a great sense of humor. His wife is just wonderful. He'll certainly be missed."

Tertyshny's wife, Polina, was four months pregnant with the couple's first child and was in their native Chelyabinsk, Russia at the time of the accident. Polina had told her husband earlier that day that an ultrasound revealed she was pregnant with a boy.

Six weeks later the Flyers conducted a private service for Tertyshny before boarding a flight to Peterborough, Ontario for training camp.

Clarke and Lindros offered eulogies in honor of Tertyshny, whose enlarged photograph rested on an easel in the front of the room.

"We all know Dmitri was a good friend, a great husband and he would have been a great father to his son," Lindros said. "We need to remember him that way."

"When you lose one of your teammates, it's a pretty high level of grief," recalled Ron Hextall. "He was such a great kid."

Clarke recalled the sudden deaths of former Flyers Barry Ashbee, Pelle Lindbergh and Yanick Dupre and shared his experience of losing Ashbee, who died of leukemia in 1977.

"A lot of us wondered how important hockey could be compared to a man dying of leukemia," Clarke recalled. "After Barry died, a friend said to me, 'Are you guys dumb? Playing hockey should be twice as important. Barry is dead. He can't play hockey anymore. But the rest of you guys can. You can mow your lawns and play with your kids. You should want to do all of those things more now than ever.' It was one of the greatest life lessons I ever learned."

Eric Desjardins recalled a story from the previous training camp when Tertyshny, who understood very little English, arrived at a team meeting and was told the players were going on a six-mile run.

"He didn't know and he was sneakers with no socks," Desjardins said. "When we were finished, the poor guy took off his sneakers and he was bleeding everywhere. His big toe was all cut up and swollen. But he never complained. He always walked around with a big smile on his face."

IRON MAN DERAILED

The 1999 training camp was not a very kind one to the Flyers. It started with Rod Brind'Amour breaking his foot in a Sept. 25 exhibition game and having his iron man streak halted at 484 games.

Four days later Keith Jones underwent surgery on his left knee. Brind'Amour missed the first 34 games of the season and Jones missed the first 25.

And when the Flyers opened the regular season with the worst start in their history (0-6-1) Lindros sent a warning flair when he was asked if it was time for him to visit Bob Clarke's second-floor office and request a vote of confidence for his coach.

"I don't go up there," Lindros told a group of reporters. "I talk to you guys."

LINDROS FOR PRIMEAU?

The Flyers started off the 1999-2000 season with heavy hearts and it took them seven games before they recorded their first win.

Once they started winning they hardly stopped and were in the midst of a five-game win streak in mid-December when reports surfaced that the Flyers were considering a trade that would send Eric Lindros to the Carolina Hurricanes for holdout center Keith Primeau.

"Sounds like they're just trying to drive up the price for him," Clarke said of the Hurricanes.

Lindros thought there might be something to the rumors and wanted some assurances he was not being shopped around.

So on Nov. 27, Clarke and Neilson meet with Lindros in an Ottawa hotel room to tell him he would not be traded to Carolina or any other team during season.

"We met with Eric to tell him there's nothing to all this, he's not being traded," Clarke said. "Then we met with the team to tell them the same thing."

NEILSON IS DIAGNOSED

The Flyers had turned around a poor start and owned a 17-8-4-1 record when Roger Neilson floored them with another dose of sobering news.

Neilson, who for weeks was battling what he thought was a sinus infection, had been diagnosed with multiple myeloma, a cancer of the bone marrow. He was told he could continue coaching while undergoing chemotherapy treatments for the next three months, but would need a bone marrow transplant that would require a three-week hospital stay.

Neilson was 65 at the time and learned of his illness following a 4-2 win over the Toronto Maple Leafs. The next day he had an interesting way of breaking the news to his players.

When Neilson arrived at the Coliseum for practice he met with Rob Cookson, the team's video coach, and spliced together a humorous video that included a scene from Monty Python's Holy Grail movie immediately followed by clips of Flyers defenseman Chris Therien losing both his gloves and his stick during a harried scramble in the win the night before.

"We're watching a video of Chris Therien losing his gloves and stuff and everybody's laughing," Flyers left wing Craig Berube said. "And then all of a sudden, Roger gets up and tells us he has cancer. It was like, wow! But it didn't seem like it affected Roger. He's as tough as they come mentally and physically. If anybody can handle this, Roger can."

Lindros, who was closer to Neilson than any coach he had in the NHL, was floored as much by Neilson's delivery as the news itself.

"This is the amazing part of it," Lindros said. "He walks in the room and talks about his cancer. Everybody was taken aback by it and then he says, `Nothing's going to change. (Assistant coach) Craig Ramsay's going to take over. Cash (Wayne Cashman) is going to be here. I've got to go to the doctor. Go out and have a great practice and get ready for tomorrow."

True to his word, Neilson marched ahead and was behind the bench the following night in his hometown of Toronto, where he acknowledged a warm ovation with a wave of his hand.

"I just don't want people feeling sorry for me," he said. "This happens. I'm trying not to worry about it. I have strong religious beliefs and my faith will help get me through this. I believe God has a plan for my life. If the plan is for me to beat it, I'll give it everything I've got to beat it.

"And if His plan is not to beat it, at least there are games up in heaven where we don't have to put up with Kris King and Tie Domi."

Just like they had a few months earlier when they learned of Tertyshny's death, the Flyers pulled together as best they could. Bob Clarke tried easing the players' minds by saying he would refrain from making any trades during the three months Neilson was to undergo chemotherapy.

"I think if we stick together as a team, we can all get through this," Clarke said.

"Roger's part of our family," Mark Recchi said. "It was very difficult for Roger to put a positive spin on this. That's the way he is. We've got to do our part and win hockey games for him. We'll back him like he's backed us. If we can help him get better by playing well, that's what we'll do."

ROGER THE GIVER

About a week before Christmas Roger Neilson's cramped office inside the Coliseum was cluttered with stacks upon stacks of Christmas cards. Piled high on chairs, on his desk, on the floor, even against his VCR, they sat there waiting to be sealed.

"Probably a thousand or more," he estimated.

Neilson personally signed every one, most of them addressed to former players, coaches, managers and employees. None of them were addressed to family because after his sister died he was left with no living relatives.

Never married, Neilson had no children, no in-laws, no nieces or nephews. His friends were his family and Neilson had thousands. Like the guy who delivered him food every day from his favorite restaurant, Vito's.

During one of his daily interview sessions with members of the media, Neilson was interrupted by a knock on the door. A gentleman from the restaurant handed Neilson his bagged lunch. In return, Neilson handed the gentleman a pair of tickets to the Flyers' next home game.

"I never have to pay for food," Neilson said with a whimsical smile. "I just give him my tickets."

The barter system is kind of nice, an observer remarked to Neilson.

"Yeah, nice for him. I just gave him tickets worth $150."

DOMI THE CHICKEN

Midway through the 1999-2000 season Flyers enforcer Sandy McCarthy and Maple Leafs tough guy Tie Domi got into a war of words that far exceeded anything that happened on the ice.

When McCarthy challenged Domi to a fight during a game in Philadelphia, Domi skated away laughing. McCarthy replied by flapping his wings like a chicken and the crowd cheered with approval as the "Chicken Dance" played in the background.

Domi put up his fight in the Toronto newspapers the next morning by saying, "(McCarthy) can't speak. The only words he knows are 'fight' and 'chicken.'"

Flyers enforcer Sandy McCarthy and Tie Domi battled more in the media than they did on the ice.

McCarthy failed to come up with a return jibe, so Flyers color commentator Steve Coates rushed to his defense. Dressed as "Santa Coates" for a pre-holiday TV skit, Coates placed McCarthy on his lap and quipped: "Did you hear about the Tie Domi doll? You wind him up and he skates away."

FLYERS ADD A LEGACY

On Jan. 3, at about 8 p.m., the Flyers were warmed by the most joyous news of the season. Polina Tertyshny, the widow of Flyers defenseman Dmitri Tertyshny, gave birth to a healthy baby boy. Alexandre Valeri weighed 7 pounds and measured 21 inches.

Alexandre's face and long, skinny fingers served as lasting reminders of his father, who was killed in a boating accident in western Canada five months earlier.

Less than two months after Alexandre's birth, a touching moment took place at the Coliseum when Polina Tertyshny presented her 7-week-old son to Roger Neilson, whose face lit up with a smile.

BRIND'AMOUR TRADE 'BELOW THE BELT'

On Jan. 23, 2000, halfway into his promise that he would not trade anyone during Neilson's three months of chemotherapy treatments , Bob Clarke pulled the trigger on his biggest and most controversial trade of the season, sending Rod Brind'Amour, goaltending prospect Jean-Marc Pelletier and a second-round pick to the Hurricanes for Keith Primeau and a fifth-round pick.

"I talked to the players and they agreed that if we could improve the team, we should make a trade," Clarke said.

News of the trade made Brind'Amour sick to his stomach.

"It was one of the worst days of my life," Brind'Amour recalls. "It worked out great for me, but I honestly hoped I could have been a lifetime Flyer. I have tons of respect for someone like Bill Barber, who spent his whole career in Philadelphia, and that's what I wanted.

"And to be traded for another centerman who I thought I was better than really pissed me off. It's not like they traded me for a goalie or a defenseman. They traded me for another centerman. It was a kick below the belt.

"At that time, of the 20 guys on that team, I was the one that bled orange and black and it left a bad taste in my mouth."

Actually, the Brind'Amour for Primeau trade came more than two months after it was first discussed. Carolina Hurricanes general manager Jim Rutherford agreed to a deal with Clarke back on Nov. 11, but had it nullified by Hurricanes owner

Peter Karmanos, who wanted the right to approve the salary the Flyers were willing to pay Primeau — nearly $23 million over five years.

Rutherford went back to the bargaining table and began shopping Primeau to other teams. He struck a deal with the Coyotes for Keith Tkachuk, but Karmanos vetoed it. He came close to making a deal with the Rangers for Petr Nedved and Manny Malhotra, but the deal fell through.

So Rutherford went back to the Flyers and their offer of Brind'Amour and a deal was struck.

The man who had played in more games for the Flyers than anyone in the past decade — Brind'Amour had suited up 633 times, including 484 in a row — was gone.

At 28, Primeau was 15 months younger than Brind'Amour. At 6-foot-5, 220 pounds, he was four inches taller and 20 pounds heavier.

In the previous four seasons, Primeau had averaged 27 goals, 30 assists and 128 penalty minutes. Brind'Amour had averaged 28 goals, 45 assists and 63 penalty minutes. So why make the deal?

"We felt with the competition in our division, we needed a little more size up front," Clarke said. "In Primeau and Lindros, it gives us two big centermen, which is real important against teams in our division. As much as we like Rod — and Rod was a real warrior for our team — we think this will help us in our division."

Today Brind'Amour spends little time wondering what it would be like playing in Philadelphia. But he admits that even after winning a Stanley Cup in Carolina, he is most remembered for being a Flyer.

"Everywhere I go, those are the people who stop me," he said. "I loved Philadelphia and I loved being a Flyer. I don't know if there is a better sports town in the country."

NEILSON KEEPS BRAVE FACE

By early February 2000 chemotherapy treatments had begun to take their toll on Neilson, who was losing weight and his hair.

"They give you pills for everything else, but not for (hair loss)," he said. "The other night before a game I was taking a shower and got a handful of hair. I said to Cash (Wayne Cashman), 'Holy Geez, I got a handful of hair.' He said, 'It's been happening to Rammer (Craig Ramsay) and me since we were 17.' So I didn't get any sympathy there."

Neilson often joked about his cancer and his gallows humor was no more evident than when he was asked if his condition might work to his advantage when discussing a contract extension beyond the 1999-2000 season.

Roger Neilson's battle with cancer ultimately cost him his last head coaching job in the NHL.

"Cancer," Neilson said wistfully, "has its perks."

Meanwhile, the Flyers' coach was getting well wishes from across North America. Hand-made cards were all over his room and letters were strewn across his desk.

"I think my religious faith helps me," Neilson said. "I have no doubts that this is God's plan for my life and that's the way it is. If He wants to see me through it, He will.

"There are certainly enough people praying for me. Every day I get a hundred letters from people. It's just been great. I got a trophy from a Catholic girls school (Villa Joseph Marie in Holland, Pennsylvania). They won it and they read I didn't have a family, so they called me their second dad, all 25 of them. They signed it, Daughter Number One, Daughter Number Two, all the way down. It was pretty nice of them to give me their trophy."

On Feb. 19, Neilson coached his final game behind the Flyers bench, a 4-2 home win over the Washington Capitals, before being replaced by Ramsay. As Neilson prepared himself for a bone marrow transplant scheduled for March 10, Eric Lindros braced himself for life without his favorite NHL coach.

"Roger means a lot to me," Lindros said. "Roger means coming to the rink and knowing there is someone there who is honest with you. In a hockey sense, he kicks you in the butt when you need it and pats you on the back when you're doing well. He's never too high, never too low and he keeps things humorous. As a person, he's someone you trust, someone who's always there for support, someone you can always confide in and talk to about anything in life."

LINDROS CONCUSSED?

Eric Lindros thought it was a hit like many others he took during his career. An elbow to the jaw, compliments of Bruins defenseman Hal Gill, left him a little dazed and forced him to miss a shift.

But between the second and third periods of that March 4, 2000 game in Boston, Lindros vomited and his vision had a yellow tint. One night later, before a home game against the Islanders, Lindros was sitting on a trainer's table at the First Union Center with team physician Dr. Gary Dorshimer.

Dorshimer, who treated Lindros for a Grade 2 concussion less than two months earlier, was aware of Gill's hit on Lindros, but unaware of the vision changes and vomiting. He asked Lindros if he had had his "bell rung" the day before.

"No, I'm fine," Lindros replied.

For the next eight days, Lindros continued to practice and play despite splitting headaches. He gave himself seven to nine Advils a day.

Three weeks later, after being treated for migraine headaches and a Grade 1 concussion, Lindros was told by Chicago neurosurgeon James Kelly that he had suffered a Grade 2 concussion and would miss the remainder of the regular season.

Kelly's diagnosis seemed alarming, especially since Lindros was given "clean bill of health" on March 17 by Philadelphia headache specialist Dr. Stephen Silberstein.

"The concern we have," Kelly said, "is that he did have a concussion on March 4 and it worsened with the medication he took. There are ongoing neurological problems that prohibit him from returning."

Kelly's findings put the Flyers' medical staff on the defensive and Dr. Jeff Hartzell admitted there had been poor communication between the Flyers and Lindros.

"All of us would like to do things different if we had a second chance," Hartzell said. "I like to think I know Eric. I guess I don't know him as well as I thought I did."

Clarke sowed little sympathy for his captain. When asked if he knew the difference between having a headache and a concussion, Clarke quipped, "I don't know. I've never had a headache in my life."

LINDROS LASHES OUT

Two days after he was told he'd miss the remainder of the regular season with his fourth concussion in two years, Lindros lashed out at the team's handling of his health.

Speaking to reporters at the Coliseum in Voorhees, Lindros said he continued to play four games with a Grade 2 concussion, even hiding the injury from his father, Carl, because he felt the team needed him. He also said concussion guidelines that should have been applied to him were overlooked.

But perhaps the most revealing nugget of Lindros' soul-bearing was his admission of a deep-rooted disdain for Clarke, one which he has guarded for years, and Clarke's lack of respect for his father.

"The last time I had a concussion (Jan. 13), I didn't talk to Clarke for three weeks. What he said off the record was that my agent (Carl Lindros) was a fool and was disruptive toward the team's return-to-play guidelines."

If anyone knew the guidelines for returning from a concussion it was Lindros. In fact, they were listed in his children's autobiography entitled Pursue Your Goals. In that book, Lindros devoted several pages to concussions and lists the criteria for a player returning from a second concussion. Simply stated, players are advised to rest at least a month, followed by at least a week without symptoms before returning to action.

The feud between the Flyers and Eric Lindros intensified when he accused the club of mishandling his concussions.

"I've been through (concussions) before and I knew things weren't real good," he said. "I tried to explain through my symptoms that things were not real good, but I was not going to pull myself out of games."

Lindros said he intentionally hid his symptoms from his father because "I knew if I told my dad what went on, I wouldn't be playing and that's not a situation I wanted to have. I wanted the team to pull me, because you know what happens around here when my dad gets involved. It becomes a headache."

Lindros was not trying to be funny, especially when he blamed Worley, Dorshimer and Hartzell for not giving him a neurological test when they were aware of his symptoms.

"John Worley knew I saw everything go to a yellow tinge and that I came in after the (second) period (in Boston), that I vomited and I was having ice packs on my head and that I had a headache," Lindros said. "I have to admit I wasn't too assertive in telling him — I shouldn't say too assertive, but I wasn't pounding down the notion that I was experiencing real bad headaches because I wanted to keep playing."

Lindros said the Flyers medical staff should have recognized his symptoms and shut him down. Instead, they sent him to team dentist Guy Lanzi, who told Lindros he might be suffering from temporomandibularjoint dysfunction (TMJ), a condition often caused by excessive grinding of teeth.

Lindros said if he had been accurately diagnosed by the Flyers' staff back in early March he might have avoided a lengthy stay on the injured list.

"I'm really unhappy about the way things have been handled," he said. "Quite honestly, this last week has just been hell."

By the end of the 1999–2000 season it was clear Lindros and Clarke were heading in different directions.

The next day, Dr. Kelly furnished Carl Lindros with a letter stating the Flyers' medical staff had been negligent in their handling of Eric Lindros. The Lindros' attorney, Gord Kirke, took it one step further by suggesting Clarke's relationship with Lindros was abusive.

"If a person, even an otherwise strong person with great willpower, is harangued, ridiculed or criticized often enough or long enough by someone in a position of authority," Kirke told the Toronto Globe and Mail, "that person is much more susceptible to doing something he would otherwise know is against his interests, just to avoid further haranguing, or ridicule or criticism."

Flyers chairman Ed Snider was floored by Kirke's assertion that Clarke was bullying Lindros into playing.

"We're taking the high road on this," Snider said. "We're not honoring anything that ridiculous with a comment. Believe me, in due time we'll have our say."

REMOVING THE 'C' FROM ERI_

Three days after Eric Lindros' biting criticisms of the Flyers' training staff and one day after Bob Clarke said he saw no need to replace Lindros as the team's captain, the Flyers named defenseman Eric Desjardins as their permanent captain.

Why the sudden change of heart?

At first, Clarke and interim coach Craig Ramsay agreed the team had been through enough and that another shake-up might be disruptive.

But after hearing of Clarke's decision to keep Lindros as captain, several players went to public relations director Zack Hill and told him they wanted a change.

The next morning, Clarke met with alternate captains John LeClair, Mark Recchi and Eric Desjardins and it was decided that Desjardins would be named captain. It was Clarke who decided the move would be permanent.

"It's fair to say when a guy like Lindros comes out and criticizes the doctors and trainers, he's thinking of himself and not the team," Clarke said. "We're trying to do what's right for the team."

Lindros, who was visiting his brother, Brett, in Toronto, said he had no problem with the Flyers naming Desjardins as interim captain, but was offended they had permanently removed the 'C' from his chest, saying he took his role as captain very seriously.

Lindros also said he maintained a desire to return to the Flyers sometime in the playoffs and Clarke said he would allow it, regardless of his personal feelings.

"That'll be up to him," Clarke said. "I don't care if he likes me or dislikes me. I don't care if I ever talk to him or he ever talks to me again. It's the smallest worry in my life. His responsibility is to his teammates. We'll see how he does, if he comes back."

NEILSON'S COMEBACK FOILED BY CLARKE

About the same time Lindros was verbally cutting his ties with the Flyers, coach Roger Neilson was conducting a valiant fight for his life.

In late March, during a bone marrow transplant, Neilson wondered if he'd live to coach another game. Delirious from the chemotherapy running through his blood, Neilson lay in a hospital bed with his eyes fixed on a sterile black and white wall clock.

"Once that chemo got a hold of me, I couldn't sleep," Neilson said. "I'd just look at the clock and wonder how it could go another hour. Oh boy, it was tough. I wouldn't want to do it again."

Neilson wondered if anyone else who had experienced the same kind of treatments felt the way he did — that surviving cancer almost wasn't worth the pain it took to fight it.

So he phoned the wife of a man who worked at his summer hockey camp. She, too, was a cancer survivor who won her battle with breast cancer. He asked her if she had the same desperate moments he had, moments when the clock stood still.

"She said she would rather let herself die than do it again," he said. "That's how tough it is."

For Neilson, lying in that hospital bed with a white blood cell count of zero was like a visit to hell. It was also a starting point to his recovery, his personal ground zero.

"The chemo knocks the crap out of you," he said from a couch outside Bob Clarke's Coliseum office, his face drawn and his hair wispy thin. "You're lying there and they've got the big chart on the wall and you see your white blood cell count is sitting at nothing.

"The next morning it's up to 20 and you know it's got to get up to 8,000."

But with every day came higher cell counts. In three weeks Neilson had taken several steps forward and with Craig Ramsay in his place, so had the Flyers.

While Neilson was recovering in Bob Clarke's condo in Sarasota, Florida – "I walked three miles a day and it took me about an hour to swim 10 laps," he said — the Flyers were stringing together a season-ending four-game winning streak under his good friend and interim coach.

Neilson watched every game on Clarke's wide-screen television and witnessed the changes Ramsay was making. And there were several.

Keith Jones was moved from the top line to the fourth to make room for Rick Tocchet. Daymond Langkow replaced Peter White as the club's second-line center. Kent Manderville became the checking-line center and Gino Odjick was bumped out of the starting lineup.

Ramsay also recalled rookie defensemen Andy Delmore and Mark Eaton from the AHL's Phantoms and played them in place of veterans Adam Burt and Ulf Samuelsson.

And with one weekend remaining in the regular season, Ramsay announced rookie Brian Boucher had replaced John Vanbiesbrouck as the club's No. 1 goalie.

"It wasn't my intention to change what Roger had done," Ramsay said. "We made some changes with our roster and we wanted to instill a real team concept. That meant a lot of the veterans buying into taking shorter shifts. I think it made us a better, deeper team."

As for Neilson, he desperately wanted to put the past three weeks behind him and get on with his life as head coach of the Flyers.

"Of course I want to coach," he said. "There's nothing else I'd want to do."

Many of his players wanted the same thing.

"Roger was around the team again and I remember how happy everybody was to see him," Keith Jones said. "Rammer did a great job during that run, but we all looked at Roger as our coach and we wanted to play well for him. We wanted to get to the Stanley Cup and win it because of what Roger meant to us."

ABBY WHO?

Two days before the start of the 2000 playoffs, the Flyers' locker room took on the look of a bad soap opera scene.

With Eric Lindros seeing teammates for the first time since dropping his bombshell and Roger Neilson on the ice for the first time in almost two months, players were getting grilled by nosey reporters.

Did Eric Lindros apologize to the team?

Who would you rather have as your coach, Roger Neilson or Craig Ramsay?

"Ever see the movie 'Young Frankenstein?'" asked John Vanbiesbrouck to no one in particular. "Abby Normal? That's what we are, Abby Normal."

CLARKE SAYS NO TO NEILSON

The Flyers rolled over the Buffalo Sabres in five games in the first round of the playoffs and with Neilson feeling as though he could withstand the rigors of coaching, he thought it was the perfect time for him to make a request.

"I'm sitting in my office and Roger comes walking in," Clarke said. "Anybody who has gone through what he went through looks awful. And he says, 'Rammer's going to be the assistant again and we're getting ready for tomorrow's game.' And I knew from the doctor that he couldn't coach.

"I said, 'Rog, you can't coach, you're a sick man. We'll find you something to do to help out.' Of course he got really mad and it turned into a mess."

To this day, Clarke says he made the right decision to retain Ramsay as coach and keep Neilson as an associate coach in the press box.

"There was not even a decision to be made there," Clarke said. "To keep Roger going and fighting, Dr. Brodsky kept saying, 'You can get back to coach this year.' Roger's girlfriend (Nancy Nicholls) kept saying, 'You can't say that to Roger, because Roger is going to want to coach and he's not going to be healthy enough.

"We were criticized for the way we handled Roger. But I gave him two coaching jobs (with the Panthers and Flyers). We used Snider's private plane to fly a nurse around with him so he could get his chemo. He stayed at my place in Florida. We were the ones who looked after him and took care of him."

ROGER ANSWERS BACK

As the 65-year-old son of a Christian minister, Roger Neilson was never very good at telling half-truths. So when Neilson was asked on a Toronto talk-radio station whether his relationship with Eric Lindros played a role in the team's decision to relieve him of his head coaching duties, Neilson told it like it was.

"I don't think they want a cancer patient who is a friend of Eric Lindros behind the bench right now," Neilson said from his Coliseum coach's office.

A few hours later, Neilson stood by his comments, saying "I believe that situation (with Lindros) certainly has come up and it could be tied in some way."

Clarke reiterated that Neilson's relationship with Lindros had nothing to do with his decision.

"We're just waiting for (Lindros) to get healthy and play."

But there was more to Neilson's anger than Clarke's decision to replace him. In a meeting the day before Neilson and his agent, Rob Campbell, contended that the framework for a two-year contract extension for Neilson was in place with the Flyers in February and that Clarke agreed they would speak again when Neilson was released from the hospital.

When Neilson asked for some clarification of that agreement, Clarke told him to wait until after the playoffs.

"We didn't get any encouragement on a contract extension," Neilson said.

Clarke stood by his stance.

"Whatever Roger's got to say, I'm sure he's going to tell you," he said. "But I think it's not the right time. We'll wait until the playoffs are over and see what he thinks and we'll tell you what we think."

FRANCIS LESSARD LEAVES HIS MARK

Francis Lessard never played a regular season game for the Flyers, but the 6-foot-3, 224-pound defenseman certainly left his mark on the franchise.

On the morning of May 4, 2000, Eric Lindros woke up headache-free for the 12th straight day and decided to take part in a 4-on-4 game of shinny with several members of the Phantoms. Afterward he planned on catching a flight to Chicago for a checkup with neurologist James Kelly.

Lessard changed those plans when he bowled over an unsuspecting Lindros.

"I was standing still," Lindros said. "I was only out there seven minutes when it happened."

Lindros suffered a cut above his lip that required 20 stitches to close.

"I'm not worried about my face," he said. "I'm just nervous about the headaches."

About six hours after the collision Lindros was lying on his couch with an ice bag on his head and still experiencing headaches. His trip to see Dr. Kelly, and his hopes of returning for the start of the third round of the playoffs, were postponed.

"It's unbelievable," Lindros said. "I was supposed to get a firm date on when I could come back."

Some members of the Flyers wondered why Lindros put himself at risk before getting clearance from Dr. Kelly.

"He wasn't supposed to have contact," Ed Snider said. "And from what I understand, the contact was accidental. It's a shame he keeps running into all these obstacles."

PIZZAS, POWER BARS AND PEDIALYTE

The Flyers' wait for Lindros seemed short compared to the longest game in franchise history.

Game 5 of their Eastern Conference Semifinals against the Pittsburgh Penguins started at 7:30 p.m. on May 4, 2000 and ended when Keith Primeau deked around Darius Kasparaitis and beat Ron Tugnutt with a high, hard wrist shot at 2:35 a.m. on May 5, 2000.

So just how long was the game?

So long that Penguins fans were asleep in each other's arms at the time Primeau scored.

So long that an 18-year-old kid from suburban Pittsburgh named R.J. Umberger was able to move down from the cheap seats to the third row and still keep his eyes open for the full six hours, 56 minutes.

So long that one diehard Flyers fan, Mike McCarthy of Collingdale, Pennsylvania, didn't have a ticket for the game and when he was kicked out of

Keith Primeau put an exclamation point on the longest game in Flyers history.

a bar across the street following last call, he simply walked across to Mellon Arena and witnessed the final two overtimes.

The best way to appreciate the game was to take a walk around the cramped visitors' locker room inside Mellon Arena.

Scattered among the rolled-up balls of black tape and empty Gatorade cups were countless wrappers from power bars and chocolate gel packs. Dozens of empty bottles of Pedialyte were strewn on the floor.

All that remained on a table in the middle of the room were three uneaten snack bars, all of them peanut butter chocolate, and six power gel packs, all of them chocolate flavored.

Flyers center Daymond Langkow stepped through the room as if it was a mine field, wearing only a towel and holding a cold slice of sausage pizza. By now, it was 3:20 a.m. and the feeling of what the Flyers had just accomplished was beginning to sink in to everyone who witnessed it.

"It was actually comical," Primeau said of the scene between each of the eight periods the Flyers endured before his shot ended the third-longest game in NHL history at 152 minutes, 1 second of playing time.

"Guys were looking for pizza and trying to figure which end (of the rink) we were going to next and what period it was and what time it was and who was still up watching."

Right wing Keith Jones was asked if he lost any weight throughout the game.

"You know," Jones said, "By the end of this series I might be in shape."

According to Craig Berube, that would have been pretty tough to pull off since Jones hardly took a shift in overtime.

"When it was his turn for a shift Jonesey came off the bench, put one foot on the ice and came right back and said, 'Boys, I'm done. Rammer, don't put me out there again.'"

"It's true," says Jones, who was the only player who failed to record a shot in the game. "I cramped so bad I couldn't skate."

As the game rolled from one scoreless overtime to the next, players wondered just how long their minds and their legs could function.

"Guys were out there fighting and clawing and scratching and hacking and spitting and slashing," Penguins forward Matthew Barnaby said. "After a while, you went past the point of exhaustion. Then you got a second wind and a sixth wind and a ninth wind."

Players wolfed down pizza, power bars and popcorn and hydrated themselves with water, Gatorade and Pedialyte. A few players, including Simon Gagne, were hooked up to IVs.

The Flyers found enough energy to celebrate their victory in front of a sparse crowd that included Penguins fan R.J. Umberger.

"After a while, guys were saying, what period is this?" said Tugnutt, who stopped 70 of 72 shots. "The sixth, no, it's the eighth. Your mind starts playing tricks on you."

Writers in the press box were getting so punchy that as the game spilled into its seventh period of play, one writer observed, "This game might go on so long, Eric Lindros will come back and play in it."

Jones, the team crack-up, joked that if the Flyers won, he would see to it there would be no practice the following day.

Thanks to rookie goalie Brian Boucher, there wasn't.

"We always kept in mind how important the game was to us," said Boucher, who stopped 57 of 58 shots. "You just keep telling yourself they're as tired, if not more tired, than we are."

When the seven-hour war was finally won on Primeau's perfect wrist shot at 2:35 a.m., the Flyers collected each other and engaged in one sweat-soaked embrace.

"It definitely was one of those bonding things," John LeClair said. "It was everybody. You can't play two or three lines. You need every single guy out there and everybody did the job."

The five-overtime game is the NHL's longest in modern-day history and ranks as the best game Umberger has ever seen.

"I was at the edge of my seat the whole time," recalls the former Flyer, who attended the game with his father, Richard. "When the Flyers scored it was a big disappointment."

Umberger got home around 4 in the morning that day and skipped school. His dad, a construction worker, went straight to work.

The Flyers? They just wanted a little shut-eye.

"We'll sleep a lot tomorrow," a baggy-eyed Simon Gagne said as he left the Igloo. "Or is it today?"

COOL HAND LUKE

Bob Boughner has laid out a few opponents with big hits over the years, but the Flyers got a measure of revenge in Game 5 of their second-round series when defenseman Luke Richardson knocked him out with a slap shot to his chest.

"I was wrestling with Boughner at center ice and I feel the puck whiz by my ear," Jones said. "It hit him straight in the chest and knocked him out. Luke could try that 100 times and I guarantee you every time the puck would go in the corner."

Penguins coach Herb Brooks wasn't amused.

"I'd go back in his family tree," he said of Richardson. "Maybe he's a direct descendant of the guy that shot Jesse James in the back. You know, the coward that shot Jesse James in the

Luke Richardson was popular in Philadelphia, but not in Pittsburgh, where Herb Brooks likened him to the man who shot Jesse James.

back. It must be in his family tree. There's a code for tough guys in the league. This was way past the code."

ONE WIN AWAY

Buoyed by their marathon win in Game 4, the Flyers swept the Penguins out in six games and Boucher was spectacular against the New Jersey Devils as the Flyers grabbed a three games to one lead in the Eastern Conference Finals.

Boucher's signature save of the playoffs came in Game 3 at the Meadowlands when Patrik Elias sprung free for a shorthanded breakaway. Elias deked right and had Boucher hung out to dry. But just as Elias shot into the empty net, Boucher rolled over on his back and stretched his glove across the crease. The move jarred Boucher's mask off his face just as Elias shot was smothered by his glove.

Elias skated away in disbelief and the Devils, who outshot the Flyers 29-21, never recovered.

"He continues to amaze me," Primeau said of Boucher. "He continues to get better and he keeps getting his confidence up higher and higher."

When the Flyers won again in North Jersey in Game 4, fans began booking flights to Dallas for the Finals. The star-crossed Flyers seemed to be a team of destiny.

"I think a lot of us thought this might be our last chance," Jones said. "Tock, Desjardins, Chief, we all were nearing the end of our careers."

Instead of rubbing out the Devils like a cigarette butt, the Flyers allowed them back in the series with a poorly played 4-1 loss at home in Game 5.

"We just didn't come out in Game 5," Berube said. "Even if we had played good and lost it would have been OK."

Tocchet agreed.

"We played a terrible game in Game 5," he said. "In my opinion that's when we lost the series."

BIG E'S BIG RETURN

The 1999-2000 season presented the Flyers with some heavy decisions, but none seemed heavier than when Eric Lindros walked into Craig Ramsay's office and proclaimed himself ready for duty between Games 5 and 6 of the Eastern Conference Finals.

A pair of concussions had kept Lindros sidelined for the past 73 days. He had criticized the team's medical staff and had been stripped of his captaincy.

"I hate to tell you, but when Eric had that concussion and took off to Canada, he pretty much walked out on the team," Rick Tocchet said. "All of a sudden he shows up for Game 6 of the Conference Finals and says he's ready to play."

Actually, Clarke says that was not Lindros' original plan.

"He was going to make his grand entrance in the seventh game if there was a seventh game," Clarke recalled. "And the players told him, 'If you don't play in the sixth game, we don't want you in the seventh.'

"I remember talking to the coaches saying, 'This is going to be a nightmare. We can't bring him back. Our team is playing good.' Without him everybody had their role. I think what happens when a player like Lindros comes back, the other players have less responsibility."

Torn with the decision that had been placed on his shoulders Ramsay decided to poll his players, which made the decision even more difficult.

"We all got called in and we were asked how we felt about having Eric back," Tocchet said. "Now I don't know a lot about Eric Lindros as a teammate, but I said we better figure this out quick because we just played like our heads were somewhere else (in Game 5).

"I never got to know the guy that well, but I remember saying if he's healthy enough to play, you have to put him in there. But the room was divided. For whatever reason, a lot of guys didn't like Eric."

Ramsay said he was satisfied Lindros was coming back for all the right reasons – "As I suspected, he's very sincere about his desire to come back and be a part of this team," he said – and penciled Lindros into the lineup for Game 6 at the Meadowlands.

"I don't think it came down to us," Berube said. "It came down to the coaches. If he's healthy I think you've got to play him."

Lindros said he was ready to take on the dangers of playing against Scott Stevens, who earlier in Game 2 had given Daymond Langkow a concussion.

"This is what it's all about, to play hockey," Lindros said. "Any time you play the game at this time of year it's exciting. My timing will improve as we go along."

With Clarke cheering him on in the press box, Lindros was one of the best players on the ice in Game 6, scoring the Flyers' only goal in a 2-1 loss that set the stage for a decisive Game 7.

'ANGER IN HIS EYES'

On the night of May 26, 2000 there was enough electricity in the First Union Center to curl Ben Franklin's hair.

With Lindros about to make his long-awaited return to Philadelphia, the building shook with anticipation as the Flyers and Devils readied themselves for battle.

"Just before we went out on the ice, Johnny LeClair said to Eric in the locker room, 'E, careful cutting across the middle. Stevens is looking for the big hit,'" remembers Boucher. "Talk about foreshadowing."

When the Flyers hit the ice, they were greeted with thunderous applause that grew even louder when anthem singer Lauren Hart, who was recovering from non-Hodgkin's lymphoma, belted out a video duet of "God Bless America" with the late Kate Smith.

"The Flyers wanted me to keep singing, even with my hair falling out," recalls Hart, who was in Cherry Hill West High School when she first sang the national anthem at a Flyers game. "I actually think it helped me turn the corner in my recovery."

To this day, Boucher said he has never heard a building as loud at the First Union Center that night.

"The place was just nuts for the first five minutes of the game," he said.

But at the 7:50 mark all of that changed.

When Lindros was taken off the ice early in Game 7, most knew it would be his final time in a Flyers jersey.

Lindros carried the puck through the neutral zone and as he picked up a head of speed and deked past Scott Niedermayer at the blue line, Scott Stevens moved toward him.

"I could see Stevens coming and I could see that anger in his eyes," Keith Jones said. "I yelled, 'Get your head up!'"

It was too late. Stevens lowered his shoulder and drilled Lindros in the face, sending his stick flying and his body crumbling to the ice.

"When he got hit, you could hear a pin drop," Boucher said. "I thought he could be done, like he could be dead. He was hit that hard."

"It was like, 'Wow! Did that just happen?'" Tocchet said. "Nobody knew what to do. We all just sat there staring. I looked on their bench and they were just as quiet as us. The whole building got quiet."

Lindros was helped off the ice, where it was quickly determined he suffered his fourth concussion of the season.

"Bundy and I were on the bench and we couldn't believe it," Berube said, referring to Chris Therien. "But we're hockey players and that stuff happens every game. We just blew it off and kept playing."

The Flyers went on to play a strong game but Patrik Elias scored the game-winner when he lifted the stick of Dan McGillis and deposited a rebound past Boucher for a 2-1 victory.

Stevens said he had trouble playing the remainder of the game but was not remorseful for the hit, which did not draw a penalty.

"Coming into Game 7, I'm thinking there is one player on that team that can win that game," Stevens said, "and it could have been him."

Clarke said Lindros should have been aware of Stevens the moment he stepped on the ice.

"He skated about 20 feet or more with his head down," he said. "If you're not aware that Scott Stevens is on the damn ice … you know he's going to come through the middle and hit you if you've got your head down. I don't even think it was a challenge for Stevens."

Jones said he thought Lindros, who was 27 at the time, had just played the final game of his career.

"I never imagined he'd go on and play another six or seven years," Jones said. "I thought he'd be walking around like the old boxers, wearing trash bags instead of gym shorts."

Jones isn't sure the Flyers would have fared any better if Lindros had not returned, but said his presence certainly changed the dynamics of the team.

"I think we had this mentality of, 'Let's beat all the odds.' And I think him coming back changed the complexion of the team," Jones said. "Now don't get me wrong. He was our best player in Game 6 and it's not his fault we lost the series. But it definitely changed how we thought about ourselves."

To this day, Clarke believes the Flyers would have been in the 2000 Finals if Lindros had not returned.

"We would have beaten the Devils if he didn't come back, I believe," Clarke said. "Even after Stevens hit him in the seventh game our team got better instantly. As soon as he was gone we were a way better team."

So why didn't Clarke simply keep Lindros out of the lineup?

"How do you say no when he's your best player?" Clarke said. "He's a hockey player and he wants to play and he had doctor's clearance. That would have been foolish on my part to stop him. I wouldn't do that to any player."

CHAPTER 10

A BROKEN FAMILY

(2000–2002)

A year-long stalemate between the Flyers and the
Lindros family is followed by the hiring and
mutinous firing of Bill Barber.

CLARKE PAINTS AN UGLY PICTURE

AS A GENERAL MANAGER IT WAS NOT UNCOMMON FOR
Bob Clarke to invite reporters into his office a week or so after the season and speak
candidly about which players were returning the following season, which were
not, and why.

On June 5, 2000, 10 days after the Flyers' crushing Game 7 loss to the Devils,
Clarke took the word "candid" to a whole new level when he described the tangled
relationship between Eric Lindros, his parents and the Flyers.

"Over the years I think there have been way too many controversies," Clarke
said. "Every time something happens, Eric's parents would get involved. (They'd
say) coaches would have to be fired; trainers would have to be fired; players would
have to be traded; this guy can't play with Eric. … He's 27 years old. He can't have
his dad going to every doctor's appointment. He gets hit (in Game 7 of the Eastern
Conference Finals) and his father and his butler are running around the locker
room.

"I saw (defenseman Eric) Desjardins get all his teeth knocked out and I didn't
hear from his mom and dad. They didn't go to the doctor with him. He got his teeth
fixed and played. (Forward John) LeClair got his face torn open for 40 stitches and
we didn't hear from his mom and dad."

Clarke's biggest gripe with Lindros was the controversies that surrounded each
of his injuries. In his eight seasons as a Flyer, Lindros missed 140 games due to
injury or illness. Following his collapsed lung in Nashville in 1999 Clarke said Carl

The split between Eric Lindros and Bob Clarke became painfully public in the summer of 2000.

and Bonnie Lindros accused him of trying to put their son on a plane back to Philadelphia knowing that the air pressure of the flight could put Lindros' life in danger.

"Eric brings all the problems on himself," Clarke said. "It's pretty hard to believe John Worley wouldn't treat Eric properly. Or I'd put him on a plane to try to kill him. This kind of stuff never ends and it's hard on a hockey club. It's disruptive.

"And as hard as it's been on all of us on this team, it's been a lot harder on Eric. You can't tell me a 27-year-old man could have his dad speaking for him, taking him to the doctor, showing up in the locker room after an injury. You do that to a 14-year-old and he's embarrassed."

Clarke admitted in that meeting with reporters that his relationship with Lindros, once considered very strong, had deteriorated to a point where the two had not spoken for months.

"Eric won't talk to me," Clarke said. "For whatever reason, the family decided I was the enemy — myself and John Worley. They've created all these scenarios that aren't true. I like Eric, at least I did at one time. I pity him now. Who wants to be 27 and have their mom and dad around? If he comes back, he can't have his dad calling us."

In that meeting with reporters, Clarke described in detail some of the conversations he had with Carl Lindros.

"We shouldn't trade for this guy (Chris Gratton) because Eric doesn't like his agent (Pat Morris). This guy (Mikael Renberg) shouldn't be playing with Eric because he doesn't pass the puck enough to Eric. Go get somebody to (fight) Mike Peca because Peca's taking runs at Eric. This is his dad talking. This is pro sports. If you were coaching a 14-year-old Little League team and a parent said that, the parent would be considered the biggest ass in the world. We're talking about an NHL team where a guy is making 8 million dollars, and his dad's calling me telling me these things. How sad is that?"

Clarke said he had been so distraught over how to handle Lindros' parents he consulted psychologists experienced in dealing with similar circumstances involving professional tennis players and their meddling parents.

"They tell you that sooner or later the athlete says to his mom and dad, 'Thank you very much. I'm my own man.'" Clarke said. "You can't tell Eric that. Every time he gets hurt, he runs to Toronto to see a massage therapist or an acupuncturist. Come on. We don't have acupuncturists or massage therapists in Philly? Give me a break."

Clarke also was angered by Lindros' assertion that the team would not allow him to travel to Pittsburgh during the second round of the 2000 playoffs.

"He wasn't even coming to the ... games here in Philadelphia, and all of a sudden he decided he's going to Pittsburgh to be with his teammates?" Clarke said. "That's a crock of bullshit. He was going to play golf with (former Penguin) Jay Caufield. We weren't hauling around injured players anyway."

Clarke also explained that it was Lindros — not someone else in the organization — who removed Lindros' nameplate from his locker stall at the Coliseum the day the Flyers packed their bags after Game 7 against the Devils.

"I mean, really, how childish is that?" Clarke asked.

With all of that toothpaste out of the tube it was painfully clear to everyone that Lindros had played his final game as a Flyer. Everyone but Clarke, who left the door open for Lindros' conditional return.

"If he comes back, it's going to be as his own self," Clarke said. "We don't want his mom and dad. We've had enough of them. We want Eric to come back. The majority of players will tell you that he's a good team player until his dad gets involved. (Eric) gets all confused and nobody knows what the hell's going to happen."

Clarke pointed out that with Lindros, Daymond Langkow, Keith Primeau and Kent Manderville down the middle the Flyers would have the best group of centers in the NHL in the 2000-01 season if Lindros decided to come back on Clarke's terms.

"His dad always says how much Eric is the most competitive guy we've got and how much he wants to win a Stanley Cup," Clarke said. "Well, take a look at our lineup with him in it. There's a pretty good chance he could compete for the Stanley Cup for a long time with those four guys down the middle. I don't know why he would want to leave if he wants to win the Cup."

Asked if he spoke with Lindros about the possibility of him returning in 2000-01 Clarke said he hadn't.

"He didn't come to the team medical or the team party," Clarke said.

During his hour-long meeting with reporters Clarke said several times how sorry he felt for Lindros and how he regretted the fact the two could not repair their relationship.

"I really don't think Eric is egotistical," Clarke said. "His parents think he is a king and we're all here to help him be successful. When you put someone up so high, he can't live up to their expectations — no one can. Just be what you are — be a good player. I think that's all Eric wants of himself."

Despite all of the ill will between Clarke and the Lindroses, Clarke gave Lindros a qualifying offer of $8.5 million on July 1, 2000 to retain his rights and open the door for an eventual trade.

"There's a part of us that thinks he should just go somewhere else and it would be better for him to get a fresh start," Clarke said. "The other side is, did we fail this guy so much? If we had this guy, we would have the best center in the league. There are all those benefits.

"I think some ways we haven't done a good job. And in a lot of ways, he hasn't either. It's not always our fault. Eric has created situations. It's a never-ending problem."

When Clarke was asked point-blank if the Flyers were prepared to trade Lindros, he relented.

"I think we'll call around," he said, "and see who's interested."

NEILSON SENT PACKING

Three days after exposing to the world the dysfunctional relationship he had with Lindros and his family, Clarke created yet another controversy when he named Craig Ramsay as the Flyers' permanent head coach and cut the team's ties with Roger Neilson.

"There will be a job for him here if he needs one," Clarke said. "He won't be an assistant coach. There are plenty of jobs in the organization for a hockey man."

Hurt by Clarke's refusal to retain him as head coach, Neilson refused Clarke's offer and later was hired as an assistant coach by the Ottawa Senators.

Today Clarke says Neilson's close bond with Lindros ultimately worked against him.

"When Roger was in New York he went to war with (Mark) Messier and got fired," Clarke said. "He made sure he was close to Eric, but I think that ended up hurting Roger because the other players felt like Eric was in his office all the time. Roger was making sure the star player was on his side.

"I think Roger was a really, really good coach and was really good to the players and we had a chance to be a good team, but all the problems with Lindros just destroyed it."

SHOULD 'E' STAY OR SHOULD 'E' GO?

As promised, the Flyers made Lindros a qualifying offer of $8.5 million in the summer of 2000, but when Lindros rejected the offer, many in the organization were left stunned.

"I was really surprised that he would walk away from that kind of money," Keith Jones said. "But I think it makes it pretty clear how bad things got. This closes the door on the whole situation.

"Any time a cloud hangs over a team, it's good to get it over with. We need to concentrate on getting back to work next season without any distractions."

Defenseman Chris Therien agreed with Jones that it was time for Lindros and Bob Clarke to part ways, but made it clear that Lindros was never despised by players in the locker room.

"By no means did anyone hate a guy like Eric," Therien said. "He's a good guy. He and Clarkie just couldn't see eye to eye. Being a player here and seeing what happened last year made playing difficult. But at the same time, I think it brought us closer and made us tougher as individuals."

"It's nothing we held against Eric," Jones said. "But there was always some controversy hanging around him. I played with Peter Forsberg (in Colorado) and there was never any controversy with him. Same with Mark Recchi. As a player, you want to enjoy going to work every day."

Therien believed Lindros underestimated the bond players have with their athletic trainers and that he could have healed several relationships by apologizing for his criticisms of John Worley.

"As a team, we wanted Eric to apologize," Therien said. "We felt John Worley was a member of the team, too. He's a good person, just like Eric is a good person. The time wasn't right for Eric to say what he said. At that time, I think a lot of us felt no player was bigger than the team. I think that's when the real problems started."

LINDROS ASKS TO BE A LEAF

In late November, with the Flyers scuffling along just above the .500 mark, Eric Lindros set the tone for a season of bickering when he said he would like to play for the Toronto Maple Leafs.

"It's a great organization, a great city and being from here, it just seems to be a good fit," Lindros said after an on-ice workout at York University in Toronto.

Bob Clarke wanted to draw more teams into the bidding and seemed perfectly content to let Lindros sit until the NHL trade deadline in March.

"Eric may want to play in Toronto, but that may not happen," Clarke said. "First of all, Toronto has to say they want him, and they have to give us compensation for him, and they have to be able to sign him.

"If someone comes along — whether it's the Rangers or somebody else — and offers us more than what somebody else has offered, we'll go with the best deal for the club."

Lindros indicated that Clarke told him to put a deal together with the Maple Leafs for his consideration but Clarke denied ever talking to Lindros.

"He's a free agent. I certainly wouldn't let him put a deal together," Clarke said. "I wouldn't let anybody put a deal together for our team. He can talk to any team he wants, but he's not putting a deal together for us."

A BAD HAIR DAY FOR FRASER

Referee Kerry Fraser could fill his own book with the things he has seen and heard on the ice over the past 30 years.

Like the time he officiated a minor-league game featuring former Maple Leafs ruffian Eddie Shack, who was at the end of his career as an NHL enforcer.

Shack took one look at the baby-faced 5-foot-6, 150-pound Fraser and grunted through his handlebar mustache, "Hey kid, did you bring your nurse with you?"

A long-time resident of Voorhees, New Jersey, many of Fraser's stories involve the Flyers.

Like the time in the late 1980s when the normally mild-mannered Tim Kerr had a goal disallowed by Fraser. Before the game, Fraser read in the press notes that Kerr had gone 12 games without a goal. So when he ruled Kerr kicked in his goal, he was prepared for a reaction.

"He went ballistic, just absolutely bonkers," Fraser said. "So much so I would have given him a misconduct. But I had read he was struggling. So I opened my hands and got away from him. I let him vent and we got out of it without a penalty.

"The next shift he apologized. He said, 'I'm sorry I snapped.'"

There have been times — more than he cares to mention — when Fraser has had to do the apologizing. Like on the night of Dec. 6, 2000 in a game between the Flyers and Tampa Bay Lightning.

Flyers center Kent Manderville had gone 99 straight games without a goal when he swooped in on a loose puck and scored into an open net.

Fraser emphatically ruled no goal, saying the goaltender had batted the puck away, constituting it as a change of possession.

"It was questionable, it really was," Fraser said. "The fans are going crazy and Mandy comes over and says, 'Kerry, what did you blow the whistle for?' And right away the light went on and I said, 'Did you score that?' He said, 'Yeah.'

"I told him I was sorry and he said, 'Well, you gotta get me a box of cookies or something.'"

A few weeks later, before working a game between the Flyers and Rangers in New York, Fraser bought a box of gourmet cookies and a bottle of wine, placed them in a Nike shoe box, wrapped it up with hockey tape, and handed it to Manderville.

Kent Manderville set a Flyers record for futility, but got a box of cookies to show for it.

"That's part of the fun of the game," Fraser said. "If we take things too seriously, you lose out on the fun. You have to laugh at yourself sometimes because that's what keeps you sane."

Fraser recalled another game in Edmonton between the Flyers and Oilers early in the 1980s. Bobby Clarke was a hard-nosed but aging center and Wayne Gretzky was establishing himself as the greatest player in the game.

"Gretzky was diving all night and I got stubborn," Fraser said. "He wasn't getting a thing. The fans were booing and he wasn't getting the calls because he tried to fool me early."

Late in the game, after a routine save by the Flyers goaltender, Gretzky flopped to the ice in an attempt to unravel Fraser.

"There was nobody within eight feet of him," Fraser said. "He jumped up in the air, threw his hands and feet out and flopped right on his stomach. We thought there was a sniper in the building. Clarke skated over to him and said, 'Get up you … baby.'"

Fraser skated over to Gretzky and asked what he was trying to prove? Gretzky responded, "It wouldn't matter, you wouldn't call it anyway. You haven't called a thing all night."

Replied Fraser: "You're right, and I'm gonna start right now.' And I went – BING! — unsportsmanlike conduct penalty."

GOODBYE, RAMMER, HELLO BILLY

Any momentum the Flyer built during their incredible playoff run of 2000 vanished quickly the following season.

Keith Jones was forced to retire with chronic knee pain eight games into the season.

"I feel like I'm attending my own funeral," Jones quipped, "only I get to shake hands with the people who walk by."

John LeClair suffered a herniated disc while training in the offseason. And the sharpness and flare Brian Boucher showed the previous spring disappeared.

As a result the Flyers started the 2000-01 season with a 1-5-2 record and when the losing continued they turned to Roman Cechmanek, a 29-year-old veteran who was tearing up the American League with the Phantoms.

Cechmanek won his first four starts and established himself as the Flyers' new No. 1 goalie. But when the Flyers were badly outplayed in a 5-1 loss in Detroit on Dec. 8, leaving them with a 12-12-4 record, Ramsay's short-lived reign as head coach ended.

"We've become an easy team to play against," Bob Clarke said. "And we don't find that acceptable."

Exit Craig Ramsay. Enter Bill Barber.

"We've got to identify ourselves a little better," Barber said after ending his long wait to be Flyers coach. "There's nothing wrong with being aggressive. There's no issue of fighting. We can be more physical by having guys dive in front of pucks, taking hits and going hard in the corners."

CLARKE GOES 'GOOFY'

Already on his fourth coach in three years and with the Lindros drama still unresolved, Clarke began feeling some heat from hockey critics across North America.

He didn't help matters in late December when he tried defending his firing of Roger Neilson in a television interview with TSN's Gord Miller.

"The Neilson situation - Roger got cancer - that wasn't our fault," Clarke said. "We didn't tell him to go get cancer. It's too bad that he did. We feel sorry for him, but then he went goofy on us."

To his credit, Neilson took the high road, saying he wanted to leave his issues with Clarke in the past and acknowledging that he was, indeed, too weak to coach in the 2000 playoffs.

SNIDER QUIETS TRADE TALKS

By mid January, it was clear Lindros and the Flyers had dug in.

Lindros would accept a trade only to the Maple Leafs, who were offering center Nik Antropov, defenseman Danny Markov and a first-round draft pick.

The Flyers wanted defenseman Tomas Kaberle as part of the package, but more than anything they wanted more trade partners.

"We've been talking to them for a month and a half and they've offered us absolutely nothing for Eric," Ed Snider told a Toronto radio station. "Toronto thinks they have us over the barrel since they're the only team we're negotiating with, but they really don't. Who they have over the barrel is actually Eric.

"I'd love to see Eric playing in the National Hockey League. He's one of the great players in the game and he deserves to play, but we're not going to give him away."

Said Clarke: "He made the choice not to play, so he had to wait for us."

LINDROS FOR TKACHUK?

As the 2001 NHL trade deadline drew near, the Lindroses expanded their list of acceptable teams to include St. Louis, Washington and Detroit, but stated Lindros would still prefer to play in Toronto.

That set off a flurry of trade talk, including a potential three-way deal that would send Blues center Ladislav Nagy, center Michal Handzus and either defenseman Barret Jackman or defenseman Mike Van Ryn to the Flyers for Lindros.

The Flyers would then send all three players to the Phoenix Coyotes for Keith Tkachuk.

That deal hinged on two conditions: Lindros passing a physical; and the Blues coming to a contract agreement with Lindros.

On the night before the trade deadline Lindros was in St. Louis undergoing a physical, but the three-way deal fell through when Blues general manager Larry

Pleau realized he could get Tkachuk from Phoenix with the same package he would have surrendered for Lindros.

The Flyers also turned down the Maple Leafs' final offer of Antropov, Dmitri Yushkevich and a first-rounder and Lindros remained in limbo.

"I'm trying to do what's right for this hockey club," Clarke said. "It has nothing to do with wanting to make Lindros sit out. We'd like to trade him. He"s basically made his own bed. He's made it difficult for us to get anything done."

Lindros was disappointed to go an entire season without playing in the NHL and wondered whether Clarke was simply spiting him.

"I don't know if Bob Clarke was going at it with the intent of trading me," Lindros said. "I think that's something that I question."

DOMI VS. CONCRETE CHRIS

With as many as six regulars out of the lineup, including John LeClair with a staph infection resulting from back surgery, the Flyers were in desperate need of some comic relief when the Toronto Maple Leafs came to town on March 29, 2001.

Tie Domi and a 36-year-old concrete worker from Havertown, Pennsylvania provided it.

With 3:36 gone in the third period Domi and Flyers defenseman Luke Richardson squared off to fight and the First Union Center buzzed with anticipation. But when linesman Kevin Collins stepped between the two to defuse the fireworks, Domi was escorted to the penalty box with an unsportsmanlike conduct penalty.

"There had been a problem with Tie before, so they put a taller piece of plexiglass, about two feet taller, behind the penalty box," recalled Flyers public address announcer Lou Nolan said. "But there was no support for it."

After Domi took a seat in the sin bin, a fan in the first row behind the penalty box began taunting him and Domi returned the favor by squirting a water bottle on him and the fans around him. The fan continued taunting and Domi turned around again and squirted water into the crowd.

That's when Chris Falcone, who was seated two rows behind the box, leaped over the glass and hung there – in suspended animation – before the glass broke and he fell into the penalty box.

"I never would have been in the penalty box if the glass didn't break," Falcone said. "I mean, there's a little kid there and an old man and he's squirting us with water? He's an ass."

Domi said fans were throwing things at him in the box and that's why he retaliated.

"He hit us with water," said Tom Foga, a 29-year-old fan from Wayne, Pennsylvania who was seated next to Falcone. "So Chris said, 'Yo! Yo! Stop that!' That's not right for a player to do that. Just ignore the fan. When he turned around and squirted us a third time, Chris has got a little bit of a temper and he went after him.

"I tried grabbing him and pulling him back, but once he went in there I wasn't jumping in."

Domi, whose only other altercation with a fan was when he punched up an opposing team's mascot when he was 15, had a slightly different version.

"They threw some stuff at me," he said. "Once was enough, the second time I told the (attendant) in the box if they hit me again I'm going to squirt water at them. I didn't plan on fighting anybody.

"Then a heavyset guy (Falcone) fell in on me," Domi said. "That's my workplace. Nobody's going to come in my work and get away with it. When he got in there he started swinging and I wasn't going to have anybody swinging at me, I don't care who it was. He got Kevin (Collins) with a pretty good one. I was trying to stick up for Kevin."

Once Falcone was in the penalty box, Domi pulled his jacket over his head and punched him several times.

"He was as surprised as anybody," Lou Nolan said of Falcone. "(Off-ice official) Joe Messina had the fan in a headlock and the fan was saying, 'Help me.' He was kind of a folk here for 15 minutes."

Falcone was taken to the security office on the main concourse of the Center, where he was treated for a cut on his forehead. A police officer in front of the security office told Foga there would be no charges pressed against Falcone.

Several players enjoyed the sideshow.

"I wouldn't want to be the guy falling over the glass into the box against Tie," Leafs goaltender Curtis Joseph said. "Tie's had a thousand confrontations. That's as comfortable to him as sitting on a couch."

Leafs winger Gary Roberts said he was impressed with the fan's gamesmanship.

"He looked like he wanted to go at it with one of the toughest guys in the league," Roberts said. "That must have been Rocky falling into the penalty box. There's a lot of guys you could fall in the penalty box with and Tie's not one of them."

CHECKO BOMBING

Despite playing 66 games without John LeClair and an entire season without Eric Lindros, the Flyers still managed a 100-point season in 2000-01. That was enough to make Bill Barber the fourth coach in Flyers history – Fred Shero, Pat Quinn and Mike Keenan were the others — to win the Jack Adams Trophy as the top coach in the NHL.

But it provided little consolation in a six-game playoff loss to the Sabres that ended with the worst playoff defeat in team history.

Roman Cechmanek, the sixth goalie to start a playoff series for the Flyers in six years –Brian Boucher, John Vanbiesbrouck, Sean Burke, Garth Snow and Ron Hextall were the others — was blitzed for five goals and the Flyers were victimized by Chris Gratton in an 8-0 drubbing in Buffalo.

Moments after the game Barber rushed to the defense of his goalie, who set a rookie record with 10 shutouts during the regular season and was a finalist for the Vezina Trophy.

"If we didn't have Roman, then we wouldn't be sitting here," Barber said. "I have the deepest respect for him and it's unfortunate that it had to end like this. But things happen for a reason."

Gratton, who was a bust in parts of two seasons in Philadelphia, recorded five goals and three assists against the Flyers in the six-game series.

"I think it's a little more embarrassing than anything," said LeClair, who had one goal in the playoffs after netting just seven in the regular season.

Even in defeat, Flyers general manager Bob Clarke was defiant, saying his inability to trade Lindros all season had not hurt his team's chances in the playoffs.

"I don't think it had any impact at all on our team," Clarke said. "In fact, I think it was positive getting that problem out of our locker room. We were forced to use different people in key situations and they responded. So I think there was a lot of positives to be taken from Lindros not having (been) on our team."

BARBER'S PRIVATE PAIN

Just before the 2001 playoffs Barber noticed that his wife, Jenny, had been battling a hoarse cough for weeks. At his urging she went for a medical examination and an X-ray showed a dark area in her lungs.

"They thought it was pneumonia," Barber recalled. "All it showed was a dark area and you just figure it's pneumonia. She took her medicine and I kept hearing her (cough) to a point where she would leave the bedroom. I knew the stuff wasn't working.

"It was going on a little bit too long for my liking. I told her to go back in there and force their hand. Run more tests and find out what the hell this is. Of course, what he found isn't want we wanted to hear."

A second round of tests revealed Jenny had a collapsed lung with a malignant tumor. Barber chose to keep the news from his players in an attempt to keep himself and his team focused on hockey.

LINDROS SAGA CONTINUES

More than a year after Lindros played his final game as a Flyer the 27-year-old center remained in limbo as the NHL draft came and went without him being dealt. Many wondered if the stalemate would ever end.

"We don't care if Eric plays in New York, and we don't care if he ever plays again," Clarke said, his tone growing more and more bitter.

"I think he'll be sitting out for another year."

J.R. ARRIVES IN LIVING COLOR

When the summer of 2001 rolled around the Flyers decided to open their wallets and sign a high-profile free agent. Their options included:

a) Brett Hull

b) Luc Robitaille

c) Pierre Turgeon

d) Alexandre Mogilny

e) Dave Andreychuk

f) Dominik Hasek …

and a 31-year-old kid from Boston named Jeremy Roenick.

They chose J.R. In fact, the Flyers wanted Roenick so badly they dealt a second-round pick to the Phoenix Coyotes just for the right to speak with his agent a few days before signing a five-year, $37.5 million contract on July 1.

"Our organization ticketed one guy as the premier guy for us to try and get and that player was Jeremy Roenick," Clarke said.

To no one's surprise, Roenick arrived in Philadelphia in style. At his introductory press conference, Roenick gave Ed Snider a big hug and said, "Mr. *Schneider*, thank you very much. You will not — will not — be disappointed."

Snider replied, "I know that Jeremy."

Then Roenick turned toward Clarke.

"Bob, you will not be disappointed," Roenick said, then turned his face back to the television cameras catching his every move. "And all you Flyers fans, let's get going, man! I want to win! Let's go!"

Roenick then stood up and hoisted an imaginary Stanley Cup over his head, hoping to foretell the team's future.

"I'm not afraid of a camera or a microphone," Roenick said. "I really enjoy it. I think the fans will enjoy my enthusiasm for the game. I am a little bit flamboyant and I do get a little flashy sometimes.

"I might throw a bunch of pucks up for kids or try to knock over somebody's beer on a ledge behind the glass," he said. "I do a

In his first press conference as a Flyer, Jeremy Roenick lifted an imaginary Stanley Cup over his shoulders.

lot of things between whistles, but when the whistle's in the (referee's) pocket and we're playing the game, I want to take somebody's head off and put the puck in the net, because that's what it's all about. This game is not for the weak at heart."

What Roenick failed to mention in that giddy introductory press conference is that he was thisclose to having a similar one in Detroit dressed in Red Wings red.

Roenick later acknowledged he and his wife, Tracy, toured the Detroit area on June 28, then were taken to dinner by Red Wings general manager Ken Holland. The Roenicks seemed sold on Detroit, but shortly after they were dropped off by Holland at a Birmingham, Michigan, hotel, Roenick received a cell phone call from his agent, Neal Abbott.

Abbott informed his client the Flyers had just offered a take-it-or-leave-it contract — with a catch. He had just 30 minutes to decide. The Flyers informed Abbott that if he didn't take their offer they would turn their attention to one of the other free agents.

"That all could have been a ploy on their part," Roenick said. "But it kind of put me in a position where I had to decide."

Roenick called former Phoenix Coyotes teammate Rick Tocchet and informed him of his dilemma. Tocchet, who was about to play his final season with the Flyers, told Roenick to choose Philadelphia, saying he'd be a perfect fit for the city.

"J.R. is a Philly-type player," Tocchet said. "He can dazzle you with moves or knock you through the boards."

Roenick took Tocchet's advice and signed with the Flyers, but not without some reservations.

"I felt bad," Roenick said of walking away from the Red Wings' undisclosed offer. "Ken Holland was more than gracious with me. But sometimes decisions have to be made — and made quickly."

FINAL-E, LINDROS BECOMES A RANGER

Nine years after arriving in Philadelphia on a wave of promise and 15 months after playing his final game in orange and black, Eric Lindros was traded to the Rangers in a river of acrimony on Aug. 20, 2001.

In exchange for the rights to Lindros, the Flyers received defenseman Kim Johnsson, forwards Jan Hlavac and Pavel Brendl and a third-round draft pick in 2003 who turned out to be Stefan Ruzicka.

The trade came with a condition. If Lindros, who had suffered six concussions in his nine-year career, suffered a head injury within the first 50 games of the 2001-02 season and was unable to play for at least 12 months following the injury, the Flyers would give the Rangers back their third-round pick and throw in their own first-round pick in 2003.

On the ice, Lindros was almost everything the Flyers had hoped when they traded six players, two draft picks and $15 million to the Quebec Nordiques for his rights in 1992. He recorded 659 points in 486 games, but played in more than 70 games just twice in his eight-year career and sat out two full seasons — one in Quebec and one in Philadelphia — because of disputes with management.

"Once we made up our minds that we weren't going to allow Eric and his dad to abuse people who work here anymore, we were fine," Clarke said on the day the deal was finalized. "They backed off."

But they never reconciled.

"He hurt this organization and I could care less about him," Clarke said. "I don't think he and I will ever have a relationship again."

Lindros took the high road on the day he became a Ranger.

"There was a tremendous amount of support there," Lindros said in his introductory press conference. "Come playoff time, that city was just rocking. Even through the many highs and lows, there was always support. ... I've got nothing but real good things to take away from what occurred as far as the players and the fans. That certainly overrides anything that took place with management."

Today Lindros' stormy career in Philadelphia receives mixed reviews from his former teammates.

"I really, really liked Eric Lindros," former defenseman Chris Therien said. "There was just so much stuff going on around him. It's disappointing to see that he never became what everyone thought he could have."

Ron Hextall said Lindros had a child's heart and was one of his oldest son's favorite players growing up.

"He loved kids and cared about people," Hextall said. "But he also had an enormous amount of pressure on him. Some of it he put on himself.

"When he refused to go to Quebec and forced that trade, he became the savior in Philly. I personally think he would have done better if he played for Quebec. They had a great young team coming together with Joe Sakic and Mats Sundin and I don't think Eric would have been asked to do as much as he had to do in Philly, where there wasn't a lot surrounding him."

Hextall said he would remember Lindros as a great player, but not as a great captain.

"Dave Poulin was the greatest captain I ever played with and was he at his level? No," Hextall said. "I practiced with Eric every day and he amazed me with things he could do. But there was a lot of maintenance with Eric and the team always had to weigh the burden of having him and the upside of keeping him. He became all anybody talked about. Something had to break and it did."

Rod Brind'Amour believes there was enough blame to go around in the Flyers' handling of Lindros.

"I think the mistake the Flyers made was making Eric bigger than the team," he said. "They made special rules for him. I don't blame Eric. He just wanted to play and he thought people wanted him to do more. They wanted him to be this great leader who would follow in Clarkie's footsteps and that wasn't Eric.

"I still think Eric took a lot of crap and a lot of it was undeserved. He brought a lot on himself, no question. It just seemed like he carried a lot of baggage with him."

Clarke agrees, but does not blame Lindros entirely for the Flyers' missed opportunities to win a Stanley Cup during the 1990s.

"We had enough players to compete for the Cup but we were short in areas," Clarke admits now. "We were always looking for another defenseman, another line that could score. Eric is a hard guy to have on a team when he's getting hurt all the time. We were always waiting for him to come back and players were getting unhappy because of it."

GAME TAKES BACK SEAT TO BUSH

The Flyers' battles with Lindros seemed trivial on the morning of Sept. 11, 2001, when every television at the team's new practice facility was tuned to the tragic events unfolding in New York, Washington and Shanksville, Pennsylvania.

Flyers coach Bill Barber canceled practice that morning, sending his players home from the Skate Zone in Voorhees, New Jersey, to be with their families.

Nine days later, during a preseason game against the Rangers at the First Union Center, the fate of a nation far exceeded the need to play a hockey game.

After a stirring rendition of "God Bless America" by anthemist Lauren Hart, the Flyers and Rangers skated to a 2-2 tie through two periods when the Flyers decided to show President Bush's much-anticipated speech to Congress on the Jumbotron during the second intermission.

With most of the 19,117 fans in their seats watching the speech and warmups for the third period about to begin, Bush's speech was taken off the scoreboard, replaced with a message advising fans the speech could be seen on the concourses.

"But when we shut it off, the fans started booing and chanting 'Leave it on!'" public address announcer Lou Nolan recalled.

The Flyers, who had handed out miniature American flags before the game, immediately put the speech back on the scoreboard and as players skated onto the ice, they all turned their attention to the Jumbotron. Some remained seated on the benches, others kneeled along the boards. Mark Recchi and Brian Boucher watched from the Flyers' goal crease.

During Bush's speech fans roared and burst into chants of "USA! USA!"

In a show of solidarity, the Flyers and Rangers shook hands following their aborted game on Sept. 20, 2001.

The biggest cheers came when Bush introduced Lisa Beamer, the widow of Flight 93 passenger Todd Beamer, who helped thwart terrorists' plans to crash a fourth plane into a Washington, D.C. landmark.

Once Bush's speech concluded, Flyers chief operating officer Ron Ryan decided to call off the remainder of the game and asked the players from both teams to shake hands in a show of solidarity.

"I'm proud of our fans, I'm proud of our team," Ryan said. "I think it worked out all for the best. These are unusual circumstances and I think it all turned out right."

Players from both teams were in complete agreement.

"I thought it was great to shake hands," said Rangers defenseman Brian Leetch, who lost a close friend in the World Trade Center collapse. "At the end, everyone was giving the President a standing ovation. It was a nice end to that game.

"It's our reality right now. It's not part of a movie, it's part of our life now. There's no denying it or trying to get away from it."

BIG E SPURS BIG BRAWL

The Jeremy Roenick era started off with a bang as the free-agent acquisition scored in his first game as a Flyer on Oct. 4, 2001.

But the hottest ticket of the season was a Nov. 14 tilt between the Flyers and Rangers at Madison Square Garden, where Eric Lindros faced the Flyers for the first time in his NHL career.

The game itself was crackling good. But the fury in the stands was even more pulsating.

"It was the best New York crowd I've seen in years," Flyers winger Paul Ranheim said.

From the middle of the national anthem until long after the game, Rangers fans showed their true colors. They were loud, obnoxious, occasionally cruel, and fiercely loyal.

Just ask the brave but senseless Flyers fans who walked around the Garden concourse wearing bright orange T-shirts with the No. 88 crossed out with black highlighters. When the Flyers scored a pair of quick goals to tie the score at 2-2 early in the third period, the fans decided it was time to stand up and be heard.

The result, of course, was more than a dozen simultaneous fist fights that captured the attention of players from both benches.

"That was wild," Flyers enforcer Todd Fedoruk said. "Those (Flyers fans) were getting hit with beers, popcorn, everything!"

The bad blood spilled down into the lower level, where grown men in suits pummeled each other with overhand rights. There was so much testosterone flowing that a post-game New Jersey Transit train carrying fans from New York to Philadelphia had to be stopped because a brawl broke out between Rangers and Flyers fans.

The source of all the venom, Lindros, hardly batted an eye.

"He seemed to be enduring it instead of embracing it," Ranheim said.

JENNY BARBER LOSES HER FIGHT

A few days before his 48-year-old wife, Jenny, took her final breath, Bill Barber tore a page off his Win The Day calendar and posted it on the Flyers' locker room door.

It read: "What lies behind us and what lies before us are tiny matters compared to what lies within us."

On Dec. 8, 2001, Barber stunned his players, not to mention a sellout crowd of 19,548 at the First Union Center, when he stepped behind the Flyers bench less than three hours after seeing his wife of 28 years quietly slip away.

Jenny Barber passed away shortly after noon and after saying their goodbyes, the Barbers' two children — daughter Kerri, who was 27, and son Brooks, who was 24 — convinced their father to coach the game.

"Billy was probably burying himself in the distraction of the moment," said E.J. Maguire, Barber's assistant coach that season. "Jenny was an absolutely wonderful person."

The Flyers rolled to an emotional 5-1 win over the Minnesota Wild that afternoon and Barber was handed the game puck by captain Keith Primeau.

"We lost a great lady, a true wife and mother," Barber said in the quiet of his coach's office following the game. "She was a champion. I'll miss her more than anyone knows. She was needed up there more than she was needed here."

Barber then pulled from under his shirt a gold charm he gave his wife when she was first diagnosed with lung cancer. On the back he had inscribed the message: "Attitude Is Everything."

"She gave it everything she had," Barber said. "Up until the very end."

BRASHEAR'S INCREDIBLE JOURNEY

On Dec. 17, 2001, the Flyers knew they were acquiring one of the most feared fighters in the NHL when they obtained Donald Brashear from the Vancouver Canucks for Jan Hlavac.

Donald Brashear says his troubled life as a foster child led him to Montreal and a career in the NHL.

What they didn't know was the kind of fight the 6-foot-2, 235-pound native of Bedford, Indiana had to get to the NHL.

The youngest of three children, Brashear was placed in a Montreal foster home at the age of five. His mother decided to keep her other two children, Lorraine, 8, and Jay, 6.

"I guess I was a lot to handle," Brashear said. "I never knew the real reasons."

Over the next three years, Brashear lived with three different foster families, all of them white and French-speaking. Brashear, who is black, said he never fit in.

"I guess not having my own mom and the love of a mom and not having my own things, I remember at one point I became real jealous," he said. "I was always looking at the other kids as if they were my real brothers and sisters because I never had the chance to grow up with my brother and sister and become friends with them."

Switching from one predominantly white school to the next brought on more difficulties. Bigger than most of his classmates, Brashear said he fought almost daily in elementary school, mostly because of racial teasing.

"I was a real aggressive person. Very, very aggressive, every step of the way," he said. "Growing up in a white environment and hearing racial slurs all the time got me pretty pissed off. Every time it happened, I would just fight."

"By the time I was in sixth grade," he said with a smile, "they were respecting me."

Brashear said his third foster family, the St. Pierres from Quebec City, sternly but lovingly guided him in the right direction, encouraging him to turn the other cheek.

"I started smiling at people who called me names," said Brashear, who lived with the St. Pierres from the time he was 8 until he was 17. "After a while, it didn't hurt."

Brashear said that while other foster families made him do chores around the house, the St. Pierres signed him up for basketball, karate and hockey. Still, there were times his aggressive behavior tried their patience.

"I used to think life sucked," he said. "I really hated it as a young kid, not to the point where I wanted to die, but I just hated every day. It was hard. To make myself better I had to realize what was going on and it took me a long time."

Brashear's most painful revelation came when he was 17 during a brave and daring attempt to reconcile his past. At the urging of his older sister, who had written him letters over the years, Brashear agreed to meet his natural mother for the first time in 12 years. The reunion was more uncomfortable than enlightening.

"I always wanted to meet her again," Brashear said. "I went to see her, it was pretty tough. It didn't even feel like my mom. I never grew up with her. It was awkward. You're sitting there and you have so many questions, but at the same time I wasn't asking any because I didn't want to start a process where I'm going to start thinking about what really happened.

"My life was getting better and I decided it was not going to be a factor in my life. I packed it all in. She actually said, 'Don't you have any questions?' I guess she was expecting to tell me more; she was expecting me to ask her a lot of questions and I didn't say anything."

Brashear said his mother revealed to him that she had 10 children with three different men, each of whom physically abused her and her children.

"She kept divorcing because they would always beat her up, and the kids," he said.

Brashear said his brief meeting with his mother made him realize that facing his past could prove to be more productive than running away from it. As his hockey career developed, so did his self-esteem and the strength of his character.

By the time he turned 18, Brashear was a hard-hitting defenseman in the Quebec Major Junior Hockey League and when he knocked out an opposing player in his first fight in juniors, Brashear was labeled an enforcer.

"When I knocked him out,' he said with a grimace, "I was like, `Oooh! I didn't know I could do that.' Just like that I became a fighter and that's not what I really wanted to do. It's not how I perceived hockey. I saw hockey as scoring goals, hitting and skating."

Today, Brashear remains one of the NHL's top heavyweights. He entered the 2009-10 season on the verge of playing in his 1,000th game and had more than 2,500 penalty minutes in his 15-year career.

THE TIBBETTS EXPERIMENT

In his 20 years as a general manger for the Flyers Bob Clarke made 177 trades, some of them very good and some very bad. One of the most controversial came on March 17, 2002 when he sent Cornell product Kent Manderville to the Penguins for troubled winger Billy Tibbetts.

Tibbetts, who was 27 at the time, had been convicted of raping a 15-year-old girl at an outdoor Massachusetts party 10 years earlier; and had twice been charged with assault and battery, the first for intimidating a witness and the second for using a BB gun as a weapon.

"I was kind of a wild kid," Tibbetts said on his first day as a Flyer. "I've tried to grow out of that. I've tried to mature as a man since being released from prison a good two years ago now."

News of the trade was met with strong resistance from the Flyers' fan base and SportsTalk phone lines lit up with angry protesters lambasting the Flyers for employing a convicted criminal.

It was not the first time Clarke faced criticism for acquiring a player with a checkered past. Over the previous four years he had added Sean Burke, who was arrested for assaulting his wife, Kevin Stevens, who was arrested in a hotel room drug raid, and Donald Brashear, who was arrested for assaulting a man at a health club.

Asked if he held a soft spot for players who had fallen on hard times, Clarke revealed a bit of himself.

"I'm not sure if it's a soft spot. I think I could have been eliminated from the NHL because I had diabetes. Someone gave me a chance. When it's happening to you, you don't forget those things. In this kid's case, he's getting a chance and it's up to him to conduct himself properly and play hard."

Ed Snider also defended the trade, saying, "I checked this extensively. The kid gets in trouble at 17 years old and soon after that he did some stupid things that tough, young kids do. But he's been clean ever since. Obviously there's a PR consideration here, but we don't make hockey moves based on PR."

Bill Barber was less optimistic about the move saying, "If the piece doesn't fit, we'll remove the piece."

As it turned out, Tibbetts career in Philadelphia lasted 23 days and included two fights, an unsportsmanlike conduct penalty for arguing with a referee, two instigator penalties, a two-game suspension, one assist, 64 penalty minutes and a minus-3 rating in six games.

Today, Tibbetts is still playing hockey as a member of the Huntsville Havoc of the Southern Professional Hockey League and his only known legal blemish was leading police on a high-speed cart chase in 2007. Manderville works for an Ottawa television network as a color commentator of the Senators.

RUMBLINGS UNDER BARBER'S FEET

Sometime around the 2002 NHL trade deadline, when the Flyers acquired Adam Oates from the Washington Capitals to fill in for injured centers Keith Primeau (broken ribs) and Jeremy Roenick (sprained knee), several Flyers began a quiet rebellion against Barber.

"There were about 20 games to go," Clarke recalls, "and five or six of them came up and they were really mad at Billy and they wanted me to get somebody else.

"I said, 'Boys, don't even bring it up. That's your ... coach and he's going to be here 'til the end of the year, so you guys figure it out. I'm not going to bring in a new coach."

CRASH LANDING

Despite their grumblings the Flyers had a 40-20-9-3 record in late March, but fell apart down the stretch, winning just two of their final 10 games of the regular season.

The emotional grind of an 82-game regular season had taken its toll on Barber, as a coach, as a father and as a widower. There were days he was angry, days he was bitter and days he was just plain exhausted.

"I'm very pleased it's over," Barber said as his team prepared to face the Ottawa Senators in the first round of the 2002 playoffs.

"I've had a tough year, family-wise. Thank God I have the team. We have a great bunch of guys who have been supportive of us. I'm glad I'm still involved with the game. The friendship they've given me is warming."

Barber began recalling all of the players and family members who had passed before their time – Barry Ashbee, Pelle Lindbergh, Kathy Kerr, Dmitry Tertyshny, Jenny Barber – and was hoping a long playoff run would help ease the burden of a trying season.

"I'm hoping we get blessed for a change and not bit," he said. "It's not just me. Everybody has their problems and I'm hoping we get some relief, we pull it all together and we see a lot more smiles on everybody.

"Every stinking year we've been stung with something. Think about it. Injuries, deaths. Enough's enough. When you really think about it, we've been hit really ...

hard. Right between the eyes. The loss of players, Jen. It's time for us to see the light at the end of the tunnel."

It was one of the few times all season Barber let his guard down, but to his players he kept a brave face.

"He kept a lot of it to himself," John LeClair said. "It's a sad part of life and it's something we've had to separate from hockey."

"There's obviously going to be a time at some point in the summer — hopefully in June or July — that it's probably going to hit him," Mark Recchi said. "It's been a tough year for him."

BETTER DUCK, CHECKO

The Flyers' playoff run of 2002 was about as short as Roman Cechmanek's temper.

After scoring one goal in their first four playoff games against the seventh-seeded Ottawa Senators, the 31-year-old Czech goalie became frustrated with his teammates after the Senators took a 3-0 lead in Game 4.

Cechmanek skated out to center ice and began waving his hands wildly at the Flyers bench. Some wondered whether he was asking Bill Barber to pull him from the game. Others thought he was trying to show up a group of experienced but unproductive forwards.

"He skated halfway down the ice and asked Billy to pull him," E.J. McGuire recalled. "Billy wouldn't go for that."

When Roman Cechmanek embarrassed his teammates in Ottawa, they returned fire at practice the next day.

Several players thought Cechmanek was showing them up and the next day at practice many of them took aim at the goalie's noggin.

"I did notice there was an inordinate amount of pucks that went off the glass that day," McGuire said with a laugh.

Clarke tried not to make too much of the incident.

"What he did was basically say, 'You're not playing and I'm the one getting embarrassed,'" Clarke said. "Of course, you don't like to see that. It was bad."

Whether Cechmanek's antics were intended to embarrass his coach or his teammates, Barber wasn't running the risk of having it happen again. He started Boucher in the decisive Game 5, which ended with a 2-1 overtime loss at home.

LOTS OF QUESTIONS, FEW ANSWERS

The Flyers' late season collapse raised all kinds of questions about the club's direction.

Did Barber devise a poorly designed system for a good team? Or, was it a poorly designed team for a good system?

After all, this was a team that was 20 games over .500 before a season-ending 5-10-4-0 freefall. How could a team full of offensive firepower get outscored 11-2 in a five-game playoff series?

"Maybe in time I can come up with some kind of analysis of why, but I don't have any for you right now," Barber said after the series-ending loss. "I have no answers at all for why we didn't put pucks in the net. It got to a point where it snowballed on us."

In truth, by the start of the playoffs the Flyers already were entrenched in a difference of philosophies.

The players wanted to play an aggressive forechecking system that best utilized their creativity. Barber wanted to install a more patient, defensive system to combat against less talented teams who would use the trap against them in the playoffs.

The result was a disorganized combination of both systems, with some players abandoning their defensive responsibilities for offensive chances and others finding themselves out of position at both ends of the rink.

Barber suggested he needed another year to convince his players the right way to play. Boucher, who won a Calder Cup as a backup under Barber wasn't so sure.

"There's going to be a lot of people who point fingers," the Flyers goalie said. "Hopefully, guys in the locker room don't point fingers at one another because there's nothing we can do about it now. If we wanted to point fingers, we should have done it weeks ago or months ago and straightened the problems out then. Doing it now does us no good."

PLAYERS TOSS COACH OVERBOARD

Ten months after being named NHL Coach of the Year, Bill Barber was fired by the Flyers in a player revolt.

Never in the history of the Flyers has there been a more public mutiny than the one that took place at the team's practice facility on April 29, 2002.

Painting Bill Barber as a hot-headed, closed-minded, unresponsive coach, several Flyers veterans met with Ed Snider and Bob Clarke, then told reporters what they had told their bosses.

Despite winning the Atlantic Division title with 97 points, they believed they were ill-prepared to win in the Stanley Cup playoffs.

"There were a lot of problems," Brian Boucher said. "Not only in the playoffs, but in the last two to three months. There were meetings about meetings and meetings upon meetings and it seemed nothing got solved. Guys made suggestions on what we felt we needed and I think, for the most part, players felt we didn't get (a response).

"I know people are saying the players are crybabies, but we're players and we need to be led in the direction the players suggested. It was frustrating because it's not something that just popped up at the end. This is something that's been growing, festering, and everybody knew it."

The biggest gripe from the players is that they never practiced any kind of system. When their power play struggled — it finished 27th in the NHL and went 1-for-16 in the playoffs — players said Barber refused to spend extra time on it in practice.

"We had the worst power play in the league," Keith Primeau said. "Why are we not practicing it?"

Mark Recchi was asked what response he was given when he went to Barber with suggestions.

"It really got blown off, more or less," Recchi said. "Basically, it was whatever. Nothing happened.

"You need somebody to grab the bull by the horns and say this is the exact way it's done. You can't have players running a hockey club. It just doesn't happen. You need one guy to lead the charge."

Primeau said Barber also created an uncomfortable environment for players to perform.

"There were tirades on the bench," he said. "All season long, we know when someone makes a mistake out there they're getting yelled at. He wants the players to make the adjustments. Well, our job is to play. I felt I was having to make the adjustments on the bench and I don't feel that's part of my job description."

Primeau was asked why he decided to air the Flyers' dirty laundry and he said it was at the request of teammates who felt they were being unfairly portrayed as coach killers.

"Everybody wants to say we're babies and whiners and we'll avoid criticism because we'll get a coach fired," Primeau said. "That's totally false. It's so incorrect. I'm tired of people who make assumptions because of what they view from the exterior.

"We're chastised in the paper and we can't defend ourselves. I'm speaking on behalf of my teammates because I'd rather walk out of this room right now with my pride intact than not."

Down the hallway from where his players were conducting the lynching, Barber and his assistants sat in Mike Stothers' office and acknowledged what they knew was inevitable.

They were all getting fired.

"And I'm not coming back," Barber said defiantly. "You can count on that."

PLAYERS GET THEIR WISH

One day after the players' mutiny, the Flyers held a press conference to announce that Bill Barber, who one year earlier was honored as NHL Coach of the Year, had been fired and offered another position in the organization.

As promised the day before, Barber refused.

After what Ed Snider called "a thorough investigation," Barber became the fifth coach in five years to receive his walking papers, joining Terry Murray, Wayne Cashman, Roger Neilson and Craig Ramsay.

"If I felt in any way, shape or form that (Barber) was being railroaded by the players and that they went behind his back, I would have taken another tact," Snider said. "I think what happened is unfortunate, but I have to tell you it was unanimous. Unfortunately, Billy lost the team."

Clarke agreed.

"We just felt there was no way of being able to heal the wounds that had developed between the coach and the players," Clarke said.

Barber refused to comment on the criticisms his players levied against him, saying he would not drag their names and reputations through the mud the same way his had been.

"Write what you know," is all Barber would say on the day he was fired.

Years later Barber says he has no room for bitterness, but had these biting words for the only NHL players he coached.

"They thought they had all the answers," Barber said. "But ask them now how many rings they own? There's your answer."

A little more than two years after his firing, Barber was being fitted for his third Stanley Cup ring, this one as the director of player personnel for the 2004 Tampa Bay Lightning.

"I give him credit for rising above it," McGuire said recently. "The shine on that ring was bright in a lot of ways."

Today, Clarke stands by his decision to fire Barber, saying the players left him no choice.

"For whatever reason he got into battles with the players," Clarke said. "The players were mad at him and he was mad at the players. It wasn't a hard decision. It was a hard decision because of who it was, not because of what it was."

CHAPTER 11

HITCHING A RIDE

(2002–2006)

With Ken Hitchcock cracking the whip and
Jeremy Roenick cracking the jokes, the Flyers
resume their flirtation with greatness.

PICKING UP THE PIECES

ON THE SAME DAY BILL BARBER WAS FIRED AS HEAD COACH
of the Flyers, veteran defenseman Eric Weinrich was gathering his belongings on
the first floor of the Flyers' Skate Zone when a reporter asked him who would make
the perfect coach for the Flyers heading into the 2002-03 season.

"A guy like Ken Hitchcock," Weinrich said. "He's a coach who was able to
convince a group of star players (in Dallas) to play one system."

Those same players staged a revolt against Hitchcock in the middle of his
seventh season behind the Stars bench, but his ability to win five straight division
titles and the Stanley Cup led the coach-less New York Rangers to pursue the out-
of-work, 50-year-old native of Edmonton.

Hitchcock interviewed with Rangers general manager Glen Sather for the vacant position, but when he never received a return phone call, he met with Flyers
assistant general manager Paul Holmgren in Sweden, where he was coaching Team
Canada in the World Championships.

Former Canadiens coach Pat Burns and former Devils coach Larry Robinson
were also believed to be on the Flyers' list of candidates, but after spending 10 minutes with Hitchcock, Ed Snider knew he was the man to point the Flyers in a new
direction.

"If we weren't successful with Ken, we were going to go to candidate No. 2,"
Snider said. "But he was far and above No. 1, and there was no sense interviewing
people just for the sake of interviewing them."

So, on May 14, 2002, Hitchcock was introduced as the Flyers' new head coach and given a four-year, "no-fire" contract with Snider's emphatic stamp of approval.

"We're not changing coaches," Snider said. "This guy is qualified, and if we have to make any changes because the team's not successful, we're changing players. We've had enough of this coaching merry-go-round.

"I know that in my interviews with the players, this is exactly the type of guy they were crying for. I'm very anxious to see how they respond."

It was the first time in the team's 35-year history that a coach was fitted with a bullet proof vest during his introductory press conference. Snider, however, was not the only person deciding if Hitchcock and the Flyers would make a good fit. Hitchcock phoned former players and coaches, including Roger Neilson, to see if Philadelphia was a good fit for him.

"Roger was very strong about coaching here," Hitchcock said at the time. "He really believes in the people here. He loves the town. He said this was his best time that he ever had. He knows it was difficult with the cancer, but he was talking very loudly that I can't afford to pass up this opportunity."

At the time, Hitchcock honestly believed he would hold a Stanley Cup in his hands before the end of his four-year contract with the Flyers.

"The window of opportunity to win here in Philadelphia is now, and I mean that sincerely," he said. "This is a veteran group of players at the right age. Four years from now seems like an eternity because this is an unbelievable opportunity right now."

BYE, BYE BOOSH

It didn't take long for Bob Clarke to make major changes to the roster inherited by Hitchcock. His biggest came in the summer of 2002 when he sent Boucher to Phoenix in exchange for reliable center Michal Handzus and unproven goaltender Robert Esche.

Boucher says now he still believes the dirty laundry he aired at the end of that 2001-02 season led to his ticket out of Philadelphia.

"It may have upset some people and I certainly realized after I said it that it was wrong," Boucher says. "I went right upstairs and apologized to Bob Clarke, Paul Holmgren and Mr. Snider. In no way, shape or form did I mean to embarrass the organization when I said those things. I was simply answering questions directed toward me and I answered them with 100 percent honesty. Sometimes you have to take a stance of political correctness because it can burn you. In that case I learned my lesson."

Apparently, the Flyers forgave Boucher because in the summer of 2009 they re-signed him to a two-year contract.

"I've grown up a lot since then," Boucher says. "When you're a 25-year-old kid you say some things when you're emotional and I was emotional. I'm still an emotional guy. But as I've gotten older I've had a lot more life experiences and you learn to not say these types of things."

HITCHCOCK'S PERSONAL TRAGEDY

Throughout his coaching career, Hitchcock's appearance often got in the way of his message. Many of his players found it difficult to respect an overweight coach who had never played hockey at a competitive level.

Those players never new the whole story of Ken Hitchcock, who kept much of his private life private.

When he was 12, Hitchcock's father, Ray, was diagnosed with a malignant tumor in his back. Two years later, at the age of 40, Ray Hitchcock lost his battle to cancer, leaving behind his wife, Janet, and their three children: 14-year-old Ken, 12-year-old Barb and 10-year-old Keith.

"For me, he was the person that drew me into all the sports activities," Hitchcock said. "He was the sportsman."

As a child, Hitchcock and his father attended junior hockey league games and supported the city's pro football team. Ken played Little League baseball, bantam football, ice hockey, golf, indoor lacrosse and was a champion swimmer.

And his father was the driving force — literally.

"I was one of those kids who never wanted to go and when I went, I never wanted to leave," Hitchcock said. "He was the guy who took me. He knew once I got there I'd stay forever. He always told me, 'You committed, you go.' I would have every excuse not to go and when I went, I'd commit."

Hitchcock also followed his father's footsteps as a hockey coach. When Ray Hitchcock coached the town's 15-to-17-year-olds, he let 4-year-old Ken hang on his pant legs as he learned to skate. Later, Ray became his son's first coach.

After losing his father to cancer as a teenager, Ken Hitchcock became withdrawn and began eating excessively.

"He coached hockey from the first day I can remember to the day he passed away," Hitchcock said. "People who knew him say I am like him, especially in the passion for instructing and teaching."

As much as Hitchcock would like to remember his father as a loving man and insightful hockey coach, the haunting image of him hanging from a hospital room traction swing devastated him.

Hitchcock was 12 years old when he secretly visited his father, boarding three different buses before arriving at the hospital. It was there that he saw a man he barely recognized.

"He looked at me with these eyes of death," Hitchcock said. "He was like a skeleton."

Five days later, Ray Hitchcock died, and so did a piece of his son.

"For me, it was a loss of direction," he said. "My dad was my direction."

Following his father's death, Hitchcock stopped swimming and golfing and playing baseball and lacrosse and hockey. He lost his competitive drive and his inactivity led to overeating. Over the next several years, his weight climbed to well above 400 pounds.

"For a long time you look around and say, 'Why me?' When you're growing up you need your parents. They're the people that mold you. I was like a lot of kids who lost parents. I was on my own and I had to fend for myself. You get over it after a while, but when I see younger children lose their parents, I know exactly what they're going through."

Fifteen years after losing his father to cancer, Hitchcock lost his mother to throat cancer. Janet Hitchcock, whom he still refers to as "Mum," was a heavy smoker when she died at 51.

Today, Hitchcock says nearly everyone he comes in contact with has been touched by cancer in some way. And as a coach in the NHL, he finds it personally painful to make hospital visits to children he may never see again.

"You go back three months or six months later and you're asking where everybody is," Hitchcock said. "Sometimes the answers you get from the doctors and nurses, you don't want to hear those answers. Every day you're hoping there's a cure and it comes quick."

HITCH'S OTHER OFFICE

Although he's done it most of his adult life, coaching hockey was not Ken Hitchcock's only profession. As a 31-year-old sales representative for an athletic equipment company in his hometown of Edmonton, Hitchcock learned a valuable lesson when he lost his first major account.

South Side Athletic Club, which sponsored the team Hitchcock played for as a teenager, took its $100,000 account and moved it across the street to another athletic equipment supplier. Hitchcock was angry, embarrassed and depressed for days. His boss finally told him to find out why he lost the account.

"I picked up the phone and said, 'I'm not going to get angry, but why did you not buy from me?'" Htchcock said. "He said, 'I thought you were telling me what I should do; you weren't listening to me. You already had all my answers.'"

Perhaps that's why, on his first day on the job, Hitchcock met with eight of his players, including captains Keith Primeau, John LeClair and Mark Recchi, in his bare office and tried to do as much listening as he did talking.

"We told him that when we make mistakes, we want him to address us, and he's not afraid to do that," Primeau said. "This is exactly what is needed."

"We have no problem with a person who holds people accountable," Recchi said. "That's what we want."

Having had five coaches in five years, several players also liked the stability that came along with Snider's "no fire" guarantee.

"We know one piece is in place, and that's not going to change," LeClair said. "There's only so many times you can point the finger in the direction of the coach before you look at other areas."

J.R. WIGS OUT

It didn't take long for the mischievous Jeremy Roenick to ruffle the feathers of his new head coach while poking fun at the Flyers' most legendary player.

On Halloween Night 2002, before a home game against Brian Boucher's Phoenix Coyotes, Roenick emerged from the Flyers dressing room wearing a blonde curly wig, long, black Cooperalls and a Flyers jersey with No. 16 and CLARKE stitched on the back. He even skated around for warm-ups wearing fake gapped teeth.

"He loved it," Roenick recalled. "I couldn't even put pads on under those pants because they were so tight. I got a chuckle out of him that night and the fans loved it."

Of course, there was nothing Roenick wouldn't do to get a rise out of fans. One night during warm-ups he noticed a fan's beer resting on the ledge behind the glass.

"I pointed a finger at the guy's beer and said 'No. no. no.' He gave me a look like, 'Why not?' So I skated over and checked the glass and his beer fell to his feet.

"He looked at me like, 'What the (heck)?' So I told (equipment manager) Harry Bricker to take five bucks out of his pocket. He gave me a five-dollar bill and I shoved it through the glass and I said, 'Buy another beer on me.'"

Jeremy Roenick celebrated a Halloween game in 2002 by dressing up as Bobby Clarke.

Roenick enjoys interacting with the fans as much as they love watching him do spin-a-ramas. When he was playing in a game in Toronto as a member of the Blackhawks Roenick noticed a fan eating a bucket of popcorn right next to the visitors' bench.

"I reached back and put my hand in his popcorn and started eating it," said Roenick, who once leaned over and kissed teammate Mark Recchi on the head when their faces were shown on a Kiss Cam in an opposing arena. "I'm a true believer we play the game for the fans."

Roenick's love affair with the lighter side of hockey dates all the way back to the time he was 7 years old and attended a Hartford Whalers practice to see Gordie Howe.

"I was standing up against the glass and Gordie scooped up a stick full of ice and dumped it on my head," Roenick said. "He acknowledged me. I thought that was the coolest thing of all time. It happened 32 years ago and I still remember it as if it was yesterday. Gordie didn't think anything of it, but I did. That's why I make sure that every time I'm on the ice I try to give two seconds to as many people as I can. Whether it's throwing pucks over the glass, making eye contact or giving a wink, I acknowledge as many people as I can. I want them to know we're there playing for them."

FRIDGE DEFROSTED

One of the bravest and most lovable fighters in Flyers history was also one of the unluckiest. Todd Fedoruk stood 6-foot-2, 240 pounds and earned the nickname "Fridge" from Bill Barber when the two were with the Phantoms.

Despite his girth, Fridge was incredibly athletic and could do a standing back flip. But in a Nov. 12, 2002 fight with 6-foot-6, 243-pound Islanders defenseman Eric Cairns, Fedoruk's face could not get out of the way of an ill-intentioned fist and it changed his life forever.

Fedoruk started the fight with an impressive one-punch knockdown, but the aggressive native of Redwater, Alberta wanted more. He pulled Cairns back to his feet and began inflicting more pain before Cairns caught him with a punch on the left cheekbone.

The next day Flyers physician Guy Lanzi needed to repair two fractures to the orbital bone surrounding Fedoruk's left his eye socket, another in his left cheek bone and a fourth in his upper jaw.

"Todd had the bones placed back into normal anatomic alignment through an incision in his left eyebrow," Lanzi said. "An incision was also made underneath his left eye in the skin of the face, and he had one other incision inside the mouth in the left cheek. Through these incisions the bones were put back together and they were held in place with small titanium plates and screws. They're designed to stay in forever."

SNOW STORM

Before becoming politically correct as an NHL general manager with the New York Islanders, goaltender Garth Snow was the Don Rickles of post-game interviews and very few opponents were immune to his barbs.

During a 3-1 win over the Flyers as a goaltender with the Islanders, Snow drew three goaltender interference penalties and a rash of criticism from the Flyers, including Mark Recchi and Jeremy Roenick, who accused Snow of flopping to the ice like a one-footed penguin.

"Number 8 there is sitting on top of me complaining to the ref," Snow shot back. "I finally had to push him off while he was crying like a baby."

Roenick jumped right into the verbal fray, accusing Snow of being cowardly.

"It's not babysitting out here. C'mon, he's the one with the facemask on, let him get hit."

Snow, a fellow Massachusetts native who attended the University of Maine, had this response for Roenick: "He should worry about playing the game, not innovating the game," Snow said. "He thinks he's Brett Hull or something. You should remind him he didn't go to college. He was a junior (hockey) guy, so he's not that bright."

Zinger delivered.

Ten months later, when Snow and the Flyers faced each other again, Roenick was given a chance to replay and he did with this verbal volley: "It's not my fault Snow didn't have any other options coming out of high school. If going to college gets you a career backup goaltender job, and my route gets you a thousand points and a thousand games, and compare the two contracts, it doesn't take a rocket scientist to figure out whose decision was better."

OH, BABY! RECCHI DELIVERS

The Flyers ended the 2002-03 season with a club record 24 road wins, but fell one point short of an Atlantic Division title and drew the fifth-seeded Toronto Maple Leafs in the first round of the 2003 playoffs.

The Leafs opened the physical series by winning two of the first three games, getting game-winners from former Flyer Mikael Renberg and an overtime winner by Tomas Kaberle in Games 1 and 3.

That set the stage for the second-longest game in Flyers history and one of the most memorable nights in Mark Recchi's life.

Standing in the basement of the Air Canada Centre following his dramatic triple overtime game-winner, Recchi was about to call his wife, Alexa, who was scheduled to deliver the couple's third child later the same morning.

"What time is it?" he asked a reporter.

"Twelve thirty."

"Maybe I shouldn't," Recchi said, putting his cell phone back in his pocket. "She might be sleeping."

A little more than seven hours later, at 8:15 a.m., the

Hours after delivering an overtime goal in Toronto, Mark Recchi witnessed the birth of his third child.

Recchis welcomed a baby boy into the world. Austin Recchi, who weighed in at 7 pounds, 3 ounces, would some day have an incredible story to tell about the day he was born.

He'd tell how his 35-year-old father skated down the right wing and snapped a 30-foot wrist shot through the pads of Toronto Maple Leafs goaltender Ed Belfour, ending a physically and emotionally draining game that lasted 3 hours, 42 minutes.

"We were running out of (hockey) tape, running out of dry underwear. We were looking for stuff to drink, stuff to eat," said Flyers captain Keith Primeau, who three years earlier ended the longest game in club history. "A couple guys started dehydrating. Just before the goal, Rex said his legs were starting to cramp."

His weren't the only legs burning. Left wing Simon Gagne also began cramping up midway through the third overtime.

"When I saw that goal go in," Gagne said, "my body was pretty happy."

Roenick said the Flyers finished off three or four 20-gallon Powerade jugs and went through nearly a case of power bars.

They must have worked because the Flyers unleashed a club-record 75 shots on Belfour, hitting him with 72 of them. The Leafs, on the other hand, managed just 38 shots on Flyers goaltender Roman Cechmanek.

The Flyers went on to win the series in seven games, delivering a convincing 6-1 knockout punch in Game 7 in Philadelphia. With three overtime games and a total of 28 periods of hockey, the 2003 conference semifinals remains the most hockey ever played by the Flyers in one playoff series.

THE CURIOUS CASE OF CHECKO

Whether it was head-butting pucks out of the rink, bending down to pick up his catching glove while an opponent was shooting, or skating halfway down the ice to berate his teammates, no one could quite figure out the wheels turning under the mask of Roman Cechmanek.

"Roman has a great sense of humor," Ken Hitchcock once said, "if you can understand what he's saying."

In three seasons with the Flyers, Cechmanek twice won the Bobby Clarke Trophy as team MVP and his regular-season goals-against average of 1.98 still ranks as the best among starting goalies who wore orange and black.

"I'm not the best goalie," Cechmanek once said. "I never was the best in the Czech and I never was the best in the National Hockey League. I play for myself and for my pleasure. I like hockey and I play for me."

Goalies in Philadelphia are ultimately judged in the playoffs and Cechmanek's inability to get the Flyers past the second round led to his demise. Each of his victories against the Ottawa Senators in the second round of the 2003 playoffs were by shutout, but he allowed 16 goals in the Flyers' four losses and that was enough to turn Clarke against him.

"I think it will be very difficult to bring Roman back," Clarke said one week after the Flyers' six-game elimination by the Senators. "I don't think he wants to come back, really. Talking to his agent, I think he feels this is not a good place for him. The agent doesn't feel that he really wants to come back. He wants a fresh start somewhere, so we'll try to do that for him."

Interestingly, Cechmanek's agent, Petr Svoboda, did not remember the conversation the same way Clarke did, saying the 32-year-old goalie wanted to honor the two remaining years on his contract.

"I never told Bobby Roman doesn't want to come back," Svoboda said. "I never said anything like that in our conversation. I'm not the one to make those decisions. If Bobby says he doesn't want to have him back, that's up to him and we'll deal with it. But Roman was very happy in Philly."

Hitchcock was equally perplexed by Clarke's intention of trading his No. 1 goalie.

"I'm surprised the plug got pulled so quickly," Hitchcock said. "Look, this is between the agent and the GM. What am I going to say? I just know what took place. In my conversation with Roman there was a complete understanding of what went right and what went wrong. That's the part that bugs me, that really bothers me."

Still, there was no convincing Clarke that Cechmanek, who went 43-22-10 with a 1.96 GAA in the regular season and 9-14 with a 2.33 GAA in the playoffs, could return to the Flyers.

"He shuts a team out one night and then, when you get down to the nitty gritty and you let a soft goal in, it takes so much out of your team emotionally," Clarke said. "When you give up goals at the wrong time, the players themselves lose confidence in the goalie.

"When some scary-type goals go in and you're losing, obviously, he's got to take the blame for it."

Svoboda stood by his goaltender, saying he became an easy target for the team's inability to beat the Senators for a second straight year.

"It seems to me everybody in Philly is trying to create a goat, a guy to blame," Svoboda said. "No one wants to play with a gun to his head. I agree with Bobby Clarke that the situation was not the best. He has the right to have his assumptions. But that's all they are, assumptions."

Two weeks later, Clarke traded Cechmaenk to the Los Angeles Kings for a second-round draft pick. He played just one season in L.A. before returning to the Czech Republic.

JEFF (CAN'T) HACKETT

With Cechmanek in their rear view mirror the Flyers bypassed free-agent goaltender Curtis Joseph a second time and signed 35-year-old veteran Jeff Hackett to be their next No. 1 goalie and a bridge to what they hoped would become the Robert Esche era.

"Our scouting staff, our coaching staff, our whole organization feels that Jeff will give us the solid and steady goaltending that we will need to take a run at the Stanley Cup," Clarke said after signing Hackett to a two-year, $6 million contract.

Many questioned whether Hackett (156-234-50) was an upgrade over Cechmanek (92-43-22) and were wary of his injury history, which included more than 100 games missed due to strained groins and hamstrings, a fractured finger, a sprained ankle, a strained hip flexor, back spasms, an injured knee, a fractured right hand and a dislocated left shoulder.

"His health," Ken Hitchcock said, "is a major concern of mine."

Hackett began his Flyers career with back-to-back shutout victories and went 9-2-6 in his first 17 starts as the Flyers raced out to the Atlantic Division lead. But in December he lost six starts in a row and on Jan. 22, 2004 he was diagnosed with vertigo.

Less than a month later, with Esche nursing a knee sprain, Hackett was forced into retirement and replaced with veteran Sean Burke, a former teammate of Esche who had played guitar at Esche's wedding.

J.R. UNPLUGGED

For years the Flyers have felt they've gotten a raw deal from NHL referees, saying their days as the Broad Street Bullies clouded the vision of the men in stripes.

On Jan. 15, 2004, after Jeremy Roenick was suspended one game for spitting blood at the feet of referee Blaine Angus and tossing a water bottle in his direction, he went on an expletive-laced tirade that, if recorded, would have been drowned by bleeps.

"I'm not going to go unheard," Roenick said after being informed he'd lost $91,463.41 in pay. "They took money out of my pocket for getting my face maimed, and I'm going to get my money's worth.

"Let's be honest," Roenick said. "There are referees out there who hate the Flyers ... hate the way we play, hate the way we bitch, hate the way we moan and

Jeremy Roenick clowns around with Comcast reporter Scott Hanson following a Flyers Halloween game.

complain, so they purposely call the games against us. That is not right. So how do you expect us to react when we see blatant favoritism against us?"

Roenick was referring to an incident one night earlier when his lip was sliced open on an accidental high-stick by teammate Sami Kapanen. He said he barked at referee Dan Marouelli for not making a call, then apologized when he realized it was Kapanen's stick that cut him. But when Roenick's cut was re-opened on a high stick by Sabres defenseman Rory Fitzpatrick in clear view of Angus, Roenick said he was incensed at the no-call.

"I made eye contact with Blaine Angus and it was almost like he said, "(Bleep) you, I'm not making a call," Roenick said. "I was bleeding like a stuffed pig, so I threw a water bottle. I just lost it."

Roenick was asked if spitting blood at the feet of Angus might have triggered his gross misconduct penalty.

"I don't think so," Roenick said. "I didn't spit on him."

At the time, Roenick's face looked like a botched med school experiment with seven stitches in his lip and another 26 under his eye, the result of being struck in the face by a Mark Recchi slapshot one week earlier. He said he played the game the way it was meant to be played and was literally paying the price for it.

"(NHL disciplinarian) Colin Campbell didn't get his lip sliced up and is unable able to eat today," Roenick said. "They don't have enough respect for me to give me the benefit of the doubt. They're just saying, '(Bleep) J.R.'"

Bob Clarke agreed, saying the suspension was "way too severe."

"It's my opinion they encourage the player to roll around on the ice and put his hands over his face hoping to draw a penalty, or to go after the player who hit him, and Roenick did neither," Clarke said. "He took it like a man, the way hockey players are supposed to take it."

"I'm not one to flail around the ice like I've been shot," Roenick said. "If that's what it's going to take to get a penalty called, I might as well retire right now because I'm not going to do it. I'm not going to fall to the ice and cry like a baby."

Roenick said he'd like to see referees fined and suspended for their actions, just like the players.

"If they want to be known as a pussy-foot, wimp league that doesn't make any of their refs accountable, the game is never going to be successful," he said. "I cannot believe referees don't get fined or suspended for having subpar performances. I get fined and suspended. They take money out of my pocket, but they're too Neanderthal to make themselves better."

REX AND THE TOOTH FAIRY

Hard as this is to believe, Mark Recchi played hockey for 30 years before losing his first tooth and it happened in the summer of 2003 when he bit into an ice cube.

"Can you believe that?" he said. "An ice cube!"

Recchi broke the same tooth midway through the 2003-04 season when a slapshot in Boston deflected off a stick and into his mouth. But one of the scariest injuries in Recchi's career occurred later that same season when in a game in Carolina he needed more than 30 stitches to close two cuts in his neck from an opponent's skate blade.

"I knew it was around my neck and I got to the bench right away for them to take a look at it," he recalled. "There was no blood spurting so I knew it was no big deal. It took a while for them to stitch me, but I came back with 15 minutes left in third period."

Recchi boarded the team flight back to Philadelphia, but the cabin's air pressure loosened the stitches in his neck.

"A vessel wouldn't stop bleeding all night and all morning," Recchi said. "So, the next morning I got stitched up again. I needed eight or 10 more to make sure it was secure."

J.R.: JAW RECONSTRUCTION

Tracy Roenick was on a ski vacation in Aspen, Colorado with her two children when her cell phone rang a little before 10 p.m. on Feb. 12, 2004.

"Are you watching the game?" Flyers senior director of communications Zack Hill asked.

Tracy Roenick said she wasn't.

"Well, you might want to turn on ESPN," Hill said. "Jeremy's hurt."

Tracy Roenick immediately grabbed the remote and saw her husband lying motionless in a pool of his own blood, the victim of a slapshot to the face by New York Rangers defenseman Boris Mironov.

"What scared me the most was that Jeremy wasn't moving," Tracy Roenick recalled. "A million thoughts run through your head."

Among the first was whether her husband had played his final NHL game.

Roenick's career-threatening ordeal began late in the second period of the Flyers' 2-1 win in New York when he awoke to scarlet red ice shavings sticking to his lower lip. He wasn't sure of the severity of the injury until he was helped to his feet.

"I was coming off ice and Worls (Flyers trainer John Worley) had his hand on my jaw and I felt it shift," Roenick said. "I started passing out again."

As Roenick was helped off the ice he raised his hand in appreciation of the standing ovation he received from the Madison Square Garden crowd.

"I was so overwhelmed with the fans standing and cheering, I had to do something as I was going off the ice," Roenick said. "That's why I waved to them, my way of saying thank you.

"I thought the next morning that if I did retire, what a way to go out. Getting a standing O from (bleeping) Rangers fans. Now that would be (bleeping) impressive. It was one of the best feelings I've had as a pro athlete."

After being helped off the ice, Roenick was placed on a stretcher and taken to St. Vincent Hospital in Manhattan. Before he left, he insisted on taking off his hockey equipment and changing into sweat pants and sneakers. He also asked for his cell phone.

"Anybody that knows me knows I can't go anywhere without my cell phone," he said.

Roenick called Tracy to let her know he was OK and that he was leaving for the hospital.

"I just asked you not to get hit in the face anymore," Tracy said to her husband.

"I've got to stare at you every day. What am I going to do with you?"

"She was upset," Roenick said. "She was really nervous."

In the ambulance, Roenick asked repeatedly for something to drink but was denied.

"I was really thirsty because I swallowed a lot of blood," he said. "But they said I couldn't drink anything because I was going to need surgery. No water, nothing."

Roenick was in good spirits when he arrived at the hospital. In fact, when a nurse began gently wiping blood from his lip, he let out a big scream, just to see her reaction.

"She screamed and started jumping all over like she'd seen a dead man come alive," Roenick said with a laugh. "I was trying to lighten up the situation."

Roenick had broken the right side of his jaw in a 1999 collision with Derian Hatcher and knew he would require surgery to repair the left side. But it wasn't until he saw the X-ray that he realized the severity of his injury.

A series of fractures started in the left side of Roenick's chin and, like a crack in a windshield, spider-webbed all the way up to his ear line. The break was so extensive that the bone fragments needed to be sewn together.

"They took needle and thread and stitched all the pieces together," Roenick said.

A large steel plate was inserted at the point of the puck's impact and was secured with tension wires and screws.

Roenick left St. Vincent one day after the surgery and attended the Flyers' next home game just two days after the injury, receiving a standing ovation when he was shown on the JumboTron.

Roenick's first goal as a Flyer was reason to celebrate.
But a broken jaw in 2004 made him contemplate retirement.

"It's one thing to say you're OK," he said, "but it's another thing to let them see you and know you care. Hockey players are tough. They do things other people won't do."

A few days later, Roenick left for his home in Paradise Valley, Arizona, saying he did not want to be the center of a "media circus" in Philadelphia and be a distraction to his teammates.

Once he arrived in Arizona, Roenick visited Dr. Reed Day, the same surgeon who repaired his jaw five years earlier. In an X-ray, Day noticed that a piece of Roenick's jaw was protruding and that it would likely heal that way, leaving him with a facial deformity.

"So he said, 'J.R., I want you to push on it as much as you can,'" Roenick said. "I'm out with him having a cup of coffee. I'm sitting there and I'm pushing and pushing and all of a sudden it goes c-r-r-runch. I went, 'Holy (bleep)!' I said, 'Reed, Reed, my jaw just broke again.' I could feel all the pieces of bone move. It was a really weird feeling. I felt the whole thing shift. He said, 'It did? Good, that's the part I was telling you about. I think you just pushed it up.' He took an X-ray and, sure enough, I pushed it right up."

Although Roenick was able to manually rearrange his jaw like a jigsaw puzzle, it was his concussion symptoms that concerned him most. One week after the injury he was still experiencing severe nausea and dizziness and began talking about walking away from the game.

"I never believed it for one second," said Tony Amonte, who attended high school with Roenick at Thayer Academy in Boston. "I know Jeremy and hockey is all he knows. He wasn't ready to hang them up. He knew he had a chance to win a Stanley Cup ring and he wasn't going to pass it up."

To make sure his symptoms were not out of the ordinary, Roenick decided to visit the Barroughs Institute in Phoenix for neurological testing before flying back to Philadelphia the following day. Instead, a neurologist told Roenick to cancel his flight because a cloudy spot showed up on the MRI.

"What's that mean?" Roenick asked.

"Well, it could be a small aneurysm," Roenick was told.

Tracy Roenick had just left Phoenix for Philadelphia thinking her husband would join her the following day.

"I had to call her on the phone and tell her," Roenick said. "She cried for three days."

With an angiogram scheduled for a few days later Tracy Roenick flew back to Phoenix to be with her husband and discuss his future. Many of those discussions went long into the night.

"I can honestly say that it was the first time in 16 years I've truly seen him scared," Tracy Roenick said. "He was like, 'I gotta retire.' When the doctors told us it could be an aneurysm, Jeremy and I looked at each other like, 'It's over. It's definitely over.' It was the first time I ever saw that look on his face."

As if the days leading up to the Roenick's angiogram weren't painful enough, the actual procedure was worse. Roenick was sedated for 2? hours and was injected with a dye the doctors cautioned would feel very hot.

"The dye goes through you and it's like your face is burning off," Roenick said. "You feel fire going up through your head. Afterward, you have to lay six hours on your back and you can't get up.

"I had one of those headaches you read about. I just laid there for six hours rubbing my head. That last half hour I didn't take my eyes off that ... second hand rolling around."

The pain, Roenick said, was worth the news that followed. An unusually small artery leading to his brain had caused the shadow on Roenick's MRI. Doctors were uncertain if Roenick was born with the small artery or if it was the result of a head injury, but they agreed Roenick's brain stem, while abnormal, was functional.

That was all Roenick needed to hear. He booked a return flight to Philadelphia for March 1 to begin his rehab. Tracy, however, was not so eager to see her husband back in the line of fire of 100 mph slapshots.

"I knew the doctors in Philadelphia wanted to see him," Tracy said. "And I was worried they might pressure him into thinking he was good enough to play."

Roenick said the scene at the Phoenix airport could have been a goodbye scene from a bad movie.

"Tracy was saying, 'When is enough enough? When are you going to realize the next blow to your head is the next one that kicks off something bad? You've played 16 years and you've done a lot of good things. You don't have to go. You can stay here.'"

"She knew that if I got on that plane, I was going to play again. And that scared her."

Tracy said all she wanted was for her husband to be emotionally available to their children, who at the time were 9 and 6.

"It's been an awesome experience," Tracy said at the time, "but I have way more than 16 years to live with this guy. This might sound selfish, but I want to be with my husband when we're 80 and 90. I want him to be able to be with our kids' kids when he's 60 or 70. Of course, I want him to play. He wants to win a Stanley Cup. And believe me, if he had already won the Stanley Cup, I would have stomped my feet a little harder."

Roenick returned to the Flyers and after having the wires removed from his jaw, he began skating and ignoring the question every hockey player who has ever suffered a concussion faces.

"What if this happens again?" he wondered aloud. "It might happen again. But I might walk down the street, have a car run a red light and run me over. You can't let chances stop you from doing something you love.

"This is what I was born to do. I was born to play hockey. My wife knows I'm too competitive to walk away now. And that I want a championship worse than anything. I know there's more to life than winning a championship. So I gotta do what I was born to do. And that's play hockey. You just can't take that away from somebody when they're not ready. And I'm not ready yet, not with this team."

THIS AIN'T NO DISCO

From the rubble of Jeff Hackett's premature retirement emerged a guitar-picking, unshaven goaltender from upstate New York who loved country music and hated losing as much as anyone who ever wore the orange and black.

But it wasn't until the final weekend of the regular season that Ken Hitchcock decided Robert Esche and not Sean Burke, would be his playoff starter. Esche's engaging personality belied the fact that he had lived through some personal tragedies.

Five years before joining the Flyers Esche lost his older brother to suicide.

Esche was 16 when he left his home in Whitesboro, New York to play junior hockey near Ottawa. At the time, his parents' marriage was breaking up, affecting each of his four siblings in different ways.

Three years after Esche left home, his older brother, Eliot, a 22-year-old profes-

Having lost his brother, Robert Esche dedicated himself to hockey and became the Flyers' starter in 2004.

sional artist, hung himself. It was reported later that Eliot Esche suffered from clinical depression.

"I was trying to search for reasons why those things happened, trying to figure out why he did it," said Esche, who was 19 and playing in the Ontario League at the time of his brother's death. "But there are no reasons. That was his form of cancer, and that was the way he chose to go."

Esche said he began drinking "quite a bit" after his brother's death but somehow kept his focus on hockey and was taken by the Coyotes in the fifth round of the 1996 draft.

"Believe it or not, I was a big fan of Ron Hextall," Esche said. "I even used his Vic sticks because I wanted to handle the puck just like him."

Esche developed his game in Phoenix under the wing of Burke, a classic rock fan who roomed with Esche on the road. Burke had images of Eric Clapton and Jimmy Page painted onto his goalie mask and Esche copied the idea, having country-music greats Waylon Jennings and Hank Williams, Jr. painted onto his. He added cowboys on horseback along the chin line to identify himself with the Coyotes, then replaced them with the Philadelphia skyline as a Flyer.

"I'm just a redneck that likes country music," Esche said.

Every once in a while Esche would slip a Willie Nelson CD into the locker room stereo, only to have Roenick pop it out.

"There ain't no country-and-western stuff coming in here," shouted Roenick, who actually kept a disco ball in a locker room cabinet. "He can have it on his mask all he wants; it's not going to be on the radio, I'll tell you that."

SENATORS EAT THEIR LUNCH

The most penalty-filled game in NHL history occurred on March 5, 2004 at the Wachovia Center when the Flyers and Ottawa Senators slugged their way to record 419 penalty minutes.

But to get the whole story, you need to go back one week earlier to Feb. 26 when Senators forward Martin Havlat took a two-handed stick swipe at Mark Recchi's head during a 1-1 tie in Ottawa.

"He's cheap," Recchi said after that game. "And he's known for it. He does stupid things like that."

Ken Hitchcock went one step further when he promised Havlat would "eat his lunch" the next time the two teams met. As luck would have it, that opportunity came eight days later in Philadelphia.

When Havlat took his swipe at Recchi Flyers enforcers Donald Brashear and Todd Fedoruk were watching in street clothes with knee sprains. Brashear and

Ironically, one of the few players not involved in the penalty–filled fracas was the man who precipitated it, Martin Havlat.

Fedoruk, who had combined for 269 penalty minutes at that point, issued the Senators fair warning the day before the March 5 rematch, for which Havlat was being listed as questionable with the flu.

"The Philly flu?" Fedoruk asked with a laugh. "Guys get a little braver and play a little chippier when Brash and me aren't in the lineup. You'll see when we're in there how some guys shy away and are quiet."

Brashear warned that Havlat should not be the only Senator with his head on a swivel.

"They all have to watch over their shoulders," Brashear said.

Fedoruk sat out of the game, but as promised, the Flyers pounded the Senators on the scoreboard by taking a 5-1 lead, then participated in one of the wildest hockey brawls in decades.

Wth 1 minute, 45 seconds remaining and the game already decided, the following events took place:

Brashear bloodied the face of Senators enforcer Rob Ray with several overhand rights. As both fighters skated off the ice, Brashear shoved Ottawa defenseman Brian Pothier, and all hell broke loose.

"There has to be a big suspension for that," Senators center Jason Spezza said. "The linesman was taking him off the ice and (Brashear) suckered somebody. He was throat-slashing on the bench and saying things like, 'You're dead.'"

"I didn't sucker punch him," said Brashear, who received a double game misconduct for his shenanigans. "If I'd have sucker punched him, he would still be laying on his back."

Brashear's antics started an ugly chain of events.

Before you knew it, fights broke out all over the ice, and goalies Patrick Lalime and Robert Esche were no exceptions, although none of their punches landed with much force because of their bulky equipment.

Three seconds after all the sticks and gloves were picked up and order was restored, it happened again. Senators enforcer Chris Neil went after Radovan Somik in one fight, and Zdeno Chara hammered the Flyers' Mattias Timander in another.

"Neil had no business going after Somik," Recchi said of his passive teammate. "That's what set us off."

"Does that mean Chris Neil has to sit back and not touch anybody?" Ray wondered. "He had nobody else to fight. Once it gets in that condition, it's out of control anyway."

Brashear said Neil got awfully brave once he left the ice.

"When I was around him," Brashear said, "he wasn't saying a word."

Three seconds after those players were escorted off the ice it was Round 3. This time it was Michal Handzus taking on Ottawa's Craig Fisher.

Order was restored again, but it was obvious by now that the only thing missing was a ring girl holding up Round 4. Public address announcer Lou Nolan said every time he tried to announce a penalty, another fight broke out.

Esche joined in on the fun by fighting Ottawa goaltender Patrick Lalime amidst a sea of gloves.

"You just knew they were going to go again, and they did," he said. "That was unbelievable."

Twenty-four seconds after the next face-off, Recchi and John LeClair dropped the gloves and fired away at the heads of Bryan Smolinski and Wade Redden.

But wait, they still weren't done. Three seconds after the following face-off – ding, ding! - Flyers rookie Patrick Sharp punched up Spezza.

It was painfully clear after the third set of fights that messages were being sent by both Hitchcock and Ottawa coach Jacques Martin.

"That," Hitchcock said, "stays on the bench."

Which was practically empty. When the final horn sounded just three Flyers skaters were on the ice and three more were on the bench. The Senators were down to three skaters and two subs. And who was safely tucked in the penalty box while all of this knuckle-chucking took place? Martin Havlat, who was serving Lalime's fighting major.

Bob Clarke was so incensed after the game he called Martin a "gutless puke" and issued this warning: "They have to come in here one more time. They won't be able to hide (Daniel) Alfredsson and (Marian) Hossa and all those guys then."

When all was said and done, the Flyers set a club record with 213 penalty minutes and the Senators set their own team mark with 206 penalty minutes. Brashear was the most penalized player in the game, racking up 34 minutes in the sin bin.

Brashear's busy night fell well short of the NHL record set by Kings enforcer Randy Holt, who received 67 penalty minutes in a game on March 11, 1979. Dave Schultz holds the NHL record for penalty minutes in a playoff game. He served 42 minutes with two fights, an elbowing minor, a 10-minute misconduct and two game misconducts in an 8-5 playoff loss to the Maple Leafs on April 22, 1976.

P.O'D IN T.O.

After disposing of the New Jersey Devils in five games in the 2004 Conference Quarterfinals, the Flyers returned to Toronto for the second straight spring and the rabid puckheads in T.O. were waiting for revenge.

A Toronto radio station muddied the line between humor and gamesmanship when radio host Todd Shapiro encouraged a listener to bang on the hotel room door of Esche at 5 a.m., saying he ordered room service.

"I knew what was going on, so I didn't even bother answering it," Esche said. "I put the Do Not Disturb on the phone and they still patched it through. Childish, but it's actually funny when you look at it."

Ed Snider and Bob Clarke didn't find it amusing. Snider called it a "disgrace" and Clarke called it "harassment."

Roenick had a similar incident happen to him the previous year in Toronto, but he looked through his door's eye hole to see someone holding a plant. He quickly filled a bucket of water from his hotel room sink and threw it on the unsuspecting prankster.

Shapiro's antics were not confined to the Flyers' hotel. He followed Ken Hitchcock and his assistants, Craig Hartsburg and Wayne Fleming, into a Tim Horton's doughnut shop and ridiculed the Flyers coach over a bullhorn live on radio.

"He just burst in and started yelling at them and tried to sit at their table," Clarke said.

Hitchcock was also verbally abused by a rabid Maple Leafs fan as he made his way from the Air Canada Centre to the team hotel a block away.

"A car pulled over to him and this idiot sticks his head out and screams, 'You're lucky you weren't walking in the road, you (bleep), or you would have been run over,'" Clarke said.

ONE HAPPY KAPPY

In 311 career games with the Flyers Sami Kapanen recorded 44 goals and 66 assists, but the true measure of the 5-foot-nothing winger from Vantaa, Finland came in Game 6 of the 2004 Eastern Conference Semifinals when he recorded his gutsiest assist as a Flyer.

With the score tied in overtime and the Flyers trading scoring chances with the Maple Leafs in Toronto, Kapanen, who volunteered to play defense in place of the injured Vladimir Malakhov, pinched along the right wing boards and kicked the puck ahead just before Darcy Tucker crashed into him at full speed.

Kapanen fell to the ice, then looked like a disoriented fan who had just participated in a spin-around bat race at a minor-league baseball game.

On his first attempt to get up, Kapanen dropped his stick and fell

Sami Kapanen's dazed return to the bench in Game 6 in Toronto led to Jeremy Roenick's overtime game winner.

to his knees. On his second attempt he staggered in the wrong direction, his back to the bench, and fell again. Finally, with the help of teammate Keith Primeau's stick, Kapanen managed to gain enough equilibrium to crawl over the boards and into the arms of trainer John Worley.

"We were screaming at the ref to blow the whistle," Primeau said. "We wanted a stoppage. The most dangerous thing is you don't know how bad Sami's hurt."

Kapanen's ability to get back to the bench actually allowed Roenick and Tony Amonte to break in on a 2-on-1 on Eddie Belfour. Roenick used Amonte as a decoy and ripped a shortside shot over Belfour's glove to send the Flyers to the Conference Finals.

While Roenick danced his way into the arms of 18 of his overjoyed teammates, Kapanen bobbed from side to side on the Flyers bench, his head still spinning from one of the most vicious checks you'll ever see at a hockey game.

"You're thinking right away, 'Blow it dead! Blow it dead! The guy's hurt!'" John LeClair said. "But Kappy sucked it up, went to the bench and it ended up being the difference. The guy's got a huge heart."

Thirty minutes after the game a surprisingly lucid Kapanen said he saw Tucker coming, but wanted to kick the puck into the offensive zone before taking the hit.

"It was that reason I got the blow to my head," he said. "Even though it is the playoffs I thought that was a charge, but there was no call. Enough is enough. Even in overtime there has to be some kind of rules. The refs looked the other way."

As for getting back to the bench, Kapanen said, "I just knew I wanted to get back on the bench because I knew my legs were not carrying me at that time."

Kapanen composed himself enough to participate in the post-game handshake, but said nothing to Tucker as the two shook hands.

"And he didn't say one thing either," Kapanen said.

For the second year in a row the Flyers had ended the Maple Leafs' season.

"There's nothing like seeing that team have to shake hands with us on their home ice," Esche said. "Two down, two to go."

CAPTAIN FANTASTIC

Keith Primeau will best be remembered in Philadelphia for two heroic feats – scoring the game-winner in the fifth overtime in Pittsburgh in the 2000 Conference Semifinals and being an absolute force in the Flyers' failed bid to reach the 2004 Stanley Cup Finals.

Primeau entered those 2004 playoffs having missed 28 games of the regular season because of a broken thumb and a concussion, limiting him to just seven goals and 15 assists as a checking-line center.

But in the post-season, he was Captain Fantastic. After leading the Flyers to a surprisingly easy five-game waltz over the Devils and telling his teammates to "jump on for the ride" during the Conference Semifinals, Primeau was at his dominating best against the Tampa Bay Lightning in the Conference Finals.

In Game 4, with the Flyers trailing the series two games to one, Primeau was a 6-foot-5, 220-pound wrecking ball, hitting the Lightning with thunderous checks, setting up John LeClair's game-tying goal in the first period and scoring the game winner with a short-handed breakaway midway through the second. The Flyers prevailed 3-2 and teammates marveled at Primeau's transformation.

Phil Esposito called Keith Primeau's playoff performance in 2004 the most dominating he had ever witnessed.

"He was a one-man wrecking crew," observed Kapanan.

Hitchcock compared Primeau's development as a leader to some of the game's greatest captains.

"It's where (Steve) Yzerman went. It's where (Derian) Hatcher went. It's where (Mark) Messier went. It's where (Mike) Modano went," Hitchcock said. "You gotta go there. You gotta give up yourself."

Even irascible Lightning coach John Tortorella was rendered speechless by Primeau's Game 4 performance.

"I'm not talking about Keith Primeau," Tortorella said in his post-game press conference. "If you have a question about my team, I'll be more than happy to talk to you about that."

Three nights later in Tampa the Flyers fell behind in the series for the third time when the Lightning scored a 4-2 victory in Tampa setting a must-win Game 6 at the Wachovia Center.

Again, Primeau rose to the occasion.

With the Flyers' season 109 seconds away from extinction, Primeau used his long wingspan to tuck a Mattias Timander rebound past Tampa goaltender Nikolai Khabibulin for his ninth goal of the playoffs.

By scoring the goal, his second of the game, Primeau became the first NHL player with 100 or more playoff games (there were 234 of them at the time) to score as many goals in one playoff season — nine in 17 games — as he had in his entire playoff career — nine in 110 games.

But Primeau's work was not done.

In a pressure-packed overtime period dominated by the Flyers, Primeau dug a puck out of the corner and pushed it toward Roenick, whose jam attempt caromed out to Gagne, who fired a shot off Khabibulin and into the net.

Gagne's goal came at 10:49 p.m. and the resulting explosion of 19,910 fans in orange T-shirts shook the Wachovia Center to its core.

"I played in buildings in the past at this time of year where people go south on you when things start to get hard," Primeau said. "Tonight they rallied and they stayed right with us. I wish we could take all 20,000 with us to Tampa."

The Flyers' dream of going to the Stanley Cup Finals for the first time since 1997 ended two nights later in Tampa in a crushingly close 2-1 loss in front of a record crowd of 22,117 at the St. Pete Times Forum.

"I think we emptied the tank in Game 6," Hitchcock explained in a quiet voice. "They won a lot of board battles and we weren't able to sustain our normal pressure. We had a lot of people who emptied it to get where we got. Those are the risks you take when you have to mount comebacks all the time. We had to mount a furious comeback in Game 6, and we paid for it in 7."

For the veteran core of players in the twilights of their careers – LeClair, Roenick, Recchi, Kapanen and Primeau — the pain of the Game 7 loss still lingers.

"There was no better shot than that year," said Roenick, who went his entire 21-year career without ever winning a Stanley Cup. "That's why it hurt so much."

Primeau, who finished the series with four goals and four assists in seven games and led the Flyers in playoff goals (nine) and points (16), said he tried to find something left inside of him for Game 7, but did not find much.

"I didn't get it done tonight," he said in a solemn dressing room, "so this one will stay with me for a while and haunt me. "We needed everything tonight and it wasn't there. We thought we had enough. We thought that somewhere, somehow, some way we were going to find a way. That we'd kick in a goal if we had to. Tonight it didn't fall."

After the game, Lightning general manager and Hockey Hall of Famer Phil Esposito paid Primeau the highest of compliments, saying Primeau's performance was the most dominating he had ever seen in a playoff series.

"More than Orr, Howe, Gretzky, or anyone."

Three weeks later, the Flyers rewarded their 32-year-old captain with a four-year, $17 million contract.

"I don't think you have any chance of being good without top leadership and Keith is a great leader on this club," Clarke said. "The players that are around him respond to Keith. His on-ice performance was obviously above anybody else in the playoffs. Had we made it to the Stanley Cup Finals he would probably have won the Conn Smythe Trophy as MVP of the playoffs."

The Flyers could not have imagined then that Primeau would play in just nine games after signing that contract.

WAITING FOR RICO

He will go down as one of the best all-around defensemen in team history, but it seemed whenever the Stanley Cup was within the Flyers' reach, injuries kept Eric Desjardins at arm's length.

Four games into the 2003 playoffs Desjardins fractured his foot and missed the final eight games of the playoffs.

The following season, Desjardins fractured his right forearm in a January collision with teammate Jeremy Roenick and Maple Leafs center Mats Sundin and had a steel plate inserted that was expected to allow him to return for the playoffs.

Desjardins returned to the lineup for the final three games of the regular season, but after taking a series of hard slapshots after practice he began feeling pain.

"I'm listening to the radio and they're saying I hurt myself having a catch with my son," Desjardins said later that same day. "It makes me look irresponsible. That's not what happened."

Not exactly, anyway. Desjardins said that after he returned home from practice he tossed a baseball with his 6-year-old son, Jakob, and when he reached to catch the ball, his wrist bent and he felt another twinge of pain. He went inside his house and reached to put something on a shelf and when he felt another sharp pain, he realized something was seriously wrong.

"I could feel the bone was moving, I didn't want to believe it at first," Desjardins said. "I asked my wife (Manon) to look at it and she told me to call the doctor and have X-rays. That's how I found out the plate had given. The X-ray showed my bone was completely broken in half."

Dr. John Taras, who performed the original surgery in January, said he told Bob Clarke that if a plate had not been used, it would have taken five or six months for Desjardins' bone to completely heal and that the decision to insert a plate carried with it the risk of re-injury.

Desjardins underwent a second surgery to stabilize his forearm and missed the entire 2004 playoffs. He was, however, prepping for a return if the Flyers advanced to the Stanley Cup Finals.

"I was very disappointed," Desjardins recalled. "Especially with the way the team was playing and the chance we could go all the way. I wanted to be part of something special."

They didn't and Desjardins played just one more season with the Flyers before retiring at the age of 37.

ARMAGEDDON ON HORIZON

Following their third-round exit from the playoffs, Flyers chairman Ed Snider took a look at the two teams left standing – the Tampa Bay Lightning and Calgary Flames – and wondered if spending $70 million on his club's payroll was worth it.

The Lightning and Flames had payrolls in the $35 million range and with a potential NHL labor dispute brewing, Snider knew it was time to start playing hardball with his players.

"The two teams surviving are teams that don't have gigantic payrolls, teams that didn't sign free agents," Snider said. "We have to look at that and say, hey, let's look at ourselves. That is not an indictment of Bob Clarke. It's just the facts. Those two teams are doing it with younger players."

The Flyers certainly had a mountain of over-aged, over-priced veterans. John LeClair was 35 with two years and $18 million remaining on his contract; Jeremy Roenick was 34 with two years and $15 million remaining; and Tony Amonte was 33 with two years and $11.6 million remaining.

Primeau announced he wanted every one of his teammates back for another run at the Cup, "but I also know the reality of professional sports and the reality of the Collective Bargaining Agreement. We just never know where we'll come out on the other side."

When the clock struck midnight on Sept. 15, 2004, the NHL officially locked its doors, closing business for what would amount to an entire season.

Stating that 20 of the league's 30 teams lost a total of $340 million the previous season, NHL commissioner Gary Bettman said the league would remain suspended until the players' union accepted some form of salary cap that would reduce the average player salary from $1.8 million to $1.3 million.

The players weren't accepting it.

"We have to get to the point where the owners are willing to negotiate and not try to force a $31 million salary cap down our throats," Primeau said.

Said Amonte, "We're prepared for the worst."

HELLO FOPPA, GOODBYE J.R.

When the NHL's 2004 labor dispute dragged into 2005 and wiped out an entire season for the first time in league history, every team wondered how the work stoppage would impact its fan base.

The Flyers never imagined theirs was about to get an infusion of optimism. At the July 22, 2005 draft, which was belated because of the lockout, Bob Clarke told agent Don Baizley that if Peter Forsberg was interested in testing the free-agent market, the Flyers would be interested in having him.

One week later, when the free agent bell sounded at noon, the Blackhawks, Penguins and Rangers already had offers in to Baizley, who phoned Clarke and told him that if he was serious about signing Forsberg he better act quickly.

"We had from noon until 4 o'clock to clear some space under our $39 million cap," Clarke said.

Clarke immediately phoned Jeremy Roenick, who at $4.94 million represented the highest salary on the Flyers' payroll, and asked him if he'd accept a trade.

"I said, 'JR, give me your preference of teams. I may not be able to send you there, but let me know who you're interested in,'" Clarke said.

Roenick gave Clarke five teams he would play for — the Kings, Sharks, Coyotes, Mighty Ducks and Blackhawks — and encouraged him to make the deal for Forsberg.

With Baizley still waiting by the phone, Clarke called Ed Snider to see if he would approve the signing of Forsberg, even though a trade involving Roenick had not yet been made and Forsberg's salary would push the Flyers more than $2 million over the NHL's new $39 million limit.

"You know Mr. Snider," Clarke said with a smile. "He's got lots of balls and he took that gamble. He said, 'Sign Forsberg.'"

At the time, Snider said he had no idea the Flyers were even interested in the 32-year-old Swede.

"I was stunned," he said. "Bob did a masterful job. He was under the gun and we decided to take the gamble. In the final analysis, things like this only happen once in a lifetime."

Once Clarke and Baizley agreed on a salary for Forsberg — $11.5 million over

Fourteen years after being drafted by the Flyers, Peter Forsberg reunited with the club as a free-agent.

two seasons — the final decision came down to Forsberg, who was taken by the Flyers with the sixth pick of the NHL draft 14 years earlier.

"It's a great organization, and as soon as I heard they called I got pretty excited," Forsberg said. "I was happy it worked out." Roenick, who was sent to the Kings for future considerations, wasn't quite sure how to feel. Two weeks earlier he had tried talking the Flyers into keeping him for the final year of his contract.

"My heart hurt," said Roenick, who recorded 67 goals and 106 assists for 173 points in 216 games with the Flyers. "It was a tough place to leave because it's one of the best organizations in pro sports. They have the best owner (Ed Snider) in all of pro sports. It hurt a lot.

"But when asked to help out the Flyers, I had to oblige. They had done nothing but wonderful things for me. Clarkie went out of his way to make sure I was well taken care of. That's something you don't get in professional sports. Usually, when you're traded, it's 'Thank you and have a nice day.' Clarkie went out of his way to get me to a place I wanted and for that I will be grateful forever."

Despite their differences, some of them public and some behind closed doors, Hitchcock said he appreciated Roenick for everything he gave the Flyers in three seasons.

"He was a warrior," Hitchcock said. "When I look back, I really appreciate what he brought to the ice."

Roenick said the feeling was mutual.

"He taught me how to be a complete player," Roenick said. "He taught me how to overcome a lot of mental adversity. Even though it seemed like we butted heads all the time, my respect for him is immense. He was hard on me and it made me a better player."

TEN–HUT!

When the Flyers opened their 2005 training camp, 13 players who participated in their thrilling playoff run in 2004 — forwards John LeClair, Mark Recchi, Jeremy Roenick, Tony Amonte, Alexei Zhamnov, Todd Fedoruk, Radovan Somik and Claude Lapointe, defensemen Vladimir Malakhov, Marcus Ragnarsson, Mattias Timander and Danny Markov and goaltender Sean Burke — were no longer with the club.

Replacing them were forwards Peter Forsberg, Jeff Carter, Mike Richards, Mike Knuble, Turner Stevenson and Jon Sim, free-agent defensemen Derian Hatcher, Mike Rathje and Chris Therien and goaltender Antero Niittymaki.

With so many new faces, Ken Hitchcock scheduled a two-day visit to the U.S. Military Academy in West Point, New York, where the Flyers went through the paces of a true military unit. Players ate meals together in a dining hall, ran in place together while holding M-14s in front of them, and heard real-life war stories that made their own sacrifices seem trivial.

The story that most resonated in their hearts and minds was that of cadet Derrick Hines, a young man some of them had met during their tour of the U.S. Military Academy two years earlier.

Hines, an Army Ranger and an alternate captain on the Army hockey team, was killed during a gunfight with insurgents in Baylough, Afghanistan, on Sept. 1. He was 25. According to his hockey coach, Brian Riley, Hines kept firing at insurgents after taking a bullet that proved fatal.

Donald Brashear, who had met Hines two years earlier, said the Flyers left West Point with this message: "No matter who you are, no matter what size you are, no matter what your personality is, we need you. One or two or three guys isn't enough. We need a little part of everybody to be successful."

WHAT'S A CONCUSSION?

Many believed that with Forsberg, Richards, Primeau and Michal Handzus, the Flyers were deeper down the middle than any team in the NHL. That, and the course of their season, all changed when Montreal Canadiens rookie Alexander Perezhogin caught Primeau with an elbow to the head.

Primeau played two more games on the Flyers road trip, but when the headaches he experienced throughout the lockout year returned, the Flyers shut him down.

"I thought maybe it was just dragging a lit bit," said Primeau, who was 33 at the time. "But I was deteriorating and not getting better."

The concussion was the fourth documented brain injury of Primeau's career, but he estimated his actual number of concussions was far greater.

"How many have I had? " he asked. "If you look since I've been playing when I was 5, a hundred? In all honesty, I love when I hear J.R. has had 11 documented concussions. Documented? C'mon. In talking with other guys in the last 15 or 18 months, it's not just one hit (that results in a concussion). Look back at the tapes of the last 80 to 100 games and every time that player gets hit or gives a hit, he's rattling his brain. It's a constant pounding."

With Primeau sidelined indefinitely, the Flyers recalled R.J. Umberger and relied heavily on Richards and Carter to play big minutes as rookies. The two newest members of the Flyers had led the Phantoms to a Calder Cup title the previous spring – Carter with 23 points in 21 playoff games and Richards with 15 points in 14 playoff games.

Hitchcock demanded more of the same.

"He was on them and I think he wanted to make them tougher," Derian Hatcher recalled. "He might yell at me for a second or two, but he would yell at Richie or Carts for 10 seconds. It was tough on them and it definitely made us uncomfortable.

Ken Hitchcock's abrasive style with rookies Mike Richards and Jeff Carter often rubbed his veterans the wrong way.

"That was Hitch. What he believed in was the way we were going to do it. You could go in and talk to him and say, 'Let's try this.' But at the end of the day he was sticking to what he believed. He was very staunch. He wanted the perfect game. We all know there is no such thing as a perfect game, but that's what he expected."

DEUCES ARE WILD

When Hitchcock assembled a top line of Peter Forsberg (No. 21) between Simon Gagne (No. 12) and Mike Knuble (No. 22) the print media fumbled around in an attempt to come up with a great nickname for the explosive trio.

Through their first 12 games, Forsberg (4 goals, 21 assists), Gagne (15 goals, 8 assists) and Knuble (7 goals, 7 assists) piled up 62 points, putting themselves on pace for a 424-point season.

To put that into perspective, the LCB Line of Reggie Leach, Bobby Clarke and Bill Barber set the club record with 322 points in 1975-76. And the Legion of Doom of Eric Lindros, John LeClair and Mikael Renberg was next with 255 points in 1995-96.

"It's a long way to keep up this pace the whole season," said Gagne, who at the time was on pace for 101 goals. "I guess if we try to give our best every night, you never know what could happen."

After a few fruitless attempts – the "Three Nations Line" and the "Foppa Express" didn't make the cut – the Forsberg-Gagne-Knuble line was dubbed Deuces are Wild and the Flyers marketing staff jumped at the opportunity for a giveaway night, handing out black ties decorated with aces, deuces and Flyers logos.

Through 21 games Forsberg, Gagne and Knuble had accounted for 44 percent of the Flyers' offense and Forsberg was tied with Jaromir Jagr with a league-best 39 points. However, groin injuries to Forsberg and Gagne kept the line apart for more than a month, erasing any possibility of catching either the Legion of Doom or the LCB lines. Gagne (47 goals) and Knuble (34 goals) finished with career-high goal totals, while Forsberg netted a team-high 56 assists. By season's end the Deuces had combined for a respectable 219 points.

SID THE KID

As part of a classroom assignment when he was attending elementary school in Cole Harbour, Nova Scotia, Sidney Crosby wrote a letter to the Philadelphia Flyers asking for a few autographed photos and hockey cards.

Much to his delight, they appeared in his mailbox a few weeks later.

Crosby's love and appreciation for the Flyers ended in his first visit to Philadelphia on Nov. 16, 2005 when players and fans chided him.

"I'd lean over the bench and say to him,' 'You know what, Sidney? Even your teammates hate you,'" Chris Therien recalls. "He'd look at me like, 'Wow, I hope that's not true.'"

Derian Hatcher left Crosby with a lasting reminder of his first visit to South Philly when he stuck him in the mouth, sawing off three of his front teeth and turning his coverboy smile into a box of Chiclets.

Crosby fell to the ice and curled into a fetal position and since there was no call on the play, everyone in the Wachovia Center mocked him with chants of "SID-NEY!" When Crosby showed the referee his bloody mouth it was clear Hatcher had sent a message to the precocious rookie.

But after a Flyers doctor sewed up Crosby's lip, the 5-11, 200-pounder went right back at the 6-foot-5, 235-pound veteran and drew a penalty, only to negate it with his own unsportsmanlike penalty for complaining to the referee.

The front of his jersey still stained with blood, Crosby came back to score two goals that night, including the game-winner in overtime for a 3-2 Penguins victory.

Just like that, Crosby became the youngest sports villain in Philadelphia history.

WHO WANTS TO BE A CAPTAIN?

Once it appeared clear Primeau would not be returning to the lineup, Hitchcock approached Simon Gagne and twice asked him to take over the Flyers' captaincy. Each time, once in late November and again in late December, Gagne refused.

"It would be an honor to be captain of this organization," Gagne said at the time. "But right now, I look around and see some different people having more experience than I do, guys who have been there before. I have two persons in front of me: Rico (Eric Desjardins) and Hatch. Those two guys were, in my mind, the best persons to have that job. That was something I wasn't comfortable with."

By late January the Flyers were in a 2-5-2 tailspin that included a somnambulant 6-0 loss to the Lightning and Bob Clarke wasn't happy. He called Primeau into his office and asked him to surrender his captaincy, at least temporarily, to Derian Hatcher.

"He said that the team is kind of a lost ship at sea right now and kind of floundering and we need some direction," Primeau said of his conversation with Clarke. "As good as the guys have been to find ways to win hockey games, right now we're at a tough patch and we need that direction."

Clarke and Hitchcock decided Hatcher would be the 13th captain in Flyers history and named Gagne and Sami Kapanen permanent alternate captains.

Derian Hatcher was not enthusiastic about accepting the Flyers' offer to replace Peter Forsberg as captain.

"They asked me and I said fine," Hatcher said. "It's not that I didn't want it, but there was a lot of stuff going on at the time. Preems was hurt and I was Hitch's captain in Dallas and in my mind there was a lot of B.S. going on. I didn't want to be perceived by my teammates as Hitch's guy. I took it and we lost in the first round of the playoffs, so there you go."

Primeau, who was named captain during the 2001-02 season, made it clear that transferring his "C" to Hatcher did not mean he was giving up on returning.

"The team is more important than my pride at this time," he said. "It's the right decision. Hatch is a strong person and he'll demand a lot from the guys. That's what we need right now."

FORSBERG VS. SNIDER

Two weeks before the 2006 Winter Olympics in Turin, Italy, Peter Forsberg was sidelined with a groin injury and Robert Esche (groin) and Joni Pitkanen (sports hernia) were coming off the injured list.

Realizing that sending all three players to the three-week tournament could increase the threat of re-injury and jeopardize his team's chances in the playoffs, Ed Snider made a public plea for all three to stay home.

"I'm a believer in the Olympics and I think it's good for the NHL to participate in them," Snider said. "Having said that, the people who participate should be the ones who are absolutely healthy.

"Peter Forsberg, for example, isn't absolutely healthy. Esche and Pitkanen just got back from serious injuries and the Olympics are just around the corner. Peter is under tremendous pressure in Sweden and I understand that, he's their top player. I feel bad for Peter, but if he was my son, I would tell him to just say no."

Forsberg had other ideas. He hoped that by returning to the Flyers' lineup two games before the Olympics, he'd quiet all of the concerns by Snider. But when his injury lingered right up to the Olympic break, Snider put his foot down again.

"It would be ridiculous for him to play in the Olympics," Snider said.

Five days later, Forsberg boarded a flight for Italy.

"I'm going to fly over and see how it goes," he said. "It's still not 100 percent and I'm going to rest a few more days and see how it goes."

Snider, who doesn't often lose such battles, was left no choice but to cross his fingers.

"Listen, he's a pro and I don't want to put any more pressure on him than he already has. I think Peter is a professional and I'm sure he'll handle things properly. He'll make his decision in the best interests of himself and the Flyers."

Forsberg wasn't the only Flyer to defy Snider's wishes. Esche also made the trip to Turin, joining healthy teammates Derian Hatcher and Mike Knuble (Team USA), Simon Gagne (Team Canada), Antero Niittymaki (Team Finland) and Michal Handzus (Team Slovakia).

Pitkanen and Sami Kapanen removed themselves from Team Finland because of nagging injuries and Kim Johnsson told Team Sweden he would not play because of the impending birth of his second child.

After defying the Flyers, Forsberg defied logic by playing in six Olympic games and recording six assists, including the gold medal game-winner by Nicklas Lidstrom. After the gold medal victory, which came at the expense of Finland goaltender Niittymaki, Forsberg and his teammates flew to Stockholm and joined in an all-night celebration before catching a flight to New York and joining the Flyers for a game against the Devils at the Meadowlands.

"It was fun," Forsberg said. "It was a short amount of time there, but it was great. It was good getting back there and seeing the support."

Asked if his gold medal vindicated his controversial decision to play in the Olympics, Forsberg credited Sweden coach Bengt Gustafsson for his patience in waiting for him to be healthy.

"I couldn't ask for anything more," Forsberg said. "I came back healthy and I came back a winner."

NITTY OR ESCHIE?

While Robert Esche served as a backup for Team USA, Antero Niittymaki returned from Turin as a silver medalist and the tournament's MVP with three shutouts.

That turned the Flyers' goaltending picture, already fuzzy to begin with, even more blurry.

"I know you guys are dying for there to be the goaltending controversy of old,"

Esche said, referring to either the Ron Hextall-Garth Snow duel of 1997 or the Brian Boucher-Roman Cechmanek battle of 2002.

"I can't go out there and cut the guy's skate laces or go out there and slash the guy's tires. The truth of the matter is you're either going to win or you're not."

PREEMS CALLS IT A SEASON, OR DOES HE?

While the Flyers battled for playoff position in the final two weeks of the 2005-06 season, Keith Primeau battled with himself over whether to return to the lineup despite persistent concussions symptoms.

On March 30, after skating with teammate Kim Johnsson, who was also sidelined with a concussion, Primeau denied a radio report that he was attempting a comeback, saying, "At this time, I can unequivocally state, 100 percent, that I am not returning for the playoffs."

He must have consulted with a linguistics lawyer, because "at this time" tends to change by the minute.

Eleven days later Primeau participated in his first full practice with the Flyers and said, "Obviously, I feel better than I have. It's a huge hurdle for me and I feel really good. By no means does it change anything that I stated earlier. I'm just taking it one day at a time."

Four days after that, Primeau seemed resigned to call it a season. "It's just too dangerous," he said. "Besides that, when I took on this challenge, I promised my family I wouldn't play unless I was a hundred percent. I just don't think I'm capable of a hundred percent."

And, one day before the end of the regular season, Primeau came off the ice and gave this report: "I feel not bad today, so I'm in a good mood. I can't say it's been that way over the last two or three days, but I'm just trying to push through it. I'm trying to put myself in a position where I can be as close to being ready as I can. If that's one week or two weeks or four weeks or six, I just hope they're still playing when I get the chance."

They weren't, and he didn't.

With Forsberg playing on a sore groin and Johnsson and Primeau sidelined with concussions, the Flyers could not keep up with the faster Buffalo Sabres in the first round of the playoffs, getting outscored 27-14 in the series, including a 7-1 drubbing at home in the sixth and deciding game.

As the final minutes ticked off the clock, fans who stuck around to witness the wake-in-progress amused themselves with chants of "Bob (Clarke) Must Go!" and "E-A-G-L-E-S!"

"That was probably the single most embarrassing moment I've had in my career," said Hatcher, who along with Mike Rathje looked like statues compared to the speedy Buffalo forwards.

Mike Knuble agreed.

"If it's a heartbreaker in overtime, that's one thing," Knuble said. "But 7-1? It's really tough to sit there and send our fans home and watch the building half empty with 15 minutes left in the game."

One day after the lopsided loss, which matched the worst home defeat in the club's playoff history, Ed Snider wanted answers on how a team that recorded 101 points could be so badly outplayed in a first-round playoff series.

"I've asked for written reports from our key people and I'll be prepared to answer at a later date," Snider said when asked if the Flyers made gross miscalculations by building a team too slow to compete in the new NHL, where a premium is placed on speed.

Snider said he was as "shocked" by the Flyers' season-ending performance as the 19,967 fans witnessed it.

"The only difference between me and the fans is I couldn't leave early," Snider said.

CHAPTER 12

WORST TO FIRST?

(2006–PRESENT)

From the ashes of the worst season in club history arise
a new general manager and a brash, young team led
by throwback captain Mike Richards.

SUMMER BEFORE THE SWOON

THE SUMMER OF 2006 BEGAN WITH PETER FORSBERG NEEDING
radical surgeries on both feet and ended with the retirements of Eric Desjardins
and Keith Primeau. It also marked the beginning of the end of Bob Clarke's man-
agerial career.

In his post-season news conference Clarke faced a rash of criticism for com-
mitting $24.5 million to a pair of slow-footed, 6-foot-5, 235-pound defensemen
whose best playing days were behind them.

Clarke blamed the "new NHL" for contributing to the Flyers' problems, saying
the crackdown on stick infractions had neutralized the strength of his team.

"Do we have some problems that have to be addressed? Of course," Clarke
said. "But the Sabres knew nothing more than we did until they got the letter in
training camp about how the game was going to be called. We certainly didn't have
time to make adjustments then. But we do this summer and we will."

Clarke also pointed out his team missed a combined 388 games because of injury in 2005-06 and despite the efforts of Hitchcock, never came together as one.

"We were a team without a personality," Clarke said. "We were just a bunch of
guys playing hockey. It falls on all of us: myself, Hitch. But I think the real cause of
it was so many different players every night."

FOPPA'S TWO LEFT FEET

Despite a radical surgery to reconstruct his foot, Peter Forsberg had trouble skating throughout the 2005–06 season.

Shortly after the Flyers' premature exit from the 2005 playoffs, Forsberg met with ankle specialist Robert Anderson in Charlotte, North Carolina and was told that his persistent groin problems were the result of abnormal arches in both feet, a condition he had lived with since childhood but could be corrected with reconstructive surgeries.

The 32-year-old center had been through 36 different pairs of skates the previous season and reluctantly agreed to have both feet broken, re-set and the ligaments tightened, even though the painful procedures would sideline him for the first half of the 2006-07 season.

"Not only do they have to tighten the tendons," Forsberg said, "my feet are crooked and they'll have to go in and crack the bones in my feet."

On May 15, Forsberg underwent a complicated three-hour procedure to modify the arch in his right foot and tighten the ligaments that were too loose to hold his foot in his skate boot. Two months later Forsberg talked his way out of having a similar surgery on his left foot and by the first week of September he was skating, three months prior to the original prognosis.

RICO'S TEARFUL GOODBYE

Eric Desjardins woke up on the morning of Aug. 10 and rehearsed the painful words he knew he needed to say. A few hours later, when he sat down in front of a dozen or so reporters on the second floor of the Skate Zone in Voorhees, New Jersey, he took a deep breath and began to cry.

"I had something prepared," he said, "but I didn't think it would be this hard. This is the hardest time I've ever had to meet you guys."

With Clarke by his side and former teammate John LeClair watching from a nearby hallway, Desjardins walked away from the game with the same class and dignity he showed in his 12 years as a Flyer.

"I just want to thank the Flyers for taking care of me and my family the way they did," Desjardins said between dabs of a tissue. "I want to thank the fans of Philadelphia. They've been really good to me for all these years."

At 37, Desjardins probably could have played one or two more seasons in the NHL and

turned down an offer to finish his career where it began, with the Montreal Canadiens. Seven major surgeries had taken their toll on him, both physically and emotionally, and he couldn't bear the thought of another lengthy rehab.

"You always try to come back to where you were, but it never comes back to the same level," he said.

Desjardins walked away from the Flyers with a record seven Barry Ashbee Trophies as the club's top defenseman and ranked second among all Flyers defensemen in scoring with 396 points in 738 games. Only Mark Howe recorded more points (480) and only Joe Watson (746) played in more games as a Flyers defenseman.

"He was one of our greatest players ever," Snider said. "He exemplified what a professional athlete should be and we will certainly miss his presence in the locker room."

PRIMEAU WALKS AWAY

Five weeks after Desjardins hung up his skates, Keith Primeau ended the second-longest concussion saga in team history when he reluctantly called it quits on Sept. 14, 2006.

"If not for (Flyers athletic trainer) Jim McCrossin, I'd still be trying to play," Primeau said recently.

With the 2006 training camp a week away and final rosters due on Oct. 1, Clarke wanted a definitive answer on Primeau's playing future and neither McCrossin nor Primeau could provide one.

"Jim said he wouldn't feel comfortable ever giving me clearance," Primeau said during a news conference to announce the end of his 16-year NHL career. "He couldn't live with the repercussions of me getting hit again."

Although the elbow by Alexander Perezhogin was the final blow for Primeau, he firmly believes the cumulative effects of multiple concussions – and his stubbornness to play through them — ultimately cost him his career.

The killer hit, he says now, came in Game 6 of the 2000 Eastern Conference

Semifinals in Pittsburgh. Forty-eight seconds after the opening faceoff, Penguins defenseman Bob Boughner spotted Primeau with his head down and dropped him like a 220-pound sack of rocks.

"He was out cold," recalled Simon Gagne, who was a rookie forward with the Flyers at the time. "I said to myself, 'There's no way he's coming back. He's done for at least two weeks.' The next day it was like it never happened."

Primeau spent that night in a Pittsburgh hospital, returned to Philadelphia the next day and talked his way into taking a baseline test. Remarkably, he passed.

"I just focused,' he said. "At the end of the day it was my call and I wanted to play."

Today, Primeau believes players are far more educated on brain injuries and their cumulative effects, yet still turn a blind eye during the playoffs.

"Unfortunately, I believe we've begun to digress," he said. "We almost have that gladiator mentality. Whether it's bravado or stupidity, I don't know. But we try to play at all costs."

Even now, Primeau is paying for his bravery, still experiencing light-headedness every times he exerts himself. It is one of the reasons he has agreed to donate his brain to the Sports Legacy Institute in an attempt to aid future studies on head trauma.

Primeau saw a story in the New York Times and followed that with numerous conversations with former WWE wrestler Chris Nowitzki, who founded SLI and is devoted to studying the brains of athletes that suffered from multiple concussions.

"If we're going to make a difference, we've got to start somewhere," Primeau said. "It's been pushed to the backburner, but the reality is the most vital organ in an athlete is the head."

Primeau said studies by the Sports Legacy Institute indicate a correlation between multiple concussions and premature death and he hopes that by donating his brain, scientists can better understand the effects of head trauma.

"I wish I was around to see what they find out," Primeau said with a laugh. "Hopefully, it's a long time from now."

CAPTAIN PETER

It didn't take long for the Flyers to transfer the "C" from Hatcher to Primeau to Forsberg. One day after Primeau announced his retirement, the Flyers introduced Forsberg as their 15th captain. The Flyers had wanted to make the announcement one day earlier, but the soft-spoken Forsberg, who had never been an NHL captain, asked for a day to consider.

Perhaps the idea of being the conduit between Ken Hitchcock and some restless teammates gave Forsberg pause for thought.

Or maybe it was the heavy reading requited for the job. Hitchcock had prepared for Forsberg a Commitment Code that outlined his responsibilities as a captain, addressing everything from setting a strong work ethic on the ice to organizing team functions off it.

"He'll be the one closest with the coach," Clarke said. "If there are problems in the locker room, he has to take care of them before they get to the coach. If he can't, he'll be the guy who talks to the coach about it."

It almost made you wonder if Clarke had sniffed out some underlying problems between his coach and his players. Regardless, Forsberg seemed excited.

"I'm definitely flattered and honored," he said. "It's something I definitely wanted to do. I have played a long time in the league and it's going to be great. It's a classy organization and I feel great about it."

'THE WHOLE DAMN TEAM STINKS'

When the Flyers assembled for the 2005-06 training camp, some of them arrived with real concerns about the team's makeup. Not only had they lost Desjardins and Primeau, Clarke's summer acquisitions were suspect as well.

Clarke added forwards Kyle Calder, Geoff Sanderson, Brad Tapper, Randy Robitaille, Mark Cullen, Daniel Corso and Boyd Kane and rolled the dice on defensemen Nolan Baumgartner, who had spent most of his pro career in the minors, and Swede Lars Jonsson.

"I think privately, guys new it going in," Derian Hatcher said. "No one ever says anything, because you're going to go out and play hard anyway. But we kind of knew we didn't have the players."

The Flyers looked lost in a season-opening 4-0 loss in Pittsburgh, but it was a 9-1 beating in Buffalo two weeks later that sent Ed Snider over the edge and ultimately led to Clarke's dismissal.

"We had an opening game and we weren't ready for it," Snider said, his blood beginning to percolate. "How can you not be ready for a season opener?

A 9–1 loss to the Buffalo Sabres put Ed Snider over the edge and triggered a massive organizational overhaul.

"And did you see last night's game?" Snider continued, now in a raging boil. "A performance like that will not be tolerated. More important, when a team is playing as bad as we are, how do you evaluate new talent when you can't evaluate old talent?

"The whole damn team stinks."

Snider later apologized for his biting comments, but there was no hiding from the truth. The Flyers had become a bad team and drastic changes were needed.

In his 40 years as chairman of the Flyers, Snider had shown unyielding support and loyalty to Clarke, both as a player and as a team executive. But the sight of that 9-1 drubbing in Buffalo put that loyalty to the test.

When asked if Clarke had assembled a team capable of winning in a faster, more skilled NHL, Snider replied with a terse, "No comment."

"I can tell you this," Snider said. "The only good part is that it's early in the season. If this was happening toward the end of the season, it would be horrible. But I'm going to get to the bottom of it and I'm going to fix it. This is just the start. I don't know how quickly we'll get out of this, but we will, because the buck stops here."

SUNDAY, BLOODY SUNDAY

On Sunday, Oct. 22, 2006, with the Flyers off to a 1-6-1 start, Snider orchestrated one of the most monumental purges in team history when a "burned out" Bob Clarke resigned as general manager and a "tuned out" Ken Hitchcock was fired as coach.

Clarke, who spent 35 years in the Flyers organization and parts of 19 seasons as a general manager, was replaced on an interim basis by assistant general manager Paul Holmgren. Hitchcock, who went 131-83-40 in parts of four seasons behind the Flyers bench, was replaced by assistant coach John Stevens, who led the Phantoms to a Calder Cup in 2005.

In a hastily called news conference at the Wachovia Center, Snider made it clear the firing of Hitchcock was a reflection of the team's record, but that Clarke's resignation was not.

"I personally am very fond of Ken Hitchcock. I think he's an outstanding coach," Snider said. "He's done wonderful things for this organization and it's very difficult to let a coach of his caliber go, especially under these circumstances. But I can assure you it wasn't done frivolously or without great thought and investigation."

Snider began his investigation by phoning Clarke, Holmgren and Hitchcock following the team's 9-1 loss to the Sabres. He said he learned in those conversa-

After 19 years as a general manager, Bob Clarke said he lost his zest for the job. "I don't know what happened to me, but it was time."

tions that players had tuned out Hitchcock and a change behind the bench was needed.

As for Clarke, he said he first entertained thoughts of walking away from the Flyers months earlier when he felt like a "bystander" at the NHL draft. He began asking Holmgren to make many of the moves he no longer wanted to make, like removing longtime equipment manager Turk Evers, who had been with the team for parts of three decades.

"I had enough of the daily grind," Clarke says now. "Twenty years is a long time to be doing what I did. It can get monotonous at times, like any type of business. I was avoiding anything controversial or anything I'd walk away feeling crappy about. I no longer wanted to fire people. It had just run its course with me. I don't know what happened to me, but it was time."

Clarke said he thought he would feel energized when the 2006-07 season started and when he didn't he brought his concerns to Flyers president Peter Luukko after the fourth game of the season.

"I've known Bob so many years and I was shocked," Luukko said. "But at the same time I thought that maybe he just wasn't happy about the way things were going with the team.

"In a way, it was typical Bob. Right or wrong, Bob always knows what he wants to do and he convinced me it was time. He's the ultimate Flyer, the ultimate warrior. And when Bob Clarke says it's time, it's time."

When it was suggested Clarke might have taken out of Snider's hands the hardest decision he'd ever have to make as Flyers chairman, Snider nodded.

"This is why I respect Bob Clarke so much," he said. "I have always known I would not have to fire Bob Clarke, that he would fire himself."

On that fateful Sunday, there was a finality in Clarke's voice, a sense that he was going out on his terms, never to return to his role as Flyers general manager.

"For me, it's been a privilege to work for the Flyers for this many years and I deeply regret not being able to win the Stanley Cup here," he said. "We've been to the Finals a number of times (1985, 1987, 1997) and we came close, but our responsibility is to try to win the Stanley Cup and I didn't deliver.

"I hope with a new face on the organization, and all the good young players that are on this team now and the ones coming up, this team will win the Stanley Cup. I think they will, but it won't be under my direction."

HITCHCOCK'S FAREWELL

While Snider, Luukko and Clarke were in Philadelphia saying Clarke's resignation was not tied to the dismissal of Hitchcock, Hitchcock was in Voorhees wondering if he'd still be coaching if Clarke had remained the team's general manager.

"I know what went on and I feel that's an unfair statement," Hitchcock said in a news conference he organized at the Wingate Inn across the street from the Skate Zone. "You can find people to say that anyplace, anywhere, anytime. But you have to look a lot deeper if you're willing to do it. I know exactly what went about and I knew how we were going to come out of it. And we ran out of time.

"I'm disappointed, but I'm tied to Clarkie and this is Homer's team now."

Several players faulted themselves for Hitchcock's firing and many disagreed with Snider's assessment that they tired of his message.

"I've heard people say we tuned him out, but I don't think so," Mike Knuble said. "He had an open door; it wasn't his way or the highway. You can't tune somebody out when they're actually listening to you like that."

Hatcher agreed with his former coach, saying Clarke's is what doomed him.

"Plus, I don't think Homer liked Hitch too much," Hatcher said.

HELLO, MR. CAMPBELL?

When Paul Holmgren was given an "interim" tag by Ed Snider on the day Bob Clarke resigned, he fully understood the implications. A search for a new boss of the Flyers would ensue and likely would result in him being out of work.

Maybe that's why Holmgren remained in his corner office overlooking the Phantoms practice rink while Clarke's office down the hallway remained vacant.

"I know the process that Mr. Snider and the organization are going through and no, I don't think it's awkward," Holmgren said. "That's part of the process and I'm fine with that."

That "process" included Snider calling NHL Director of Hockey Operations Colin Campbell and offering him the job of Flyers general manager. Campbell told a Canadian reporter about the Flyers' offer, leaving Snider angry and embarrassed.

"Colin recently contacted me to inform me that he appreciated our conversation, but at this time he did not want to be a candidate for the position," Snider said in a prepared statement. "Paul Holmgren will continue to be the interim general manager. There will be no other statements concerning this issue."

Holmgren made it clear he wanted the opportunity to prove he could manage the Flyers, but was resigned to the fact Snider wanted to move in a different direction.

"Would I like it to be under different circumstances? Absolutely," Holmgren said. "It's a big decision for Mr. Snider and the organization and I'm sure he wants to do what's right. The fact I'm in the position I'm in now to me is a statement that I can do it. He's just not sure if that's the way he wants to go yet and I'm OK with that. I don't think any assurances are necessary. We're all aware of what's going on. It's part of the business."

Despite his uncertain future Holmgren received unwavering support in the Flyers' dressing room, especially from captain Peter Forsberg, with whom he had established a strong relationship.

"I hope Homer stays put, but we'll see what happens," Forsberg said.

Sami Kapanen agreed.

"The interim part leaves the door open a little bit, but I think everyone here feels he's the one," Kapanen said. "I think everybody has the feeling that Paul is the one running the ship right now."

On November 11, 2006, three weeks after Clarke's resignation, Snider lifted the interim tag from Holmgren, saying he would remain the team's general manager through the remainder of the regular season. Three weeks later, Clarke returned as the Flyers' senior vice president.

"It was a tough decision that I made, but it was the right decision," Clarke said of relinquishing his managing duties. "But you still don't want to be left out of the team. The way it is now, whatever Paul wants me to do, I'll do. If he wants me to do scouting I'll do that. If he wants my opinion I'll offer it. But I'm not looking to do anybody else's job. I'm there if Paul feels he needs help."

Today, Clarke is perfectly happy in his advisory role with the Flyers but is not ruling out the possibility of someday returning to managing.

"I might want to go back, I'm not sure," he says. "If somebody came along and asked if I wanted to manage again I would certainly think about it. But last year was the first year in my life that if I wanted to go to Florida for a week I could. If I wanted to go skiing I could. When you're in this job you miss so much. It's 24/7, twelve months a year. You're getting texted on the golf course.

"(Former Bruins general manager) Harry Sinden said he went through the same thing. Is it burnout? I don't know what burnout actually is. But it's a tiredness you have. I could do it because I have the experience to do it. But I don't feel like it."

FOOTLOOSE FORSBERG

Any stability that might have been perceived by the re-hiring of Clarke and the temporary pat on Holmgren's back was uprooted by a hurricane of uncertainty surrounding Peter Forsberg.

Frustrated by a reconstructed right foot that felt like it belonged to someone else, the Flyers captain spent the entire 2006-07 season flying around the world in search of a glass slipper no one knew how to make.

He saw foot specialists in North Carolina, Ohio and Arizona and saw skate experts in Sweden, Montreal and Colorado. He tried wedges, inserts and ankle ribbing. Everything but Super Glue.

"It's not the skate, it's the foot," Forsberg said after sitting out the second half of a December practice. "The foot is definitely not a normal foot. That's the problem. It's functionally normal, but it does something weird."

Forsberg said his right foot felt as though it was pulling out of his skate and was preventing him from making the tight turns that he relied on as one of the game's best playmakers. And his numbers showed. Through his first 22 games in 2006-07 Forsberg had seven goals, nine assists and was a minus 6. At the same junction the year before he had nine goals, 31 assists and was a plus-14.

"It's tough when you can't do the things you want to do out there," he said. "I've had 400 turnovers and one takeaway."

His teammates, who were losing games whether their captain was in or out of the lineup, eventually grew tired of Foppa's foot follies.

"Anytime anyone's hurt, you just move on," Hatcher said. "But because it was Peter and he was trying new things every day, it kind of wore on us as a team. The whole season was miserable. It couldn't get any worse. It was the worst season I ever had playing. It just wasn't fun to come in."

In early February, Holmgren offered Hatcher an opportunity to escape the misery of a lost season, saying the Sharks, Red Wings and Ducks were interested in adding him before the NHL trade deadline.

"He asked if I wanted to be traded and I told him no," Hatcher recalled. "If you want to trade me, fine. But if you're asking me, my answer is no. It was a bad year, but at the time Homer had made a few deals and we started to play better. Just because we had a horrible year didn't mean we couldn't get better and I felt we could."

FORSBERG SENT PACKING

Every once in a while, a player comes along who makes everyone around him a better player. Perhaps that's why the Flyers tried so hard to keep Peter Forsberg, even though it seemed obvious it was time for him to go.

Before trading him to the Nashville Predators for Scottie Upshall, Ryan Parent and a pair of draft picks, Ed Snider, Paul Holmgren and Peter Luukko met with Forsberg in an attempt to convince him to stay in Philadelphia beyond the 2006-07 season.

"We all tried from different angles," Holmgren said. "We ganged up on him. We didn't want to do this deal, but we couldn't afford to not do it."

Forsberg met with Holmgren two days before the trade and gave him a list of teams he would agree to play for. His relationship with Predators forwards Paul Kariya and Darcy Hordichuk, along with Nashville's NHL-leading 39-16-3 record put the Music City at the top of his list.

Holmgren spent the next two days working the phones, but Snider wanted one more chance to convince Forsberg to stay.

"I was selling," Snider said. "It was a last-ditch effort."

Forsberg, who attended his own trade press conference, wasn't buying, saying he would not want to commit to another contract until he could resolve the issues with his foot.

"I have a lot of respect for Peter Forsberg. He has a lot of pride," Snider said. "He doesn't want to sign a contract just to sign a contract. He wants to know exactly what his future holds before he signs a contract with anybody and I respect that."

Forsberg left open the possibility of returning to Philadelphia once he became a free agent the following July.

"If they want me back, I'm going to hear from them and I would consider it," he said. "I liked it here. I had two of the best teammates I could ask for in Simon Gagne and Mike Knuble. I think we fit each other perfectly and it's really sad to leave them. If I was to look for a line in the future, I would love to play with them again."

Forsberg's former teammates said they would do anything to make that happen.

Said Gagne: "He swore to me that he was going to talk to the Flyers (this summer) and that might be the team he listens to first to see what they offer him."

And Knuble: "The door's always open. Come July 1st, I'm sure he'll be getting phone calls from Simon and I begging him to come back."

Hatcher admits that as much as he liked Forsberg, he didn't want him back the following season.

"He's a great guy and everyone liked him," Hatcher said. "But it was turn-the-page time. We knew this was the team we were moving ahead with."

One person in the Wachovia Center who did not believe Forsberg would ever return to the Flyers was Neil Smith. The former New York Rangers general manager Neil Smith, who was working as a scout for the Dallas Stars, said Forsberg would never return to a team so far from playoff contention.

"I would be surprised if Forsberg re-signed with Philly because obviously they have to do some rebuilding," Smith said. "I don't think they can go from where they are to a contender in one year."

TRADER PAUL

Despite managing a team that finished with the worst record in franchise history (22-48-12), the Flyers were encouraged enough by Holmgren's bold and decisive player moves to give him a two-year contract extension on March 14, 2007.

In less than five months, Holmgren had replaced Peter Forsberg, Kyle Calder, Petr Nedved, Randy Robitaille, Alexei Zhitnik, Nolan Baumgartner and Freddy Meyer with Marty Biron, Scottie Upshall, Braydon Coburn, Mike York, Dmitry Afanasenkov, Todd Fedoruk and Lasse Kukkonen.

"He showed he could lead our organization," Peter Luukko said. "He could have been in a position where he wanted to make some quick moves just to get into the playoffs, but that was totally contrary to what Paul believed."

Holmgren said it wasn't until he forged a relationship with Snider and Luukko that they began to appreciate his talents as a manager.

"In my role as an assistant to Bob, you're along for the ride," Holmgren said. "Consequently, they didn't get to know me very well. I think over the last four or five months, Peter and I have gotten to know each other a lot better and developed a real relationship and Mr. Snider has gotten to know me a lot better as well."

As for that ill-fated phone call to Colin Campbell, Snider says now he's glad Campbell rejected the offer.

"To be perfectly honest, Paul surprised the hell out of me," Snider said. "He's done a fantastic job."

FRIDGE OUT COLD

One of the uglier moments in a season full of them occurred just 21 seconds into the Flyers' 5-0 loss in Madison Square Garden on March 21 when Rangers enforcer Colton Orr clobbered Todd Fedoruk to the ice with a hard right hand to the jaw.

Fedoruk, who was participating in his 99th NHL fight despite the fact he was playing with seven titanium plates in his face, crumbled to the ice and lay motionless on his back for more than seven minutes, his hands raised at his sides.

When a backboard and stretcher were brought onto the ice, Fedoruk told Rangers medical personnel, "You're not putting me on a stretcher. Let me get up."

Flyers athletic trainer Jim McCrossin advised otherwise and Fedoruk's arms and legs were strapped together and he was carted off the ice to polite applause. Back home in South Jersey, Fedoruk's wife, Theresa,

Todd "Fridge" Fedoruk could do a standing backflip, but could not get out of the way of Colton Orr's devastating punch.

and 3-year-old son, Luke, were helplessly watching the man closest to them lying unconscious, his arms twitching by his side.

"When something like that happens she waits for the phone call," Fedoruk said of his wife. "It's either good news or bad news. I know it's stressful for her and she's done a good job dealing with that. I'm more worried about my son. He was watching it and telling Daddy to get up off the ice. He's a little too young to understand everything yet. But it's part of the game."

X-rays taken at Madison Square Garden and a CAT Scan taken at St. Vincent's Hospital in Manhattan were negative and Fedoruk was prescribed rest.

The backdrop for the showdown between Orr and Fedoruk came one month earlier when Fedoruk spent most of his shifts taking runs at Jaromir Jagr and anyone else in red, white and blue. Orr was a healthy scratch in that game.

"I initiated it by running around in New York," Fedoruk said. "I knew what I was doing. Jagr is a guy that if you play physical against him, it can get him off his game. I'm not saying he's a wimp or anything like that, but if you play physical against certain guys in this league they look over their shoulders, their confidence goes down and they won't make those plays they might normally make."

Fedoruk knew he would eventually face the music and Rangers coach Tom Renney made sure Orr was in the lineup when the teams met again.

"I looked at (Orr) and he said, 'Let's go!'" Fedoruk recalled. "He knocked me out on the way down. I guess I got my bell rung. It looked worse than it was, but if I knock Colton Orr out, it's right back the other way. Fridge is back. I mean, you can't control chaos, and fighting is chaos."

That fight against Orr proved to be Fedoruk's last in a Flyers uniform. He signed a one-year contract with the Dallas Stars the following summer for $875,000.

"Not bad," Fedoruk said, "since I was negotiating from a stretcher."

CHRISTMAS IN JULY

The Flyers ended the worst season in their history with just 56 points, marking the largest single-season dropoff (from 101 points the year before) in NHL history.

Their streak of misfortune carried from their nightmarish regular season to the 2007 draft lottery when they lost a coin flip and the chance to take Patrick Kane with the first overall pick.

The Flyers instead took big winger James van Riemsdyk, but it was Holmgren's crafty maneuvering before the draft that had other general managers buzzing. With a keen eye on potential free agents Kimmo Timonen and Scott Hartnell and enough room under the salary cap to afford them, Holmgren agreed to send the Nashville Predators the 23rd pick of the draft in exchange for the right to speak with the agents for Timonen and Hartnell.

The only stipulation was that the Flyers had just a 48-hour window to sign both players and within hours the parameters of six-year deals for Timonen ($37.8 million) and Hartnell ($25.2 million) were forged.

Just like that, Holmgren turned an untenable situation with Forsberg, who refused to sign a long-term contract, into Upshall, Hartnell, Parent, Timonen and a third-round pick.

"We are talking about the opportunity of adding two pretty good players to our team for a draft pick, a later draft pick," Holmgren said. "If (the 23rd pick) is going to play at all, he is probably a few years away for our team. So I think it is certainly worth that."

For the record, the Predators took defenseman Jonathon Blum with the 23rd pick.

But Trader Paul was just getting started. Holmgren celebrated his first Free Agent Day as the Flyers general manager by trading Geoff Sanderson and Joni Pitkanen to the Edmonton Oilers for right wing Joffrey Lupul and defenseman Jason Smith, then signing Danny Briere to an eye-popping eight-year, $52 million deal.

"We made a few pitches today and there were a lot of anxious moments waiting around," Holmgren said, acknowledging that Chris Drury and Scott Gomez, who signed with the Rangers, were also on the Flyers' shopping list. "I actually found

The Flyers made a big slash in Paul Holmgren's first summer as general manager, signing Danny Briere to a $52 million contract.

today more stressful than the trading deadline. You're dealing with a lot of what-ifs. With free agency you don't know what other teams are involved and the money involved and whether a player has you first on his list or third. There's a lot of stress."

In the end, the last-place Flyers were at the top of Briere's list, thanks to an assist from Flyers goaltender and former Sabres teammate Marty Biron.

"Even in the past few weeks, every time I thought about it, Philly came out at the top of my list," said Briere, who was coming of a career-best 95-point season. "To be honest, I was a little afraid they might not be interested in my services."

Actually, Holmgren had executed his offseason plan without a hitch (no pun intended) if you believe Simon Gagne. At the end of the regular season, Holmgren mapped out the team's plans with Gagne, saying he would specifically target Briere and Timonen.

"But I knew there were a lot of teams that would want those guys, too," Gagne said. "Now, here it is and we have them both. He's done everything he told me he'd do."

Even Ed Snider, who called the 2006-07 season his worst in hockey, was able to smile after witnessing Holmgren's summer magic act.

"To end up with the worst record in the league, not only was it embarrassing, it was unacceptable," Snider said. "I think Paul has done one of the most outstanding jobs I've ever seen in one year of retooling a team. The proof of the pudding is in the eating, but at least we know we've put together a great group of guys and we've covered all of our needs. Now it's up to these guys to perform."

BYE, BYE JONI

During his four years in the Flyers organization, no one ever questioned Joni Pitkanen's ability to skate. It's why the Flyers took him fourth overall in the 2002 draft behind Rick Nash, Kari Lehtonen and Jay Bouwmeester.

It was his inability to think the game that frustrated Flyers coaches and teammates and eventually led to his July 1 trade to the Oilers.

"I tried to talk to him several times," Derian Hatcher once said, 'but have you ever tried to talk to Joni?"

Often, Pitkanen would look into your face wide-eyed and with a grin, nodding as if he understood everything completely. But when it came time for him to respond, nothing.

"He has all the talent in the world, he's strong as a horse and he's as powerful a skater as Al Iafrate was, but he is also very immature," former Flyers defenseman Eric Desjardins wrote in a column for Montreal La Presse shortly after the trade.

"(Holmgren) knows his people and he knew the guys couldn't put up with Pitkanen anymore," Desjardins wrote. "They tried to give him support, but the youngster can't accept criticism and is very hard-headed. Even his (Finnish) compatriot Sami Kapanen had trouble with him and asked me to deal with it because he couldn't do it anymore."

Conversely, the Flyers acquired from Edmonton one of the game's most respected leaders in Jason Smith.

"I think he's a throwback defensive defenseman," Holmgren said. "From a character and heart standpoint, he's off the charts in both those areas."

It was not until his ninth month on the job that Holmgren finally rested, satisfied that his total makeover would bring brighter days.

"Now, he said, "I think we have a fighting chance."

RICHIE THE RUNNER

After a pair of mediocre seasons, Mike Richards set the tone for his third year in the NHL during the Flyers' 2007 training camp when players were timed in a three-mile run on the track at Eastern High School in Voorhees, New Jersey.

A few laps into the race Richards noticed that one of his running shoes was untied.

"He just kicked it off and ran barefoot for like the last mile-and-a-half," Biron said, "and he still beat me. That shows you the dedication and willpower he's got."

Richards, who was mockingly referred to as Zola Budd for his barefooted adventure, hardly remembers his feat as extraordinary.

"I was too tired to bend down and tie my shoe, so I kicked it off," he said. "Marty finished last and I only beat him by about two seconds."

A TEAM WITH ATTY-TUDE

It didn't take long for the 2007-08 Flyers to grab the attention of the NHL – negative attention, that is.

Midway through a preseason game against the Ottawa Senators, ornery rookie Steve Downie got up after being driven into the boards by Christoph Schubert, skated nearly the entire length of the ice and leaped into Dean McAmmond behind the Flyers net, driving his left shoulder into McAmmond's head.

McAmmond was carried off the ice on a stretcher. Downie, 20, was carried out of the NHL in a paddywagon, slapped with a 20-game suspension, the fourth longest in NHL history.

Downie, who was suspended several times during his junior career in the OHL, showed some remorse for the hit, but said his nasty style of play would continue.

"My game is hitting and finishing checks," he said. "I'm just trying to earn a spot on a roster."

Less than three weeks later Jesse Boulerice was in front of Judge Colin Campbell accepting a 25-game suspension for breaking the shaft of his stick on the jaw of Vancouver forward Ryan Kesler. At the time it was the longest single-season suspension in NHL history.

"I expected the worst," Paul Holmgren said. "Is 25 the worst? It's pretty close to what I expected."

Flyers coach John Stevens was remorseful for the two incidents, saying, "Hopefully, we don't have to go visit Mr. Campbell again this year."

Two weeks later Flyers defenseman Randy Jones was suspended two games for checking Bruins forward Patrice Bergeron from behind; four weeks after that Scott Hartnell was given a two-game suspension for driving the head of Bruins defenseman Andrew Alberts into the boards and a week after that Riley Cote was given a three-game sentence for elbowing Stars rookie Matt Niskanen in the head.

The Flyers had not even played 25 games and they had 52 games worth of suspensions. Concerned that the Broad Street Bullies had again reared their ugly heads, NHL commissioner Gary Bettman issued a warning to Holmgren.

"The question was raised about ramifications if it happens again," Holmgren said, refusing to elaborate. "Obviously, we're under watch."

Publicly, Holmgren said he was upset by his team's undisciplined play, but privately he took pride in the fact a fighting spirit was returning to his team.

That spirit revealed itself during a December practice when two of the team's smallest players, Sami Kapanen and Danny Briere, got into a scrap.

Briere and Kapanen, each of whom was listed at an exaggerated 5-foot-10, traded a flurry of punches while battling for a puck along the boards in a 2-on-2 drill before being separated by teammates.

"It wasn't much," Briere said. "It was a battling drill. I think he gave a shot to somebody and then he gave me a shot. There were some pushes back and forth."

For the record, those weren't pushes, they were punches.

Kapanen suggested there was more to the skirmish than some spur-of-the-moment adrenaline. The aftertaste of a 4-1 loss to the Dallas Stars was fresh in players' mouths. "Going into practice everyone was a little pissed," Kapanen said. "I'm frustrated with the way I'm playing. But it's not a big deal. We talked after practice and everything's fine."

A GENTLE BIRON

When Blackwood, New Jersey's Sue Nutt received a permission slip from the Overbrook School for the Blind asking if her 3-year-old daughter, Isabelle, could skate with the Flyers, she had obvious reservations.

"I thought, 'How is that going to work?'" Nutt said, moments before letting her daughter "skate" around the ice with Flyers goaltender Marty Biron. "This is the first time she's ever been on skates, but it's very exciting. Overwhelming, actually."

Born with Leber's Congenital Amaurosis (LCA), a rare hereditary disorder that leads to retinal dysfunction in infants, Isabelle Nutt had been blind since birth.

But on an October afternoon, Isabelle wore a pair of figure skates, sat on a metal folding chair and was pushed around the ice by Biron had worked with mentally and physically disabled children before, but had never skated with a visually impaired child.

"It was a unique experience," he said. "It didn't take long for Isabelle to get the idea of what it feels like to skate. She felt the snow on the ice and moved her feet back and forth like she was skating. As much as I tried to help her understand, she made her own image in her head and that was impressive."

Within 20 minutes, Biron had himself a new friend.

"It went from a little girl not wanting to go with me to the two of us sitting on chairs singing 'Wheels On the Bus,'" he said. "It was very rewarding."

Biron's infectious personality made him a popular player in the dressing room, where he'd spend hours talking about ... well, anything.

Anne Marie Biron surprised her husband, Marty, with an orange and black 1969 Camaro for his 30th birthday.

One of the few times Biron was rendered speechless was when his wife, Anne Marie, surprised him with an orange and black 1969 Camaro Z-28 for his 30th birthday.

Loaded with an original 302 engine, the car sounds almost as good as it looks.

"Almost everything is original from the way it was when it came out of production in 1969," he said. "It's a very nice collector's edition."

Biron said he changed the interior to black leather and kept the original orange and black paint design, adding black racing stripes. He said he's lusted after the '69 Camaro long before he wore orange and black.

"For years I've been saying I want the orange and black Camaro because I thought it looked cool," he said.

LINDROS RETIRES

When Eric Lindros announced his retirement from hockey in the fall of 2007, many wondered how his career would be remembered by those who played with him. Former teammate Chris Therien, who was beginning a career as a Flyers color analyst, said Lindros held a unique place in Flyers history.

"Eric's career was a fairy tale with a bad ending," Therien said.

Therien said that as a teenager he drove to a game in Oshawa to see what the phenomenon surrounding Lindros was all about.

"There were 13,000 fans crammed into a 10,000-seat arena," he said. "And another 5,000 people waited outside after the game just to get a glimpse of him."

Therien said that for the first five or six years of his career, Lindros lived up to his hype as one of the most feared players in the game and recalls vividly his annihilation of Tampa Bay Lightning defenseman Igor Ulanov during the 1996 Conference Quarterfinals.

"He just killed him," Therien recalled. "It was like, 'Here's what you get for playing me the way you did this series.' We just stood there watching. We couldn't believe it."

The following spring, Lindros and the Flyers appeared poised to be anointed champions. He led the Flyers to the Stanley Cup Finals with 26 points in 19 playoff games, but looked like a deer in headlights in a four-game sweep by the Detroit Red Wings.

Despite their differences, Bob Clarke believes Eric Lindros did enough in his career to warrant a spot in the Hockey Hall of Fame.

"In '97 I thought, 'This is Eric's calling in life,'" Therien said. "He's going to lead us to a championship. And it just never happened."

Therien described Lindros as the most talented player he ever played with and it can be argued he was the most talented to ever wear orange and black. But unlike Clarke, Parent and Barber, Lindros never realized his true potential.

"I like Eric and I'm trying to be fair to Eric, but he never lived up to that hype," Therien said. "He never delivered. Eric was a tragic case of an athlete in Philadelphia. He's the biggest 'What If' player I've ever seen."

When all was said and done, Lindros finished his career with one Olympic gold medal (2002) and one Olympic silver (1992), two world junior titles (1990 and 1991), one Hart Trophy (1995) and seven NHL All-Star appearances.

That, according to the most unlikeliest of sources, is enough to land him in the Hockey Hall of Fame.

"I believe he should be in," Bob Clarke said after Lindros' retirement. "I watched him for seven or eight years. This is the first big powerful dominant forward with the skill - not Gretzky or Lemieux, but very close. He won the MVP, he went to the Stanley Cup Final. If you eliminate the crap that surrounded him he's easily a Hall of Fame hockey player."

AN EARLY FATHER'S DAY

In the winter of 2007 the Flyers organized their first Father-Son Road Trip and from all accounts, it was a blast for both generations.

For three days in December, the Flyers' fathers slept in their houses and apartments; drove with them to practices and morning skates; played cards with them on chartered planes; roomed with them in swanky hotels and ate steak dinners with them at five-star restaurants.

"I've watched hundreds and hundreds of games," said Bill Hartnell, the father of Flyers left wing Scott Hartnell, "but this is different. It's very enjoyable to see them do what they've dreamt about all their lives.

"Not that any of us put them in hockey to make the big time. That wasn't the goal. It was to keep them off the streets on Friday nights."

A retired educator, Bill Hartnell worked 34 years as a teacher and principal of an elementary school in Regina, Saskatchewan – the same elementary attended by Scott.

"Yes, I was sent to the principal's office," Scott Hartnell said. "I always called my dad 'Dad' in the hallways, but when I got into trouble I called him, 'Mr. Hartnell.'"

In 2007 the Flyers organized their first Father–Son Road Trip and have continued the tradition ever since.

Intrigued by the history of Philadelphia, Bill Hartnell stayed in his son's apartment in Olde City, where he could tour Independence Hall, the Liberty Bell and the Constitution Center.

"(Regina) was not settled until 100 years ago," Hartnell said. "Anything that's old is ripped down. Here, everything that's old gets preserved. It's neat."

BEWARE THE PENS

After seeing his team lose to the Penguins eight straight times by a margin of 42-21 in 2006-07, Flyers coach John Stevens thoroughly enjoyed the Flyers' 8-2 rout against the Penguins on Dec. 12, 2007. Until the end, that is.

Despite Joffrey Lupul and R.J. Umberger becoming the first Flyers teammates to record hat tricks in the same game in more than 20 years, Stevens opened his post-game press conference by criticizing Pittsburgh coach Michel Therrien.

"I don't want to hear any talk about our team and how undisciplined we are," Stevens said. "That was ridiculous in the third period, in my opinion."

Stevens was referring to a third period in which the Penguins and Flyers were called for 124 minutes in penalties, including eight 10-minute misconducts. Penguins heavyweight Georges Laraque accounted for 18 of those penalty minutes by slashing Flyers defenseman Rory Fitzpatrick and taking a run at Marty Biron.

"The game got out of hand," Stevens said. "The discipline by them in the third period in my opinion is unacceptable. I mean, they're breaking sticks over guys away from the play. There's no place in the game for that. We all know that."

When told of Stevens' comments, Therrien was livid.

"Are we talking about the same team that got five guys suspended this year?" Therrien snapped. "Is that the same team? It's a lack of respect what he (Stevens) did tonight.

"At 7-2 you don't send your best power play on the ice. Even (Flyers center) Daniel Briere didn't want to go on the ice. It's a lack of respect. We got criticized last year because we didn't want to put the best players on the ice when we could humiliate the other team. You never put yourself in a position to show a lack of respect for the other team and a lack of respect on players and this is exactly what he did tonight."

Asked if he thought Stevens tried to humiliate his team, Therrien responded, "Big time. Big time," then stormed away from a small group of reporters.

During the interview Flyers enforcer Ben Eager was just a few feet away from Therrien in the hallway that separates the two dressing rooms and a reporter said he heard Eager call Therrien "a joke." Therrien spun around and shouted a two-word expletive at Eager that ended in "You!"

Mike Knuble stood up for his teammates, saying that after being humiliated by the Penguins the year before, the Flyers were on a mission to exact revenge.

"You don't have to lay off anybody," he said. "We want to show other people that when we get teams down we want to stay on top of them and not show any mercy."

RICHIE'S MEGA-DEAL

In late October of 2007 Paul Holmgren met with Pat Morris, the agent for Mike Richards, and offered a one-year contract extension for the 22-year-old center.

Morris' reply was short and sweet. "See you in the summer," Morris told Holmgren.

Morris then phoned Richards, who was scheduled to become a restricted free agent on July 1, and asked him exactly what he wanted.

"Keep me in Philadelphia," Richards instructed Morris, "as long as you can."

A month passed and Holmgren again reached out to Morris, who stunned him by asking for a 15-year deal that would allow Richards to retire a Flyer.

On Dec. 13, 2007 the Flyers announced they had come to a very expensive compromise, giving Richards a 12-year deal worth $69 million. Richards' contract, which carries through the 2019-20 season, is the second longest in NHL history behind the 15-year, $67.5 million deal goaltender Rick DiPietro signed with the Islanders in 2006.

The extension makes Richards, who will be 35 when the contract expires, the highest-paid player in team history, topping the six-year, $52 million deal Daniel Briere signed in 2007.

"I want to be here," Richards said. "I love the city. I love the organization and I'm excited to be here for the next 12 years. Nobody treats you better anywhere."

LIKE A DOG ON A BONE

The Flyers have had their share of unusual on-ice altercations over the years. In 1988 Rick Tocchet was suspended 10 games for gouging the eye of Islanders defenseman Dean Chynoweth.

But chewing on a guy's finger?

On Jan. 4, 2008, Derian Hatcher was accused of such a savage act by Devils forward Travis Zajac, who accused him of biting the middle finger of his left hand during the Devils' 3-0 win at the Prudential Center in Newark.

During a second-period scrum in front of the Flyers' net, Hatcher and Zajac got tangled up. Here is each player's version of the altercation.

"I guess my finger got close to his mouth and he bit me," said Zajac, who needed to get his finger stitched before returning to the game. "But things happen. Emotions run high. It's not really a big deal."

Asked if Hatcher said anything to him, Zajac joked, "No, he had my finger in his mouth."

Hatcher said Zajac face-raked him with his glove on.

"He almost ripped my tooth out, it's still sore," Hatcher said. "If he's cut, good. But I didn't bite him."

Hatcher said some of the Devils asked him if he bit Zajac several minutes after the incident. "Until then, I never even thought anything of it," Hatcher said.

"The league obviously has to look at something like that," Devils coach Brent Sutter said. "You've got a player that obviously bit another player in a scrum. But that will be up to the league to determine if anything comes of it. That's not something you see in a game, let alone (from) a veteran player like that."

Sutter said a video replay shows Zajac pulling his hand away from Hatcher's mouth, "and the glove is still in Hatcher's mouth, like a dog on a bone."

Proving every dog does not necessarily have his day, Hatcher did not receive disciplinary action for the alleged bite.

RICHARDS THE ALL-STAR

When Mike Richards was 18, Peter DeBoer watched him lead his Kitchener Rangers to a Memorial Cup title with 27 points in 21 playoff games.

When Richards was 19, DeBoer watched him captain Team Canada to a gold

medal in the World Junior Championships with five points in six games.

And when Richards was 20, DeBoer watched from afar as Richards led the Phantoms to a Calder Cup with 15 points in 14 playoff games.

So it came as no surprise to DeBoer when

One former coach says it's only a matter of time before Mike Richards brings a Stanley Cup to Philadelphia.

Richards was selected to play in the 2008 NHL All-Star Game at the age of 22.

"I have no doubts that before he's done Mike will win a Stanley Cup in Philadelphia," DeBoer said.

Told that similar predictions were made about a 19-year-old kid from London, Ontario named Eric Lindros, DeBoer backed up his bold prediction.

"I'm so sure I'd bet my house on it," said DeBoer, who was later hired to coach the Florida Panthers. "This kid wins championships. The days of me doubting Mike Richards ended about two weeks after I started coaching him."

That would have been in September of 2001 when Richards was a 5-foot-7, 170-pound 16-year-old who didn't appear to have any special hockey talents.

"He wasn't real fast and didn't have the greatest set of hands, but when the puck dropped he could take over a game," DeBoer said. "If we needed a big goal or a fight, he sensed it and did it without it ever being said."

DeBoer said Richards' parents, Norm and Irene, thought nothing of driving 18 hours from Kenora to Kitchener to see their son play for the Rangers, then hop back in their pickup and drive another 18 hours home the next day. Maybe that's why Richards presented his father with a brand-new pickup truck shortly after signing his hefty contract with the Flyers.

FORSBERG SAGA ENDS

In the months that followed Peter Forsberg's trade to the Nashville Predators, Paul Holmgren made several attempts to lure the future Hall of Famer back to Philadelphia. He tried in the summer of 2007 after Forsberg underwent yet another procedure on his right foot. He tried again in October, November, December and January, hoping a healthy Forsberg could infuse some much-needed offense to a team that played most of the 2007-08 season without a concussed Simon Gagne.

Finally, on Feb. 17, 2008, Forsberg, through his agent, Don Baizley, called off his attempted comeback, turning away a one-year contract offer from the Flyers believed to be worth about $2.5 million.

"Don called everybody and said Peter is not optimistic about playing this year," Holmgren said. "He's letting everybody know that if they have a Plan B go ahead and use it.

"I'm disappointed, mostly for Peter. I know how much he wanted to play. It would have been great for him and a boost for the NHL."

A week later, the Flyers executed their Plan B, acquiring Vinny Prospal from the Tampa Bay Lightning for defenseman Alexandre Picard and a second-round draft pick.

SCARE OF A LIFETIME

The Flyers have had their share of travel misadventures over the years but their experience on a February 2008 flight to Ottawa ranks as one of the scariest. The team charter took off into a storm and reached an altitude of about 12,000 feet.

That's when the plane began rocking and suddenly went into a steep dive, causing luggage and drinks to go flying. Radio play-by-play broadcaster Tim Saunders saw his laptop hit the roof of the plane and television commentator Steve Coates said a flight attendant told him she saw a distinct "bend" in the cabin.

"I went right to religion," said television analyst Bill Clement. "I passed on Norman Vincent Peale and went right to religion. Right to heavy prayer."

Clement said he turned to Coates, who was not wearing a seatbelt, and said, "Coatesy, if you're ever going to experiment with this seatbelt thing, I'm just going to suggest as a friend that you try it right now."

Five minutes after the freeefall, the plane leveled out and eventually climbed safely to 15,000 feet.

"That's when I announced to everyone that my feet were soaked," Mike Knuble said with a smile. "Nobody puked but I thought some might. Guys were a little too nervous to be puking.

Veteran Jim Dowd said the flight was enough to wilt even the toughest hockey player.

"The first bump, guys were laughing. Then it was, 'Whoa!' Then it was left, right, down. That was the first time it ever happened to me where I had to think, 'This could be it. Are you kidding me?' "

STEVENS FEELS THE HEAT

Although the Flyers' 2007-08 season will be remembered mostly for the club's lengthy playoff run, a late-season collapse that included a 10-game losing streak nearly cost John Stevens his job.

After losing 10 in a row from Feb. 6 through Feb. 25, the Flyers won five of seven, then lost four more in a row, capped by a 7-1 pounding by the Penguins in Mellon Arena on March 16.

"That was painful to watch," Holmgren said. "You've got to question a lot of things. It was a big game; we're in a fight for a playoff spot. To have that type of performance is alarming."

Asked what he questioned about his team, Holmgren said, "Preparation. We weren't ready to play in a game. The players certainly need to look in the mirror right now and I'm sure the coaches are looking very closely at their preparation."

"He's right," Stevens said. "It starts with me. I'm the head of this snake, if you want to call it that, and we have a staff here that works diligently to get this team ready to play. At the end of the day I have the responsibility to make sure these guys are ready."

The Flyers' hold on a playoff spot, which seemed a foregone conclusion when they were 30-17-5 in early February, was down to one point.

"The way we're playing right now, we're probably not going to make the playoffs at all," straight talker Sami Kapanen said. "And if that happens, some guys might get traded, they might sign with other teams and you might end up with a team that for the next six or seven years doesn't get in the playoffs at all. That's the way it is and it needs to be said."

John Stevens resorted to changing the names in the locker room to pull his team out of a late-season swoon.

In an attempt to loosen up his team, Stevens huddled up his players and asked them to describe the most memorable goals they ever scored. Then he had equipment manager Derek Settlemyre change the seating arrangements of every player in the Flyers' dressing room at the Skate Zone.

The result? The Flyers went 7-1-1 down the stretch to squeak into the playoffs as the sixth seed, where they were matched against the third-seeded Washington Capitals.

BALL BUSTER IN D.C.

Patrick Thoresen's career with the Flyers lasted barely three months, but his place in the team's playoff history was cemented in Game 1 of the Flyers' opening round playoff series against the Capitals.

With the Flyers clinging to a one-goal lead and the Capitals on the power play early in the third period, Thoresen slid in front of a slap shot by Washington Capitals defenseman Mike Green. The puck struck the Norwegian left wing between the legs with such force that it broke his protective cup.

"You're talking about a 95 mile an hour piece of rubber destroying your (protective) cup," Knuble said. "Cups can stop just about everything, but a 95 mile an hour slap shot hitting it flush?"

Thoresen remained on the ice for at least seven seconds while play continued around him.

"Clearly, the guy's in pain," Flyers tough guy Riley Cote said. "It's almost like salt in the wounds. The poor guy is laying his life on the line for the boys. I knew he was hurt. It's a tough call for the refs, but it was obvious to me he wasn't just crying wolf."

Crying, no. Howling is more like it.

"I was in the dressing room when he came off and all I heard was him screaming," Randy Jones said. "He was in quite a bit of pain. I have nothing but respect for that guy."

After the game Thoresen was taken to Washington Hospital Center, where Paul Holmgren said he faced the possibility of having one of his testicles removed.

"Right now we're not sure how serious it is," Holmgren said after the Flyers' crushing 5-4 defeat. "But he may need surgery. There is a chance they may have to remove one."

Hours later an MRI showed Thoresen had not ruptured his testicle, but would need rest and lots of ice.

"My groin area is sore and swollen," Thoresen said. "I can't really walk properly right now. It hurts."

The respect meter for Thoresen, already high, went off the charts when he returned to the lineup for Game 5. Mike Knuble was asked if Thoresen's damaged cup should be enshrined in the Hockey Hall of Fame in Toronto.

"Maybe the Flyers Hall of Fame," he said. "We'll dangle that thing in the (locker) room for motivation."

GOING THE DISTANCE IN D.C.

The Flyers grabbed a convincing three games to one lead on the Capitals in the first round, but according to Capitals forward Shaone Morrisonn, the Flyers weren't nearly as big an obstacle as their fans.

Morrisonn recalled an incident after Game 4 of the series when Flyers fans blocked the path of the Capitals' team bus as it tried to make its way from the Wachovia Center to 30th Street Station.

"People weren't moving," Morrisonn told the Washington Post. "They were mooning us, throwing stuff at us, beer bottles, whatever they had in their hands.

It's to be expected from Philly fans. Didn't they boo Santa Claus?"

The Capitals rallied back to tie the series, setting the tone for a decisive Game 7 in Washington's Verizon Center. John Stevens, who might have been fired if the Flyers blew the 3-1 series lead, had trouble sleeping the night before the game and arrived earlier than normal after a short walk from the team hotel.

When his players arrived, Stevens delivered this message: "It doesn't matter how we got to Game 7 – we're in a Game 7. That's a pretty exciting time for a hockey player."

OK, so it wasn't exactly Knute Rockne.

But when Joffrey Lupul deposited Kimmo Timonen's power-play rebound in the six-inch space between the left post and Cristobal Huet's right pad 6 minutes, 6 seconds into overtime, he carved himself a little spot in Flyers history.

Lupul's goal, which came with a broken stick he tossed high into the air, gave the Flyers their first-ever Game 7 overtime victory. While, the players poured onto the ice, celebrating in a big pile, Stevens and his staff jumped up and down behind the bench, hugging each other.

Then the red-faced Capitals fans got involved, throwing debris onto the ice as the Flyers celebrated. Scott Hartnell - never one to shy away from provoking a reaction — skated around the ice and waved goodbye, enjoying himself despite getting pelted with bottles and other garbage.

While Lupul was the star of the game, Marty Biron was the reason the Flyers lived to see another day, stopping 39 of 41 shots including all 16 in a third period dominated by the Capitals.

"After that game, my hair was standing straight up on my arms for 24 hours," Biron said. "That's what you play for."

Kimmo Timonen was just as satisfied after holding Alex Ovechkin to four goals when he could have had triple that total.

"It was tough," Timonen said. "We're talking about the MVP. He's unbelievable. But it wasn't just me. I can't take all the credit. (Braydon) Coburn was out there with me and so were Gator and Hatch."

UMBIE KILLS THE HABS

Before 2008, the only Stanley Cup playoff highlight of R.J. Umberger's career was of him lying flat on his back in Buffalo's HSBC Arena, the victim of a vicious open-ice hit by Sabres defenseman Brian Campbell.

"They kept showing it throughout the playoffs that year," Umberger said. "I was kind of sick of it."

Two years later, Umberger made a new highlight reel that left giddy Canadiens fans wondering what just hit them. Umberger scored eight of his 10 playoff goals in the Flyers' five-game annihilation of the Canadiens, making it one of the most dominating single performances in team history.

"You dream of playing in the playoffs and having a chance to win the Stanley Cup, but you don't dream of it exactly like this," Umberger said. "It's an unbelievable feeling to be here, and to be a big help in the process is gratifying."

The fact Umberger came so far from the seat of his pants two years earlier was a credit to his diligence. He struggled through a horrendous second season with the Flyers, netting just 16 goals and finishing with a career-worst minus-32 rating.

That's when Stevens suggested Umberger try a series of mental exercises under the Dore program. Named after a British doctor, the program is designed for children and adults affected by Attention Deficit Disorder and dyslexia.

Over the course of six months Umberger spent 40 minutes a day exercising his brain. He read while tossing a bean bag in the air. He looked straight ahead while focusing on an object placed to his left or right. He balanced himself on one foot, then the other — first on the floor, then on a wobble board. And while he was balancing, he'd recite the alphabet, a poem or name cities of states. Every morning for 20 minutes, every evening for 20 minutes, for six months.

"I didn't know how it would affect me on the ice, but I did it anyway," Umberger said. "It was tedious, but it helped."

Umberger went on to lead the Flyers with his 10 playoff goals and hoped his production would keep him in Philadelphia..

"It means a lot to me to stay here," Umberger said after those 2008 playoffs. "I know this city. I know how to play here and this is my home now."

THE SUPERSTITIOUS TYPE

The Flyers have had their share of superstitious players, but Jim Dowd might have topped them all.

"Superstitious?" he said. "Nah, I call it routine."

On game days, without fail, the Flyers' 39-year-old forward ate the exact same breakfast — thin pancakes, egg whites, rye toast with peanut butter – and the exact same dinner – salad, rice, green vegetables and either fish or lamb.

In fact, he had eaten those exact same meals on game day for 10 years. But Dowd's "routine" did not end with his last forkful of rice.

"I like my stall nice and neat," Dowd said. "(Former Islanders great) Butch Goring once told me that if something works, don't change it. Stick with it. Some guys say I'm a little bit of a neat freak. But I ain't changing anything."

When he arrived at an arena, Dowd would rearrange the equipment in his locker stall, put on his equipment in the same order he had for the last 16 years, and begin tapping his stick on the floor as he rattled off every teammate's name, forward line by forward line, defense pairing by defense pairing.

"C'mon, Richie!" "C'mon, Carts!" Dowd barked. And when when it came to the goalies, Dowd would say, 'C'mon Marty-Nitty!" whenever Biron started and "C'mon, Nitty-Marty!" whenever Niittymaki started.

On the bench, Dowd's "routine" continued, where between shifts he would take off both gloves, re-tie his skates, adjust his shin pads and socks and towel himself off, all in the same order.

"His gloves were on the ice more than he was because he rested them on the ledge and they kept getting knocked off," Flyers equipment manager Derek Settlemyre said.

"Everybody has their thing, and if they say they don't," Dowd said, "they're lying."

BRAVERY ON THE BLUE LINE

Patrick Thoresen was not the only Flyer with a heroic tale to tell from the 2008 playoffs.

Kimmo Timonen played with a blood clot in his left ankle. Braydon Coburn tried to play after needing 50 stitches to close a cut over his left eye. Derian Hatcher played with no cartilage in his knee and Jason Smith played with a pair of separated shoulders.

Of the four, Timonen's appeared to be the most serous. The Flyers began their third-round series against the Penguins with the news that Timonen had developed a blood clot in his ankle after blocking a shot in the previous playoff series against Montreal.

"When (the doctors) said if he gets hit in the right spot, they might have to cut his toes off or he could lose his foot, that was scary," Paul Holmgren said.

Timonen was given two choices when he met with a vascular surgeon at the Hospital of the University of Pennsylvania. He could continue taking blood thinners and wait several weeks or months for the blood clot to slowly disappear.

Or, he could continue to take blood thinners between playoff games and try playing, even though the lack of blood circulation in his left foot caused numbness in his toes and excruciating pain.

"Well, it takes only 15 minutes (of skating) and I can't feel my toes," Timonen said. "When that happens, the pain comes in. But I'm sure we've got some medicine for pain."

In other words, it was going to take a lot more than five numb toes to keep the Flyers' best defenseman out of what turned out to be the Flyers' final playoff game of the year.

Coburn, who took a puck in the face in Game 1 of the Conference Finals, could barely see out his swollen left eye, but still tried practicing in hopes of returning to the lineup if the series extended beyond five games.

It didn't. The Flyers were outclassed 6-0 in their final visit to Pittsburgh on May 18, ending a season in which their rallying cry became, "Why Not Us?"

In the basement of the Igloo after that game, perhaps knowing they had played their last games in orange and black, Holmgren paid Hatcher and Smith the ultimate compliments.

Jason Smith's ability to play with two separated shoulders in the 2008 playoffs left a lasting impression with his teammates.

"Derian Hatcher and Jason Smith brought toughness to a new level in my mind," Holmgren said. "Neither of them should have been playing."

Smith brushed off his injuries, saying he wasn't the only one playing through pain. But his teammates did not minimize what they had just witnessed.

"When Gator was in Edmonton we heard the stories about how he'd play through everything," Jeff Carter said. "But we saw it first-hand.

Derian Hatcher paid the ultimate sacrifice in the 2008 playoffs, eventually having his right knee surgically replaced.

The guy's chest was all swelled up. I don't know how he did it."

Richards said few players in hockey would quietly endure that kind of pain without a single complaint.

"You have to see it, because you're never going to hear him complain about it," he said. "When your captain is playing through what he did you can't help but be inspired. You might have a sore shoulder and you look at him and it goes away."

"He's a tough man, a tough man," Holmgren said of Smith. "His teammates worship the ground he walks on, he and Derian."

Hatcher broke his right tibia on March 15 and missed the final 10 games of the regular season. When he returned two games into the playoffs Holmgren called it a miracle.

With Smith signing a free-agent contract in Ottawa and Hatcher unable to resume his career, the two former captains would never play for the Flyers again.

WORST TO FOURTH?

The Flyers' ability to resurrect themselves from the worst team in the NHL in 2007 to one of four left standing in 2008 was nothing short of amazing.

In the process, they found a natural-born leader in Mike Richards, who justified his 12-year, $69 million contract by playing every shift in the playoffs as if it was his last.

In Marty Biron, they found a goaltender in his prime who could raise his level of play in the post-season.

In Jeff Carter and R.J. Umberger, they found two budding stars capable of producing clutch goals when the spotlight was at its hottest.

In Braydon Coburn, they found a hard-nosed thoroughbred who could anchor their blue line for the next 10 years. And in Kimmo Timonen, they found a durable two-way defenseman capable of calming every loose nerve in the dressing room.

But if the Flyers hoped to avoid another season-ending lopsided loss like the one they endured in Pittsburgh, changes would need to be made.

"Paul has done a tremendous job," Flyers president Peter Luukko said the night his team was eliminated by the Penguins. "He knows his work is not done yet. As much as this day stings, there are 26 other teams that weren't here today. That's how far Paul got us.

"As an organization we're going to do whatever it takes to win the Cup. That's always been our goal — not to just get into the playoffs or just get to the conference finals, but to go all the way. Paul and his staff will evaluate everything in the days and weeks to come."

Holmgren agreed.

"We're in this business to win the last game and when you don't, it's discouraging," Holmgren said. "Obviously, we need more depth and we need more speed."

CALLING CAPTAIN RICHIE

It seemed clear after the 2008 playoffs that the Flyers' leadership torch was ready to be passed from Jason Smith to Mike Richards.

"I don't know if he could ever be more ready," Derian Hatcher said.

"I think we all know he's the heart and soul of the team," agreed Carter.

But when Richards was asked if he'd accept the role of Flyers captain if the team asked him, he backpedaled like a defenseman trying to defend Sidney Crosby.

"I don't think so," Richards said. "I'm still learning so much from everybody. Gator is the best captain. And then there's Hatch and Kimmo and Danny. I don't feel I'm ready right now. I like the position I'm in as a little bit of a leader. But there are so many leaders in the dressing room right now that I don't think it's the right time or that I'm ready."

Four months later, the Flyers named Richards the 17th captain in team history, making him the youngest player to wear the "C" since Eric Lindros. Richards was officially presented with the captaincy before the Flyers' final appearance at the Spectrum, a preseason game in which every Flyers captain was recognized.

"I felt honored for the opportunity to shake their hands," Richards said. "To see the legends that have put on the 'C' sends chills up your spine."

"He's a natural," Bob Clarke said. "Mike's been a captain his whole life. I don't think it was a tough decision for Paul and John. He should be the captain, he is the captain and I hope he is for the next 15 years."

Bob Clarke believes that with a 12–year contract, Mike Richards will bring much–needed stability to the Flyers.

Richards' teammates agreed.

"Richie was the heart and soul of our team last year and he's got the world ahead of him," Scott Hartnell said. "Every night he gives 110 percent; he scores timely goals; he's not afraid to drop the mitts; he goes into the corners and comes out with the puck. And he's a class-act guy with a great family."

So why was Richards so reluctant to take the captaincy when he was approached about it months earlier?

"I had too much respect for Gator to say anything else," Richards said.

Perhaps, but with former NHL captains Kimmo Timonen and Danny Briere already in the locker room, Richards really did wonder if it was too early in his career to lead an NHL team with established stars.

Stevens spoke privately with Timonen, Briere and Simon Gagne over the summer to get their thoughts on the captaincy and all agreed the "C" belonged on Richards' chest.

"One of the reasons Mike is appealing is he has such respect for the veterans on our team," Stevens said. "He's not going to command them around; he's going to ask them to be his ally in the locker room."

Clarke said he tried to do the same thing as a captain and the season after he took on the role the Flyers won their first of two straight Stanley Cups.

"The captaincy is not important on every club," Clarke said, "but it has always been important on our club. You can't create the personality of a captain. You are what you are and you do what you do. Hopefully, that's enough."

SARAH PALIN'S DEBUT

After a summer of relative inactivity, the Flyers created quite a stir when they invited vice presidential candidate Sarah Palin to drop the puck in their 2008-09 home opener.

Inside the Wachovia Center there were bomb-sniffing dogs, men in dark suits with curled wires hanging from their ears and black Explorers with tinted glass parked where Zambonis usually hang out.

Palin, the world's most popular hockey mom, arrived minutes before the game sporting a white leather jacket. She strolled to center ice, kissed captains Mike Richards and Scott Gomez on the cheeks and waved to the crowd, even though many of them were booing her.

Some fans, like Brian Giordano of Olde City Philadelphia, wondered what Palin was doing politicking at a hockey game.

"Why would you want to put her in this kind of position when it's pretty evident Philadelphia is a Democratic town," Giordano said. "Trotting her out there is like feeding her to the wolves. I booed her because I'm not a fan of hers."

Tabitha Tobin of Blackwood, New Jersey agreed.

"I think it's ridiculous," she said. "I believe most people around here, regular people, are for (Barack) Obama, not for (John) McCain."

Palin received the invitation from Ed Snider when she was in Philadelphia for a campaign stop the previous month. Why the invite?

"Because she's meant so much to hockey and she's a hockey mom," Snider said. "We weren't doing this as a political statement. People should lighten up. I'm not subjecting her to anything. We asked her and she accepted."

Still, the fact that Snider reportedly contributed $25,000 to the Republican presidential campaign had many wondering if the Flyers chairman was intentionally mixing politics with sports to drum up support for McCain and Palin less than a month before the election.

"How about when they closed down the streets (around the Art Museum) and brought Bruce Springsteen in to play in the City of Philadelphia?" Snider replied, referring to a campaign concert for Obama. "What's that called?

"We hired Ed Rendell to analyze football on our Comcast SportsNet. We don't care if he's a Democrat or a Republican. If it's fun, we do it. This is fun."

APOCALYPSE NOW

Maybe the Flyers should have retained a few of those bomb-sniffing dogs for their first home win of the 2008-09 season.

It came during a smoke-filled overtime victory against the New Jersey Devils that had even the players' holding their noses.

With the score tied at 2 midway through the overtime period the Flyers thought they won it when Devils goaltender Martin Brodeur made a spectacular save on Simon Gagne.

Immediately after referee Dave Jackson waved off the goal, a fan on the second level hurled a smoke bomb onto the ice. It took a couple bounces and landed in front of the Devils bench, where Mike Richards pushed it with his stick.

At that point smoke streamed out of the bomb and Flyers defenseman Ossi Vaananen picked it up with his gloved hand.

"I figured I would carry it off quickly so we can move on with the game," Vaananen said. "Maybe I shouldn't have. It caught some flames and I thought, 'What if it explodes?' That's not funny. I shouldn't have touched that thing."

According to a Wachovia Center security guard, the fan who threw the smoke bomb quickly exited the building through the 11th Street exit. A description of the fan was given to security personnel.

"It reminded me of soccer games in Italy," said Devils forward Patrik Elias, who said the smell gave him a headache. "Maybe they should do the same thing that they do in Italy when they throw the flares. One game misconduct for fans so they can't come in."

With some of the sellout crowd still holding rally towels over their noses, the Flyers finished off the Devils when Jeff Carter scored to give the Flyers their first home win of the season.

Three months later Philadelphia police arrested Earl Greene of South Philadelphia and charged him with causing and risking a catastrophe, possession of an instrument of crime, recklessly endangering another person, and disorderly conduct.

"We want to thank the Philadelphia Police Department, as well as our fans, who came forward and helped us identify the individual responsible for disrupting our game," Peter Luukko said. "It is satisfying to know that he has been arrested as our organization does not tolerate this behavior."

BROTHERLY GLOVE

Someday, Scott Hartnell would like to be remembered by Flyers fans for something other than his wild hair and crazy decision to stop a breakaway by throwing his hockey glove. But during the 2008-09 season, the Flyers celebrated both.

Joffrey Lupul (left) and Jeff Carter (right) try to imitate the real hair of teammate Scott Hartnell.

Hartnell's glove toss came late in a game against the Lightning on Dec. 2 when, with 16.3 seconds remaining in a 3-3 game, Ryan Malone blocked a shot in the defensive zone and broke free on a breakaway. Hartnell, who had lost his stick earlier on the shift, saw the puck spring free to Malone and gave chase.

Without a stick and without a prayer to catch Malone, Hartnell threw his right glove at the puck and missed.

"I couldn't catch him at the end," Hartnell said. "It was just a desperation play, and I threw the glove. Looking back, it was kind of stupid. But Marty (Biron) came up huge and basically won us the game."

Biron stopped Malone's shot, but referee Stephane Auger awarded Malone a penalty shot, which Biron stopped with his right skate.

A few weeks later the Philadelphia Phantoms conducted a charity glove toss featuring Hartnell and the Flyers followed with their own hair-brained giveaway in which the first 5,000 kids in attendance received Hartnell wigs.

"It's pretty cool to see all those fans wearing that curly, afro mess," said Hartnell, who says he has not cut his hair since October 2007.

"I never put my hand on Hartsy's hair, and I hope I never have to," Biron said.

Hartnell says his teammates are just envious of his curly brown locks.

"I know there are 20 guys in this (locker) room that are jealous of my hair, so maybe in warmup a couple guys will be wearing them just to be like me," he said. "Maybe they'll get a little better looking if they wear it."

Biron said he thought it would be cool if every Flyer wore the wig during pregame warmups.

"We'd all look like Fartsmell," Biron said with a laugh.

Hartnell says the wigs can be used over and over again.

"I'm sure there might be a couple Hartnell renegades out there on Halloween night," Hartnell said, "mucking it up at the bars."

HIS FATHER'S SON

Before his son's meteoric rise to NHL stardom, Jim Carter's claim to fame was being selected between Mike Gartner and Dino Ciccarelli in the 1976 Ontario Hockey League draft.

Gartner and Ciccarelli went on to become NHL superstars, combining for more than 1,300 goals and 2,500 points. Jim Carter, a 5-foot-8, 145-pound forward, endured the worst season in Oshawa Generals history, hung up his skates and went to work at a local copper mill.

But that didn't mean Jim Carter would not someday leave his mark on the NHL.

Jeff Carter says his father is the biggest reason he was playing in his first All-Star Game in 2009, where he shared the Montreal ice with the likes of Alex Ovechkin, Pavel Datsyuk and Joe Thornton.

"He coached me from the time I could skate until I was 16," said Carter, who finished second in the NHL in goals in 2008-09 with 46. "It was awesome."

Jeff Carter and Ben Franklin celebrate Carter's selection to the 2009 NHL All–Star Game in Montreal.

Jim Carter said he knew his son had tremendous potential from the time he was 10 and dominating his leagues by scoring nearly a goal a game.

"He'd score 75 or 100 goals in a season," Jim Carter said. "You could tell he was a natural because things came to him fairly easy."

As a coach, Jim Carter said he stressed the fundamentals of the game with an emphasis on skating and positioning.

"If you can't skate," he said, "you can't play."

Maybe, but it's Carter's wicked wrist shot that makes him one of the NHL's most dangerous snipers.

"His shot is the hardest I've ever seen in my life," said former Flyers goaltender Antero Niittymaki. "The reality is that he can score goals from the blue line. He has a long stick and it's always tougher when you face a big guy with a long stick."

From butt end to heel, Carter's stick measures 63 inches. By comparison, Danny Briere uses a 57-inch stick.

MAKING A DIFFERENCE

For years the Flyers have prided themselves in being active members of their communities, often visiting local hospitals and schools and participating in food and clothing drives.

In February of 2009 three Flyers alumni granted the wish of Gary Seeburger, a 56-year-old fan from Fort Washington, Pennsylvania who was stricken with cancer.

A Flyers season ticket holder for 20 years, Seeburger told a friend his life would be complete if he could meet one of the "old-time Flyers." Within a few days, Joe Watson, Bob Kelly and Bill Clement were standing beside Seeburger in his Abington Hospital room, sharing stories of their days as Broad Street Bullies.

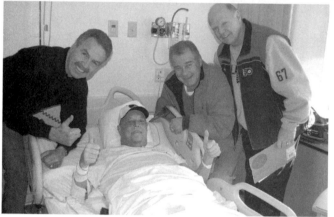

Bill Clement, Joe Watson and Bob Kelly granted a wish by Gary Seeburger by visiting him at Abington Memorial Hospital.

Eleven days later, Mr. Seeburger passed away.

"He was a phenomenal Flyers fan and I can't tell you how much it meant to him to see those guys," Seeburger's wife, Eileen, said. "We hung the pictures from their visit in the room and it's all he talked about for days. He absolutely loved the Flyers."

MOST INTIMIDATING?

In 2008 The Sporting News anointed Philadelphia as having the most intimidating fans in hockey and when the Penguins arrived in Philadelphia for Game 3 of the 2009 Eastern Conference Quartrerfinals, the Wachovia Center faithful were hungry for revenge.

Sidney Crosby was greeted with hand-man signs that questioned his manhood and Evgeni Malkin was ridiculed before the first strings of God Bless America.

Penguins center Max Talbot laughed at all the attention the Flyers' fans were given.

"They call themselves the most intimidating? That's pretty pretentious," Talbot said. "They try to be intimidating. They're all dressed in orange T-shirts and they scream a lot. Does that make the Flyers a better team? I don't think so."

The Flyers will argue they were the better team in that first-round series, but a remarkable comeback by the Penguins in Game 6 muted that argument and left the Flyers kicked to the sidewalk by Pittsburgh for the second straight spring.

Leading by three goals early in the second period, the Flyers were so gassed up it looked like they might fly back to Pittsburgh without the aid of fuel.

Back-to-back-to-back goals by Mike Knuble, Joffrey Lupul and Danny Briere had given them a commanding 3-0 lead and Dan Carcillo had just pounded Talbot to the ice like a sledge hammer to a toothpick.

The sellout crowd of 20,072 – 20 short of a Wachovia Center record – was on its feet and "Sign Man" Dave Leonardi held up a bold-faced sign that read "Old Time Hockey."

"You get a 3-0 lead, it should be over," Flyers coach John Stevens said.

It should have been. It wasn't.

Led by Malkin and Crosby, the Penguins scored five unanswered goals to pull off an incredible 5-3 comeback victory that ended the Flyers' season six games into the playoffs. It was just the third time in team history the Flyers had blown a three-goal lead in a playoff game and the first time it had ever happened at home in an elimination game.

"They took it to us and we didn't respond," said a dejected Ed Snider. "They came at us and we didn't have an answer. It's something we have to look at and figure out why."

"It was like, 'What just happened?'" Briere said. "One goal turned into two and eventually three. I think we lost our focus. We were missing that killer instinct.

"All we had to do from that point on was to play solid hockey and not give them anything. I don't know if we were looking ahead or thought we had it won at that point. You're not going to get away with that."

The Flyers didn't. The difference in the series was the play of the teams' top two centers.

Malkin (4 goals, 5 assists) and Crosby (4 goals, 4 assists) combined for 17 points, while Mike Richards (1 goal, 4 assists) and Jeff Carter (1 goal) combined for six.

"It's tough," said Carter, who finished second in the NHL with 46 goals but had just one goal on 30 shots in the playoffs.

"I had a pretty good regular season and coming in I had high hopes of myself. I'm looked upon to put the puck in the net and one goal doesn't cut it. I had some shots and some chances but you've got to put it in the back of the net. I'm not overly pleased with my performance."

After the series, it was clear the Flyers had closed the gap on the Penguins, but difficult to know how much, especially since the Penguins marched all the way to the Stanley Cup.

"Look, Pittsburgh's a young team with young stars," Snider said. "We're a young team with young stars. Right now, we've got to get a little bit better, obviously. They're a better team than us right now and we've got to catch them. This team does not need major changes."

FORSBERG IN THE MAKING?

Despite their early exit in 2009, the Flyers believe they've found a star in the making in Claude Giroux.

Snider says he reminds him of a young Bobby Clarke, saying "I saw Clarke play every game he's ever played and he sure looks the same to me."

Simon Gagne likens Giroux's game to Peter Forsberg.

Chris Therien went so far as to suggest that within two years Giroux will be one of the top five players in the NHL.

"I've watched him closely and he's a special, special player," Therien said. "I'm not taking anything away from Jeff Carter or Mike Richards, but he's ahead of where they were in their rookie year. I give him three years and he'll be a hundred-point player."

Giroux averaged 42 goals and 65 assists in his three years in the Quebec League and recorded nine goals and 18 assists in half a season with the Flyers. But his strong performance in the playoffs, where he had two goals and three assists in six games, had everyone in hockey talking.

Therien believes Giroux will someday average 40 goals and 75 assists a season, which could make him the first Flyer since Eric Lindros in 1995-96 to record 100 points.

"He plays like he has 10 eyes on the back of his head," Therien said. "And he gets his shot off so quick."

Giroux, who turned 21 in January, has gained nearly 20 pounds since the Flyers drafted him in 2006. At 5-11, 172 pounds, he is deceptively strong in the corners and is willing to make a hit just as willingly as he is to take one.

As for the comparisons to Forsberg and Clarke, Giroux said he's flattered, but will leave those comparisons to others.

"I really don't think I'm there yet," he said. "I'm not even close."

EMERY THE ANGEL

Ray Emery issued in a new goaltending era in Flyers history by wearing a cream colored suit and white shoes to his introductory press conference on June 9, 2009. The only thing missing was a pair of angel wings.

One year after being exiled to Russia because of his disruptive behavior, the NHL's most maligned goaltender quietly spoke about being a reformed man willing to prove the Flyers were right in signing him to a one-year, $1.5 million contract.

Those 30 traffic stops during his playing days in Ottawa? Ancient history.

The practice fights with teammates and team trainers? Rear view mirror.

The missed flights and wrong turns and late arrivals to practices? Behind him.

"All I can say is I really appreciate the opportunity I'm being given here," Emery said at a summer news conference celebrating his arrival. "I lost that opportunity once before and I have that in the back of my head before I do anything. When I wake up in the morning, that's what I'll be thinking about – that I have an opportunity and I'm not going to let anything get in the way of that. I'm not going to do anything to jeopardize that or make people that are giving me this opportunity look bad."

Those people include Ed Snider, Paul Holmgren, Peter Luukko and John Stevens, each of whom personally met with the 26-year-old native of Hamilton, Ontario before deciding he had the mental makeup to be the Flyers' ninth starting goalie in the past 10 years.

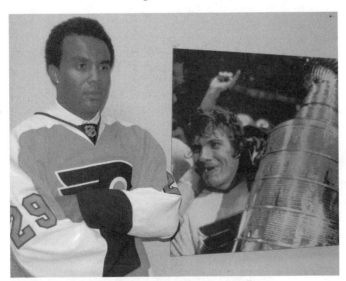

"We'd love to have Ray Emery be our goalie for the next 10 years," Luukko said. "But Ray's got to come in and prove himself. We did pretty well with a guy by the name of Hextall and I think Ray brings a bit of that element, and that's going to be exciting for the team and the fans."

The Flyers' ninth starting goalie in 10 years, Ray Emery says he's out to prove the Flyers made the right decision.

Like Ron Hextall, Emery's game is built on athleticism and attitude. In addition to leading all NHL goaltenders in penalty minutes over the past seven years, Emery took the Ottawa Senators to the Stanley Cup Finals in 2007.

"His competitiveness is huge," Holmgren said. "Sometimes the front of the net looks like an NFL line of scrimmage. The goalie's got to fight to see the puck and Ray's competitive fire gives him a distinct advantage in that area."

But what fuels Emery on the ice has often burned him off it.

His unraveling began at the start of the 2007-08 season when he arrived in Ottawa with a wrist injury. He eventually lost his starting job to Martin Gerber and became an ornery presence in the locker room, showing up late for practices and getting into fistfights with teammates.

"I came into camp out of shape and wasn't willing to work like I had in the past to earn starts," Emery said. "After that I didn't go about it the right way dealing with that disappointment. The team suffered because of it and I suffered because of it. I know this is the last chance for me and I'm excited to correct my mistakes."

The Senators placed Emery on waivers after that disastrous 2007-08 season and when no NHL team showed interest in him he signed a contract to play in Russia's Kontinental Hockey League, where he went 22-8-0 with a 2.12 GAA.

Emery made news in Russia when he charged after a team trainer who insisted he wear a baseball cap after he was pulled from a game. Emery was back in the news a few months later when he was pulled over by Ontario police after his white Hummer was clocked at more than 100 mph on Highway 416.

"He was on a back country road and he was driving too fast," said Emery's agent, J.P. Barry said. "I'm pretty sure when they see a white Hummer driving on a back country road in Ottawa they know who it is.

"Ray was very flamboyant playing in a small town in Ottawa. He likes his clothes and drives around in a white Hummer. It was a fishbowl environment in a very small town and he became the focus of attention."

Of the opinions sought by Holmgren, none might have mattered more than that of John Paddock, whose firing as Senators coach in 2008 was directly tied to his mishandling of Emery. Paddock said Emery's talent is good enough to make him a dominant goalie in the NHL, but it's his off-ice behavior that will ultimately decide how long he remains a Flyer.

"Some athletes view that as unfair, but they are more in the limelight and they do have an image to uphold more than the average citizen and they need to be accountable," Paddock said. "That's obviously another area I would hope over time he's very aware of and very conscious of."

'THE FUTURE IS NOW'

Never ones to be accused of complacency, the Flyers made the summer of 2009 another exciting one when they dealt Joffrey Lupul and Luca Sbisa, along with two first-round draft picks, to the Edmonton Oilers for mammoth defenseman Chris Pronger.

"We gave up a lot of our future in this trade," Snider said. "Sometimes in sports the future is now and we didn't want to wait too long."

The signing seemed to send a direct message to the three biggest obstacles standing in the Flyers' way of a Stanley Cup: Sidney Crosby, Evgeni Malkin and Alex Ovechkin.

So, during his introductory news conference the 6-foot-6, 223-pound defenseman was asked if there is a message he'd like to send to his new conference rivals.

"I think you know the answer to that," Pronger said with a menacing grin. "We don't want to premeditate anything, now do we?"

Suspended eight times in his 15-year career, Pronger was careful not to make himself a target for NHL officials before even pulling on a Flyers jersey. But he seems to completely understand what his new team expects of him.

"To make sure teams understand who's net it is in front of our goal," he said.

For years the Flyers have yearned for a defenseman who hit like Ed Van Impe, skated like Joni Pitkanen, passed like Mark Howe, shot like Tom Bladon and defended like Eric Desjardins. They believe they have found him in Pronger and put their money where their mouths are with a seven-year, $34.9 million contract that will expire when Pronger is 41.

"Bobby Orr and Ray Bourque could do a lot of things great, but they didn't have the meanness Pronger has," Bob Clarke said. "It's very, very rare to have all of that in one player. My own feel-

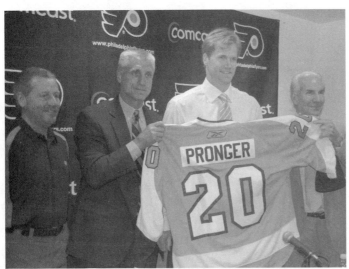

Peter Luukko, Paul Holmgren, Chris Pronger and Ed Snider are all smiles as they issue in a new era of Flyers hockey.

ing is that Pronger is better than (Scott) Niedermayer. We've never had a guy with all that come through here."

Pronger says he will earn every penny and is ready to take on any pressure that comes along with being the highest-paid player on the Flyers' blue line. Asked if he considers himself the best defenseman in the NHL today, Pronger smiled and said, "I guess we're going to find out real quick. I plan to be."

Snider believes Pronger will be worth the price if he can end his team's 35-year wait for a championship.

"Our goal every single year is to win the Stanley Cup and this is no different," Snider said. "But you can't put that burden on one guy. People say this is the piece that's going to do it, but it's unfair to him, totally unfair.

"I think we've gone a long way to closing the gap on Pittsburgh. We won't know until we get on the ice, but I like our prospects."

So does a man named Bernard Marcel Parent, who wants nothing more than to see a new generation of Flyers sip from the Stanley Cup and feel the joy of being a champion in Philadelphia.

"I'm predicting that the next seven, eight years are going to be wonderful years in Philly for all our professional teams," Parent said. "Our time has arrived. It's a beautiful time."